D0853872

Witnessing Whiteness

Witnessing Whiteness

Confronting White Supremacy in
the American Church

KRISTOPHER NORRIS

OXFORD
UNIVERSITY PRESS

OXFORD
UNIVERSITY PRESS

Oxford University Press is a department of the University of Oxford. It furthers
the University's objective of excellence in research, scholarship, and education
by publishing worldwide. Oxford is a registered trade mark of Oxford University
Press in the UK and certain other countries.

Published in the United States of America by Oxford University Press
198 Madison Avenue, New York, NY 10016, United States of America.

CIP data is on file at the Library of Congress
ISBN 978-0-19-005581-3

1 3 5 7 9 8 6 4 2

Printed by Integrated Books International, United States of America

To Calvary Baptist Church
Washington, DC

Contents

Acknowledgments

THE COMPOSITION OF this book was framed by a white nationalist march in Charlottesville, Virginia, and a white nationalist mass shooting in El Paso, Texas. Its origins lie in the shooting death of Michael Brown several years earlier. The events in Ferguson, Missouri, triggered a national racial reckoning that, by all appearances, has been curtailed by a regime of white power at the highest levels of political office and a resurgence of white supremacist violence. They also prompted a personal and theological transformation that mark the pages of this book. Of the friends who educated, guided, and journeyed with me, books would not contain all that could be written, or at least an already overly extended word count cannot. But their wisdom permeates these pages and provides the hope— or, perhaps, the right amount of hopelessness, as the reader will see—to believe that white supremacy may one day be broken.

I thank all of those people who contributed to this book through conversation and example. But I also want to express explicit gratitude to a few who provided direct feedback on this manuscript. I thank especially Chuck Mathewes and Charles Marsh, two brilliant scholars who oversaw this project in its earlier version as advisers at the University of Virginia and have guided me long after their official duties ended. Their support, encouragement, and friendship have been and continue to be invaluable. Several others read and offered insightful and critical feedback on nearly all of this manuscript—if not all of it. My gratitude goes to Paul Jones, Jim Childress, Maurice Wallace, Christina McRorie, Elijah Zehyoue, Matt Puffer, Travis Pickell, Nelson Reveley, Kyle Nicholas, and Amy Canosa, and especially to Ashleigh Elser and Joe Lenow, without whose weekly winery workshops this project would never be finished.

Anything good about this book is indebted to you. I appreciate many others who read and edited one or more chapters of the manuscript, including Paul Gleason, Greta Matzner-Gore, Matt Elia, Ross Kane, Nate Lee, Rick Elgendy, Josiah Young, Beverly Mitchell, Sondra Wheeler, Jennifer McBride, Sarah

Azaransky, and Karen Guth. I am grateful to all of you for your time, dedication, and friendship. I also thank my Center for Public Theology team at Wesley Seminary for their support and encouragement throughout this process: Mike McCurry, Irene DeMaris, Rochelle Andrews, Liz Pruchnicki, and Jon Deters for excellent editing and bibliographic work.

I was able to workshop portions of this at the Fellowship of Protestant Ethics gathering at Notre Dame, and I appreciate all of those who read and gave careful feedback. I'm also grateful to Martin Kavka and Aileen Kalbian for editing an article that would become chapter 3 and to the *Journal of Religious Ethics* for granting permission to reuse material from that article as well as *Political Theology* for permission to reuse content from my article, "James Cone's Legacy for White Christians." It has also been a pleasure to work with Cynthia Read and the editing team at Oxford. I thank them for their guidance and patience.

This book could not have been written without the generous hospitality of Stanley Hauerwas and James Cone, as well as others at various churches mentioned in this text, who allowed me to interview them. It is rare to find prominent scholars willing to be so vulnerable about their own work, successes, and mistakes. They have been two of my most important teachers. I hope this book pays tribute to them both—even in its criticism—and perhaps offers some new perspective on their work and legacies in their own words.

I also thank the students who made up two semesters of my Church, Politics, and Race class at Wesley Seminary. Your insightful questions and sometimes intensely graceful discussions gave life to this book and helped me to organize my early, inchoate thoughts on the subject. The Theology on Draft group at Calvary Baptist Church also helped me to think through the depths of Christianity's entanglements with white supremacy.

I dedicate this book to Calvary Baptist Church. This congregation breathed life into a dry soul and demonstrated a new way of being Christian in the world when this theologian was questioning if theology mattered. I am convinced that theology must arise out of the shared life of community—of the church—and the theology that emerges from these pages has no greater influence than this rogue Baptist community of all colors and quirks in the heart of Washington, DC.

Finally, I want to thank my family, especially my parents, Keith and Elizabeth, for supporting me in incalculable ways during the twenty-odd years I spent in school (!). They patiently wrote down my stories when I was young and have encouraged me ever since and especially during the composition of this book. And I thank my niece and nephew, Bethany and Wesley, for wonderful little interruptions amid writing deadlines for more important matters like dance contests and magic shows! The idea for this book began with a dissertation at the University of Virginia. I dedicated that dissertation to my dog who had passed away just three months before I finished. He was my loyal companion, sitting patiently by my side as I wrote nearly every word of it. That project, and thus this book, would never have been completed if it weren't for Mojo.

—August 2019, four hundred years after the first enslaved Africans arrived in Jamestown

—Ordinary Time, ten Sundays after Pentecost

Introduction

The slave auctioneer's bell and the churchgoing bell chime in
with each other.

—FREDERICK DOUGLASS[1]

THE CHRISTIAN FAITH begins in stories. The practices and doctrines of
the church are based on foundational narratives like "In the beginning God created. . . ." "In those days Caesar Augustus issued a decree. . . ." "He took the bread,
gave thanks, and broke it." We sing stories in our hymns and recite them with
our prayers. Even our creeds express our beliefs in narrative form. In the Baptist
tradition in which I was raised, faith took expression in personal stories we called
testimonies. "And that was when I felt Jesus in my heart. . . ." "I heard God speak
to me, and I believed. . . ."

Racism begins in stories too. White supremacy emerged as European
Christianity collided with the peoples of the New Worlds. The stories of black
and brown peoples' inferiority, their lack of rationality and religion, were brought
back by its missionaries, explorers, and entrepreneurs. These stories set in place a
new anthropological narrative and injected it with theological value. Narratives
like the myth of Ham canonized a new racial taxonomy ordered around skin color,
and story-shaped communities perpetuated racial oppression through practices
and beliefs in individualism, supersessionism, and superiority. Today, the seemingly innocuous claims of colorblindness are produced through stories that allow
white Christians to avoid the responsibility of reckoning with reality: "I'm not a
racist," "I don't see color." Stories shape social and theological imaginations and
mold ethical visions; they allow white people to see ourselves as not racist or to
believe Christianity is not concerned with social realities like race.

Stories also challenge the present reality. As theologian James Cone notes,
spirituals communicated stories about where African American enslaved people
might find freedom, the blues told stories of lament, and folk tales reminded
them of their dignity. These counternarratives offer respites of resistance to a
world and a church burdened under the regime of white supremacy. Black liberation theology provides a vision of a world and church that emerges from these

Witnessing Whiteness. Kristopher Norris, Oxford University Press (2020). © Oxford University Press.
DOI: 10.1093/oso/9780190055813.001.0001

counternarratives, yet Cone insists that counternarratives cannot stand on their own. They must connect, illuminate, and challenge the dominant stories that have shaped the white imagination and its theology.

As white theologians, pastors, and Christians—a group into which I fall—these counterstories are our own—contingently, provisionally—as they illuminate what we have failed to see. They force us to recite our own stories, but now at the foot of the cross and the lynching tree. They force us to tell these stories—and acknowledge their intersections with the counternarratives that confront us—in a new dialect of confession. And they force us to respond.

Stories make us witnesses. Whether we are witnessing the testimonies or counternarratives that others tell us or offering witness ourselves to an event or about our perspective on reality, we are unavoidably witnesses.

A major argument of this book is that white Christians have failed to be witnesses to our own whiteness. We don't perceive it, much less give an account of it, or tell its story. In fact, the stories we tell ourselves—"My family didn't own slaves," "Racism is in the past; let's just move on"—actually serve to blind us from our own whiteness, and the devastating effects it has upon the church and the world. Our theologies and church practices shield us from these realities and prevent us from rightly telling the stories of our own past and present. Our theologies and church practices fail us—and especially fail those harmed by our failure to witness whiteness—because they are entangled in white supremacy in patterns threaded so tightly that only a painful, dangerous, and necessary process of unraveling will allow us to see the horror we have inflicted (in the name of Christ) and to have any hope of redemption.

* * *

This project began when I was a graduate student at the University of Virginia. I reached out to James Cone to request an interview for a research project. I had an affinity for the Christian ethics model of Stanley Hauerwas, especially his focus on the church, attention to character formation and Christian practice, and radical view of Christian discipleship against the powers and principalities of the nation-state. I had also acquired his resistance to talking about racism, though I did not know it. When I called Cone for our interview, he was rightly suspicious of me, another white theologian trained at an institution dripping in white supremacy since its founding by a slaveholder. For most of the conversation he pressed me—dubious and testing. By the end of the call I had at least convinced him to let me come to New York and interview him in person.

I climbed the tight staircase of the Gothic tower at Union Theological Seminary to Cone's office on the top floor, a few blocks from Harlem. This felt similar to the several trips I had made to the top-floor office of Stanley Hauerwas at Duke University. Yet besides their unforgettable, nasally voices, these two theologians—perhaps the most significant American Protestant theologians of the last half century—ostensibly shared little in common. In fact, the theologian *Time* had dubbed "America's Greatest Theologian" and the founder of "black liberation theology" had never engaged one another in print and had likely only spoken once in person (a brief exchange during a conference panel, recalled by Hauerwas, years ago). Yet these two theologians represent the two most significant contemporary threads of Christian ethics and political theology. These threads go by a number of different names that denote slightly different yet overlapping circles of scholars, methods, and aims. I identify them as *postliberalism* (though this also references a scholarly group or movement that has been called the New Traditionalists[2] or neo-Anabaptists,[3] with slight modifications) and *liberation theology* (including feminism, womanism, Latin American liberation, queer theology, and of course, most significant for this book, black liberation theology).[4]

At the turn of the twentieth century, as Roman Catholics made a shift to the social encyclicals, Protestant theologians in America also began connecting evangelical fervor to social transformation. Social gospel theologians, like Walter Rauschenbusch, envisioned a process of "Christianizing the social order" to "redeem the permanent institutions of human society from their inherited guilt of oppression and extortion."[5] These aims were short-lived, however, evaporating in the trenches of world war and before the forceful critiques from Christian realists. *Realism* is exemplified best by brothers Reinhold Niebuhr and H. Richard Niebuhr, who, acknowledging the futility of attempts to convert a social order irrevocably mired in sin—a perpetually "immoral society"—held a more chastened expectation for the approximations of love and transformation that Christians could achieve in the world.[6] This expectation entailed measures of proximate justice achieved through morally ambiguous political action. Yet midcentury, in the wake of U.S. imperial aspirations abroad and growing resistance and justice movements at home, this realist theology generated two key responses signaling a "seismic shift" in Christian ethics.[7]

Christian liberationists who were dissatisfied with the realists' gradualism recalibrated the realist paradigm toward activism, underscoring the overcoming of oppression for the poor and marginalized as the core mission of Christianity. They turned to communities of resistance as sites of theological production and issued a call similarly tethered to social and political expediency, yet promoting a more hopeful and grassroots message of human flourishing.[8] For these theologians, Christian theology was in service of liberating the poor and marginalized from the yokes of oppression and injustice.

Likewise, postliberals attempted to correct for what they saw as an accommodation to the culture of liberalism and its fragmentary pretensions to universal rationality and individualism, along with a thin Christology and sense of community in the realists. They also countered with a strong communitarian commitment, to the communal-dependence of experience and thought, a cultural-linguistic understanding of tradition. Postliberalism highlights the community as a coherent and integrated sociality constituted by its own distinctive practices and funded by particular patterns of language use that grant the community a way of interpreting its foundational narrative into those practices. For them, this entailed a high ecclesiology that imagined politics as located first within the church community.

Brian Bantum helpfully describes these threads as two projects of theological and ecclesiological reclamation within ethics and political theology. He claims,

> The church today, as well as theological reflection, exists between these two tectonic shifts.... Responding to the dehumanization of certain bodies, some seek to narrate the centrality of dark and female bodies within Christ's own life. Resisting the secularization of Christian ideas, others seek to reclaim the ancient doctrines, the ideas of Christian faith considered as a "tradition." These two projects of reclamation . . . can also be seen as the centers of two distinct paradigms of theological formation that participate in the development of Christian intellectual and pastoral leadership.[9]

His two "tectonic shifts" correspond to the threads I invoked above. Postliberalism, an important representative of the "tradition" paradigm, is a retrieval of what came before liberalism—namely, tradition, orthodoxy, and community (and for Hauerwas, practices and virtues as well). Liberation theology seeks to retrieve the embodied and prophetic characteristics of the gospel that have slipped out amid the Docetic persistence of prioritizing spirituality or rationality over materiality in Western, individualized conceptions of the gospel. Importantly, these are two paradigms of theological formation (ideas versus bodies) that have influenced polarized developments within the church as well. In fact, Bantum contends, "These two theological giants have effectively marked *the* theological trajectories before the contemporary church."[10] The American church then is left with the seemingly exclusive pastoral options of focusing on minds or bodies, tradition or liberation.

As someone firmly in the traditionalist camp during graduate school, I only gradually began to see the ways the bounded ecclesial vision of the traditionalists often blinds us to the pervasive injustice within the institutional church, especially racism. Liberation theologies—especially womanist theology—have drawn attention to the multiple overlapping and intersectional issues of justice that bear upon theological ethics: race, gender, sexuality, class. While it is important to consider the ways that one issue necessarily intersects with and bears upon the others (and I try to do this when appropriate), one book can only do so much; I am not unique in judging that racial injustice was and continues to be foundational and focuses most directly on antiblack racism. (White supremacy certainly transcends many forms of racial oppression, yet history surely demonstrates something unique and peculiar about antiblack racism.) Traditionalists' centripetal focus on a unifying story holding the community together often ignores bodily difference and the ways that racial formation—both from within church and from "outside" culture—impact the formative character of the church community and its witness.

My visits with Cone, along with other experiences detailed in these pages, forever altered my theological (and personal, if one can ever separate the two) perspective on the church, character formation and practice, discipleship, the nation-state, and white supremacy. They were the beginning of this book, which is a critical reflection upon my own theological and ecclesial heritage.

1. Argument

Witnessing Whiteness analyzes the current racial climate of American Christianity and argues for a new ethics of responsibility to confront white supremacy. I uncover this responsibility ethic at the convergence of these two prominent streams in theological ethics: traditionalist and liberationist theology. Then, employing their shared resources and attending to the criticisms that liberation theology directs at traditionalism, it proposes concrete practices to challenge the white church's and white theology's complicity in white supremacy. The concept of witness, so prominent in postliberal theology, is often expressed in narrow, triumphalist rhetoric: witnessing to the gospel before a world that rejects it. Yet, as I argue in this book, drawing on the methodologies of liberation theology, that witness may be a useful tool when turned reflectively upon white theology to uncover the whiteness that so often remains unseen, as well as its devastating effects upon both church and world.

At this point, a few initial definitions are in order. By *white theology*, I mean theology performed by those who have been formed by the culture, social environment, and sociopolitical practices of whiteness. Granted, these racial terms are fluid and tricky—as is apparent with my use of them in this book—since, as examples, not only those with white skin have been shaped by whiteness, and as I discuss in chapter 4, James Cone's insistence that white people can "become black." I offer working definitions of *whiteness* and *blackness* in later chapters. For now, when I invoke *white theology* or the *white church* or *white Christians*, I mean theologians and church members and Christians like me who have internalized the normative ideology of whiteness and write and act out of that identity. This categorization includes most Christians of white skin throughout history, and surely most theology produced by scholars of European descent.

This point also raises the issue of my intended audience. I write this primarily to convince white theologians, Christians, and church leaders, especially in the American context, of the need to take responsibility for white supremacy, and to offer suggestions for how to do that work. This is work that white people need to do ourselves, drawing on resources in black theology but not burdening scholars and ministers of color with teaching us how to not be racist. Other people may, of course, look on and even have much to say or criticize in response (I hope so!). But this is intended to be a critical reflection on and intervention into my own heritage and tradition. While that includes several overlapping and concentric circles of scholars, practitioners, and ministers, those in the smallest and central circle are white postliberals, like myself, who have been influenced by Stanley Hauerwas. To this end, my argument employs concepts and language crucial to this theological perspective, in order to offer somewhat of an immanent critique and, hopefully, a compelling argument. As the circles expand, they include other traditionalists, liberals, and then all white theologians.

It would be easy to point out the explicit racism of white nationalist groups or of some conservative Christians holding on to age-old family prejudices or hopes that "the South will rise again." Calling out explicit forms of racism are often a tactic of "progressive" white folk to distance ourselves from those groups without having to interrogate our own practices and participation in systems that support those same attitudes.

This book makes a deeper and perhaps more painful inquiry: to uncover the way *all* of white theology and white Christian practice is implicated in white supremacy. The notion of white supremacy evokes not only slavery and Klan rallies, but a larger ideological, political, and religious system in which all white people are implicated that often operates in subtle and invisible ways to maintain its system of control. Examining the current manifestations of racism in American churches, exploring the theological origins of white supremacy, and reflecting on the ways whiteness impacts well-meaning, even progressive white theologians, I want to question the depths to which white theology and church practice are distorted by white supremacy, and ask if they can be redeemed. Kelly Brown Douglas begins her book, *What's Faith Got to Do with It*, with the question: If Christianity has been used for centuries to oppress black people, "Was there not something wrong with Christianity itself?" Is there something endemic to Christianity, theologically constitutive of the tradition, that is inclined toward the disregard of certain human bodies?[11] This is not a question of Christianity's complicity in white supremacy as a side project with which our faith was incidentally entangled. It is a question of Christianity's direct contribution to and role in the invention and infection of white supremacy.

Christian theology developed a "collective theological consciousness" that sanctions racial oppression, or what Willie Jennings calls a *diseased theological imagination*.[12] In other words, this problem exists within the tradition of white theology itself. It is not only a distortion in the logic that has been transmitted through the centuries, but also the ongoing process of forming faith communities and communicating the "gospel" that continues to fortify that distorted logic. This disease is an unwillingness to see what lies beneath the gentle veneer of white theology—a refusal to engage with the colonialist, racial logics that supply and shape it. This same malady continues to train theologians, ministers, and Christian leaders not to see what lies beneath.[13]

White supremacy is not something with which the white church has merely been complicit—as if it is something out there, a cultural problem that has seeped into the church or which the church has accommodated. Rather, the origin of white supremacy lies in the church's theology and practice. White supremacy is the world that the church has made. This also means that the Christian church has a particular, and particularly acute, responsibility to address it.

But white theologians have not done so. We have been inattentive to white supremacy, avoiding it for various reasons I explore in this book; we have, in fact, encouraged with our own theology. We have done this through our failure to witness the ways whiteness has inflected our theology, and often our tendency to avoid the issue; thus, we continue to perpetuate the concepts and practices that drive it. "Race is the child of racism," Ta-Nehisi Coates claims in *Between the World and Me*.[14] This book adds to that claim: racism is the child of white supremacy, and white supremacy is the child of Christianity. Now, it may not be the child of Christianity exclusively, through some twisted immaculate conception; it may be the progeny of Christianity and other cultural and scientific factors. But my point is that white Christianity cannot deny its role in producing white supremacy. It is our responsibility. The solution, therefore, does not lie in blaming sinful, "worldly" culture, nor in turning inward to the doctrines and practices of the church that have been corrupted by and through their formation in white supremacy. Any effort to confront and contest the reality of white supremacy must bear this difficult reality. It must take responsibility for the ecclesial origins of white supremacy and recognize the ways white theology has continued and continues to fund it. This requires an ethic of responsibility that draws on the methodological and conceptual resources of black liberation theology. This book, therefore, is not a retrieval project, attempting a return to some unadulterated period or aspect of Christian history before things went wrong. Instead, it interrogates white theology to uncover the elements of white supremacy in its theory and practice and develop a model for confronting and resisting it, specifically through the actions of remembrance, repentance, and reparation.

2. Outline

The book proceeds in three parts. Part I, "What Is Going On?" engages in social analysis to outline our current racial landscape and to determine how and why we have arrived in this situation. Chapter 1 examines our current racial context by addressing and defining the problem of whiteness. Drawing on the work of James Baldwin, womanist theologians, and contemporary sociology, in this chapter I describe whiteness as a process of social and identity formation currently experiencing a crisis of legitimation. This crisis has precipitated colorblindness, leading white people to see our interests and perspectives as universal and blinding us to our epistemological limitations. I conclude by arguing that whiteness presents itself as a "wicked problem" with no identifiable solution.[15] Chapter 2 offers a historical and theological narrative of how we arrived at this moment. I analyze the theological elements that both contributed to the development of white supremacy and were, in turn, distorted and continue to be malformative aspects of white Christian theology. I investigate the ways some of these elements of white supremacy show up in the work of two of America's most influential theologians, Walter Rauschenbusch and Reinhold Niebuhr. The case of these two theologians illuminates the power of white supremacy to corrupt theological personalities and systems despite their best efforts and intentions to resist it. In this chapter, therefore, I establish my claim for the white church in America to take responsibility for white supremacy by demonstrating its theological origins and continuing presence in corrupting even the most well-intentioned white theologians.

Part 2 turns from the social analysis of part 1 to theological analysis. Dietrich Bonhoeffer's question "Who is Christ for us today?" suggests the contextuality of theology and highlights the differing approaches to concrete problems, like racism, among different theological communities. In part II, therefore, I analyze the ways race factors into the two most prominent threads of contemporary Christian ethics: traditionalist and liberationist theologies. To focus the analysis, it engages with the predominantly white *witness theology* of Stanley Hauerwas and the *black liberation theology* of James Cone as representatives of these threads. Chapter 3 analyzes the ways white theology neglects race and white supremacy as topics of ethical engagement. I then offer the influential witness theology of Hauerwas as an example of a theology that fuels colorblindness through the avoidance of race. I argue that Hauerwas and many white theologians are indebted to the concept of tradition and a limited account of story, which have been influenced by whiteness and hinder our ability to see the effects of whiteness in our work. I also identify resources within Hauerwas's work that are useful in confronting whiteness, even if Hauerwas has not deployed them to this end and, in fact, misdirects them in ways that demonstrate his own whiteness. Then, using Cone as a representative of black liberation theology, in chapter 4 I analyze the narrative basis of his ecclesiology as a vision of the church untethered from whiteness. I demonstrate the ways that Cone's ecclesiology contrasts and refines Hauerwas's, and the ways his narrative theology offers more promising theological resources for rightly telling the story of white Christianity in America and offering better witness to our whiteness.

After social and theological analysis, in part III I ask and attempt to answer Martin Luther King Jr.'s famous question "Where do we go from here?" It argues for an ethic of responsibility and then outlines this ethic through concrete practices for congregations' worship and public life to confront white supremacy. The failure of white churches and theologians to reckon with the power of whiteness suggests the need for a new approach: an ethic of responsibility built upon the shared commitments of Cone and Hauerwas, and their mutual appeal to Dietrich Bonhoeffer, as well as the criticisms and corrections that black liberation theology directs at white theology. As a process of formation, an ethic of responsibility promotes incremental, communal action to confront the wicked problem of whiteness through material practices, while also recognizing the lingering challenges of whiteness within a broken and wounded body of Christ. I conclude the book, in chapter 6, by fleshing out this ethic in practical terms through three practices: remembrance, repentance, and reparation. I call the white church to remember and memorialize its invention of white supremacy, publicly repent of its continued complicity and silence, and confront the racial damage it has inflicted through concrete actions of reparation (politically, financially, spiritually).

* * *

In the aftermath of Holocaust and the Christian church's complicity in that ethnic genocide, Reinhold Niebuhr called the church to avail itself of every method of social and scientific analysis that could contribute to understanding and resisting racism. He then added, "but let it not forget its own resources."[16] That is the task I undertake in this book, to redirect and refashion the inevitably tainted resources of the Christian church to peer back at itself and recognize its own sins.

Niebuhr continued with his frustration with liberals' "habit of confessing the sins of the group from which they imagine themselves emancipated."[17] *Witnessing Whiteness* addresses a problem from which I am not emancipated. One of its central themes is that all white people, and especially white Christians, are embedded in systems of white supremacy—and the pages of this book are not immune. It is only in recognizing our captivity to whiteness, and helping one another do the same, that we can prove ourselves of any use to the cause of overcoming white supremacy.

In this book I attempt to tell a more truthful story about our faith, theology, and church practice. It is not a triumphant story; in fact, it is more of a horror story, but hopefully one that points us to the voices and stories of those best equipped to help us escape the grips of white supremacy, for the sake of the world. The book is certainly an insufficient effort, and that is all it can be. There will be errors, missteps, and more repentance to be made afterward. But I write this as one small step in the struggle for our conversion as white Christians. James Cone told me to write about race and white supremacy, and when I made mistakes, he would correct me. Cone is no longer here to do that. But I submit this work in the hopes that those who follow in his wake may do so in his honor and power.

PART I

What Is Going On?

I

Racism at the End of White Christian America

1. Charlottesville

On the morning of August 12, 2017, I watched as white van after white van pulled next to the downtown Methodist church and unloaded groups of eight to ten white men, dressed in white shirts, wearing helmets, and carrying shields and clubs (sometimes a baseball bat, sometimes a two-by-four). I had walked in the dark to a 6 a.m. multifaith prayer service; the night before, our gathering had been interrupted by a crowd of torch-carrying white nationalists marching to a statue of Thomas Jefferson. Neo-Nazis had come to town for the "Unite the Right" white nationalist rally in the park down the street, and they brought with them a menagerie of hate: a torch-wielding, club-carrying, rifle-brandishing garrison of the Ku Klux Klan (KKK) and other white nationalists.

They descended upon Charlottesville, a city famous for its slave-owning founding father, that struggles with its heritage while continuing to obfuscate it with a whitewashed rhetoric of progress. In the summer morning heat they stormed into the streets, fitted for battle, chanting, jeering, marching. As I gathered with a group of clergy, they swarmed within a barricaded park, their rage rising until it was unleashed in a barrage of pepper spray, tear gas, and eventually a car plowing through a crowd of protesters and killing Heather Heyer. Even before the violence of that day, as these men first stepped out of their vans, two things were clear—they were mostly young (college age, high school even), and they were angry. They were angry because someone told them that they were being replaced; that is, white people were losing control of the power we once enjoyed. The country was changing—white people would soon be in the minority, black protesters were in the news every night—and these young whites were angry.

Witnessing Whiteness. Kristopher Norris, Oxford University Press (2020). © Oxford University Press.
DOI: 10.1093/oso/9780190055813.001.0001

They expressed this anger, looking at us and at the black clergy standing next to me, and yelling, "You will not replace us."

Their visible hate emanated from a deeply rooted sense of fear that their regime of domination—the subjugating, hegemonic power long held by white Christian males—would soon crumble amid changing population demographics, shifting religious loyalties, and a growing consciousness of systemic racial oppression. As James Baldwin observed sixty years ago, "[Old orders] have always existed in relation to a force which they have to subdue. This subjugation is the key to their identity and the triumph and justification of their history."[1]

The white nationalist rally in Charlottesville is just one of a number of events in the past few years that have both expressed and triggered the volatile racial climate in which we now live. The election of our first black president led to the election of the man Ta-Nehisi Coates has called the "first white president,"[2] the growing visibility of racialized police violence and awareness of racist mass incarceration led to a new movement for racial justice,[3] heightened public racist and anti-immigrant rhetoric spurred an increase in hate crimes and white nationalist terrorism, and a widening perception gap between the problems encountered by different racial groups in the United States means that white and black folks cannot even agree to basic facts of our contemporary situation. Yet attempting to understand these facts as well as the racialized hermeneutical lenses that refract these facts into divergent perceptions, narratives, and conclusions is an essential task for coming to grips with the forces shaping the nation. In the 1950s Baldwin also contended that the racial problem in America cannot be discussed coherently without bearing in mind its context: the history, traditions, customs, moral assumptions, and preoccupations of the country. Because it is so thoroughly embedded within the social fabric of the nation, he says, "No one in America escapes the effects [of race] and everyone in America bears some responsibility for it."[4] To better analyze these effects and better assess what this responsibility requires, it is important to understand the recent currents that have shaped the contours of our racialized state—trends that led to the visible expressions of fear and hate witnessed in Charlottesville.[5]

This is an especially important task for Christians because the church mirrors the same racial distortions and fragmentations that one observes in society at large, and that appears integral to upholding its continued power. Therefore, when we ask about the problem of race and white supremacy in America, we are necessarily asking about the role of the church. As evident from its early debates about ethnic inclusion (Acts 15), much about the church's practices, liturgy, mission, witness, and politics emerged from the church's division and hostility along ethnic lines.

What is most striking considering the perpetual significance of this issue is the silence of so many white churches and theologians on matters of race, racism, and whiteness—what black theologian James Cone calls "theology's great sin."[6] Even in this current moment of violent white nationalism and renewed social activism, the silence of white churches and white theologians is deafening. Yet, as Toni Morrison says, "Invisible things are not necessarily 'not there.'"[7] Some absences signal; some evasions call attention to themselves. The silence of so many points to an often invisible and implicit racism masquerading as colorblindness.

The task before white theology is to unmask the racism that whiteness inflicts and hides in our churches. Cone, the founder of black liberation theology, insisted that social analysis is necessary to reveal the inner workings and implications of faith within church communities.[8] Foreshadowing the present ethnographic and ecclesial turn in theological analysis, he claimed, "There can be no genuine Christian theology without prophetic self-criticism of the Christian community that gives birth to it."[9] By observing, describing, and critically analyzing the silence and colorblindness of society and especially the church, I attempt in this chapter to uncover the racism—the whiteness—that lies beneath it, animates it, and shields it.

Following these prescriptions in this chapter and the next, I attempt to provide a deeper analysis of whiteness—in society and churches—by filtering social data through the lenses of a legitimation crisis and colorblindness in order to reveal the complexity and difficulty in disentangling the power of whiteness on social and ecclesial life, concluding that it constitutes a "wicked problem" with no easily discernible solution.

2. *Whitelash and the Death of White Christian America*

The 2016 presidential election provides another instructive example of the current climate. On election night, CNN analyst Van Jones famously called Donald Trump's election "A whitelash against a changing country." Trump himself has proven the veracity of this claim. In fact, by giving presidential voice to this whitelash on several occasions, he has bestowed legitimacy upon its leaders. A few days after the tragedy in Charlottesville, as a family mourned and officials cleaned glass and blood from the terror-stricken corridors of the city, President Trump claimed that there were bad guys, very fine people, and blame "on both sides" for the violence that erupted at the white supremacist rally. Employing the same slogans the white nationalists offered as reasons for their fire and fury—"They're trying to take away our culture; they're trying to take away our history"—Trump suggested a moral equivalency between the racists and their resisters, an attempt to resubmerge threats to the regime of white supremacy. A mass shooter targeting Latinos in El Paso in summer 2019 reflected these same sentiments. The administration's policies restricting immigration fused with a flux of voter restriction laws and gerrymandered voting districts appear to be explicit attempts to keep a dwindling white majority in power for as long as possible by finding new ways to disenfranchise voters of color under the guise of colorblind policies. For example, during the 2018 midterm election in my home state of North Carolina, the combination of these policies resulted in Democrats winning 50 percent of the vote while securing only 23 percent of congressional seats.[10]

The election of Trump and support for these nationalist policies were fueled by many whites who felt disenfranchised by a growing ethnic and religious pluralism in America and increasingly intense focus on minority rights and reveal the tight grip of the hegemonic dominance of white supremacy.[11] We've heard repeatedly the statistic that 81 percent of white evangelicals voted for Trump. But less noted is the fact that only 7 percent of black evangelicals and 31 percent of Latinx evangelicals did, confirming that the determinant common factor was not their evangelicalism but their whiteness.[12] This "disenfranchised" group peering longingly back to a monochromatic 1950s and 1960s comprises a significant homogeneity in racial, cultural, and religious identities. That is, a map of the religious identity of many U.S. counties (white evangelical) was a primary predictor of the counties that voted overwhelmingly for Trump.[13] Yet, just before the election, in the summer of 2016, data analyst Robert Jones published a book counterintuitively titled *The End of White Christian America*.[14] What Jones identified as "White Christian America" includes both mainline Protestants and evangelicals, and points to their positions of social and political power through the history of the United States, but particularly in their mutual hopes that the twentieth century would be a "Christian century." Jones describes the White Christian America of the mid-century as follows: "June Cleaver was its mother, Andy Griffith was its sheriff, Norman Rockwell was its artist, and Billy Graham and Norman Vincent Peale were its ministers."[15] While mainline Protestants enjoyed tremendous influence in the first half of the century, as their position (and membership) weakened, evangelicals positioned themselves to become the new face of White Christian America since the 1970s. Yet both groups have grown at ease in their own culturally constructed Zion, reclining on their beds of ivory while failing to grieve, or even see, the ruin that their cultural power has wrought.[16]

White Christians, especially conservative and evangelical Christians, centralized political power in the 1980s with the rise of the Religious Right and Moral Majority. Historian Randall Balmer has argued that though these groups proclaim pro-life issues as their organizing cry, it was race, and specifically school segregation, that functioned as their primary political motivator.[17] This movement began in the 1960s with the so-called Southern Strategy of the Republican Party to highlight anti–civil rights issues to garner favor among southern voters, consolidated with the rise of the Religious Right motivated by the disappointment of white evangelicals in the presidency of Southern Baptist Jimmy Carter, and reached its zenith with the growth of the Tea Party and populist rise of Donald Trump. This last development was supported by key evangelical and "alt-right" leaders, with the endorsement of leaders of the KKK. One of the best examples of the underlying racist motivation of these movements was conservative efforts to simultaneously claim that the election of Barack Obama signaled America's entry into a "postracial" era while relentlessly questioning his religious and national legitimacy.[18] NAACP leader and pastor William Barber, famous for igniting the Moral Mondays movement in North Carolina, observes that the recent events that have brought race to the national forefront are only the most discernible symptoms of a larger social and political movement to maintain white supremacy in response to Obama. In fact, it is crucial to understand that this whitelash, or what Carol Anderson calls *white rage*, is not a new phenomenon but a recurring event every time African Americans make gains toward freedom or equal justice—Jim Crow laws and lynching after Emancipation, the war on drugs after the civil rights movement, and now this whitelash after a black president and ostensible demographic changes.[19]

Barber recalls that the Republicans' Southern Strategy birthed the colorblind model of racism that hides within invisible and "postracial" structural components today.[20] He notes that Richard Nixon's Republican Party did not employ the direct racist language of the segregationists. Rather, they appealed to more nuanced, dog-whistle terms for those with ears to hear—terms like the need for "law and order" and the waste of "entitlement programs," as well as buzzwords like "fiscal responsibility," "big government," "states' rights," and the "undeserving poor."[21] In this way, "The Southern Strategy protected white political power while appearing to be color-blind."[22] Its proponents, and those individuals that propel it still today, he says, are "skilled in the mechanics of defending institutionalized racism without using the language of race."[23] On a deeper rhetorical level, Barber claims that "By using such abstractions, extremists were able to commit" what he calls "attention violence"—that is, manipulating people by distracting them from the concrete consequences of policies by employing language that appeals to their values.[24] Barber offers a keen insight: that colorblindness and the use of abstraction go hand in hand to blind white people not to actual color, but to the concrete effects that white power has on social, political, and religious institutions and structures.

This history and these examples, as well as their lingering endurance in social and political life, point to what Robert Jones has called a "racial perception gap," according to which white Americans and black Americans see and comprehend the same events or realities in vastly different ways. For example, in a 2014 survey, only 14 percent of black Americans said they believe that they and other minorities receive treatment equal to whites in the criminal justice system, whereas 47 percent of white Americans said that about minorities. And this discrepancy has remained consistent over the past twenty years, which becomes most apparent when evaluating reactions to the numerous videos of white police violence against unarmed black people. Whereas almost three-quarters of African Americans see these incidents as part of a broader pattern of abuse and inequality, less than half of whites do.[25] This perception gap is perhaps even more revealing when it comes to attitudes about the best way to bridge racial division. In a 2006 survey, 43 percent of white Americans said the most effective way to improve race relations would be to stop talking about race altogether. By 2012, that percentage had risen to 55 percent, compared to just one out of every three African Americans.[26]

Jones suggests that three factors contribute to this racial perception gap. The first is segregated neighborhoods, due to formal systems of segregation like housing codes and ordinances as well as informal desires for homogeneity. The result, Jones claims, is that whites live primarily in neighborhoods that are insulated from the difficulties facing many African Americans.[27] The second factor is homogenous social networks; most white Americans don't have a close relationship with a single person of color. Specifically, the "core social networks" of whites are 91 percent white, while three-quarters of white Americans have a completely white social network. The statistics are worse for white Christians. Many whites have trouble understanding the anger of African Americans over events in Ferguson or the election of Donald Trump because they live in neighborhoods and exist in social networks insulated from the consequences of those events. They have no one close to them able to challenge their perspectives. Third, Jones notes the lack of civic institutions poised to overcome these gaps and nurture relationships between races.[28] (This does not mean that integration is the solution to racial problems. But it does mean that opportunities for encounter and mutual understanding are a key ingredient to healing.) Here Jones points to the failures of the corporate sector and the public school system, and notably, the segregated character of churches. Eight in ten American congregations are single-race, that is, made up of an overwhelming majority of members of one race.[29] Despite the work of the civil rights movement, the claims of H. Richard Niebuhr in his 1929 *The Social Sources of Denominationalism* still ring true: American churches have accepted "the accommodation of Christianity to the caste-system of human society" and have "draw[n] the color line in the church of God."[30] A long history and many reasons account for this segregation, dating back to the church's role in and justification of colonialism before the birth of the United States.

In fact, sociologists Jason Shelton and Michael Emerson claim that Christianity actually amplifies this racial perception gap rather than providing resources to contract it. Due to the "hyper-segregated" character of American congregations—reflecting the fact that most churches are ten times more segregated than the neighborhoods they are in and twenty times more than neighboring public schools—churches only exacerbate the problem by creating racial echo chambers.[31] Churches, indeed, are making the problem worse. According to Shelton and Emerson's research, white and black Christians understand their own Christian faith through two distinct lenses, shaped by their relationship to the history of oppression and privilege in America. White Christians tend to perceive faith as an individual commitment that leads to a belief in personal merit as the primary determinant of success (think of the Protestant work ethic), while black Christians maintain more of a social view of faith and a structural account of success and failure.[32] This perspective allows black Christians to perceive the ways structural patterns and factors lead to oppression and privilege. White Christians' individualistic worldview—predicated on an individualistic perception of sin and salvation—constrains our ability to perceive these larger institutional, policy, and economic forces. Philosopher Charles Mills calls this "white myopias" and, putting it mildly, claims, "Because of racial privilege, an inherited racialized set of concepts and beliefs, differential racial experience, and racial group interest, whites tend to get certain kinds of things wrong."[33] This myopia makes it difficult, as theologian Jennifer McBride argues, for white Christians to see themselves as bearing any "responsibility to respond with concrete action."[34]

The effects of these cultural patterns are exacerbated by fears of the declining influence of (white) religion. The decline in religious affiliation and church membership in the United States is well documented and does not need to be repeated at length here. Still, this decline is most notable, significantly, in white Protestantism. In 1993, 51 percent of Americans self-identified as white Protestant; by 2014 that figure had fallen to 32 percent. During that same period, the percentage of black Protestants held steady at around 10 percent.[35] When this reality is coupled with dramatic ethnic demographic changes (the U.S. Census Bureau predicting that by 2042 the United States will no longer be a majority-white nation, and that year keeps dropping with every prediction), many whites, and especially white Christians, have begun to feel a sharp sense of dislocation, leading to a nostalgic longing for the glory days of power enjoyed in the past.[36] This is remarkably evidenced in the fact that more than six in ten white Christians believe American culture and way of life have changed for the worse since the 1950s.[37]

The anxieties that many white Americans feel sensing this loss of privilege, power, and familiarity have resulted in serious entrenchment, a psychology of ressentiment grounded in a lost sense of entitlement.[38] In light of this, Jones notes how "this anxious minority swarmed to the polls to elect as president the candidate who promised to 'make America great again'" and predicts that, despite its imminent death, "White Christian America will be survived by significant numbers of its descendants."[39] Jones calls their attempts to hold onto power at all costs "defensive offensives" in which an enclaved community recasts itself as a victimized minority and organizes to preserve its particular social, moral, and cultural values.[40] The changing realities signaling the death of White Christian America triggered the whitelash of the election of Donald Trump, growing empowerment of white nationalist groups, and violence like we witnessed in Charlottesville and El Paso. As Jones concludes, "The waning numbers of white Christians in the country today may not have time on their side, but as the sun is slowly setting on the cultural world of white Christian America, they've managed, at least in this election, to rage against the dying of the light."[41] Thus, the landscape of our segregated society and radically fragmented perceptions of reality fueled by the long domination of White Christian America have set the stage for the last, and sometimes violent, gasps of this dying hegemon. The social and political stronghold of white Christianity is weakening, but its death does not come as a whimper.

3. The Legitimation Crisis of Whiteness

The preceding cultural description requires a more specific analytic frame to uncover the deeper rationales and prerational reactions fueling this whitelash. One way to make sense of these current cultural and ecclesial trends is in terms of a legitimation crisis of whiteness. Melvin Rogers writes that recent events make clear that a "sizeable segment of the population rejects an American future that is more diverse, more inclusive, and potentially more equal. It rejects, in other words, precisely the vision to which Black Lives Matter gave expression."[42] This rejection is an attempt by white Americans to address what they perceive as a cultural "legitimation crisis." By this Rogers means, "They can no longer trust their racial identity to secure for them the entitlements (including economic ones) that it previously had." The recent attention to race brought about through Obama's presidency, the Black Lives Matter movement, and increases in protest and resistance is seen as a loss of primacy, privilege, and prestige. In this way, Rogers helpfully invokes a concept that will more fully develop the phenomenon we are currently experiencing.

The concept of a legitimation crisis originated with sociologist Max Weber and his work on "legitimate domination."[43] Jürgen Habermas has interpreted the concept for contemporary social realities and claims that all social systems and institutions have a need to justify the norms they employ or demand in order to accomplish the integration of any social or political order and induce the loyalty of its participants, subjects, or citizens. This process of legitimation "explains" the institutional order by ascribing cognitive validity to the social meaning it prescribes—in a sense, justifying the institutional order by granting normative dignity to its practical imperatives.[44] In other words, legitimation explains why a member of some collective or system should perform a particular action as well as explaining why things are what they are within any system—and here Habermas refers primarily to cultural, economic, and political systems and institutions. However, when "the legitimating system does not succeed in maintaining the requisite level of mass loyalty," Habermas claims, it falls into a form of identity crisis he calls a "legitimation crisis."[45] "Crises arise," he asserts, "when the structure of a social system allows fewer possibilities for problem solving than are necessary for the continued existence of the system."[46] According to Habermas, when problems outstretch all available resources to solve these problems, a crisis ensues.

All cultures are internalized symbolic universes, what he defines as "world-maintaining interpretive systems."[47] As symbolic and normative realities, these systems need to have an apparent relation to truth—or at least perceived truth even in the form of a constitutional myth (such as that the United States is a white Christian nation). When dramatic changes like the impending loss of white-majority status call this truth into question, a crisis of legitimacy occurs, and those in power employ strategies and mechanisms to maintain these symbolic universes.[48] Building on the work of Habermas, sociologists Peter Berger and Thomas Luckman contend that when a symbolic universe breaks down in the midst of an especially potent legitimation crisis, those in power employ specific procedures of relegitimation, or what they call "conceptual machinery for universe maintenance." When such situations arise, Berger and Luckman argue that "custodians of the 'official' definitions of reality" employ "repressive procedures" to shore up and re-concretize the universe.[49] Common "conceptual machinery" of maintenance includes mythology, theology, philosophy, and science—residing primarily on the discursive, symbolic level but occasionally taking coercive or violent means.[50]

The whitelash that Van Jones observed, the last gasps of White Christian America desperately trying to overcome its crisis of legitimacy, comprise the violently repressive measures designed to retain the old racial order of white domination: Muslim bans, border walls, asylum restrictions, immigrant family separations.[51] Recall Baldwin's observation that orders always exist in dialectical relation to a force they must subdue. This subjugation not only shapes their identity and legitimates their history, but "it is also on this continued subjugation that their material well-being depends."[52] This machinery takes many obvious forms, like immigration bans and vilification of black activists, but also more complicated and subtle forms. The use of conceptual machinery is even easier in our social media age as stories, philosophies, and certainly theologies can easily be deployed and disseminated to shape the social imaginaries of those hell-bent on maintaining control. It works in the shadows, slightly adjusting public policies, shifting language, tightening institutions, redrawing voter districts, insinuating voter fraud to create imagined and structural resistance to any racial progress.[53] Melvin Rogers insightfully recognizes, "Just as the logic of white supremacy involves valuing white lives more than others, it leads to the presumption that white Americans are thus (a) accurate when they describe the context in which they engage nonwhites as threatening and (b) are therefore legitimate in their display of force to extinguish the source of fear"[54]—and we might add, to maintain the cultural hegemony of their "universe."

But the machinery persists at an even deeper, if less perceptible, level.

4. The Problem of Colorblindness

In 1965 *Ebony* magazine published an issue with the title "The White Problem in America." This issue contained an essay written by James Baldwin on white guilt, in which he wrote, "History, as nearly no one seems to know, is not merely something to be read. And it does not refer merely, or even principally, to the past. On the contrary, the great force of history comes from the fact that we carry it within us."[55] History endures like an apparition haunting the structures and attitudes of the present. History does not go away, but simply morphs; racism shapeshifts from chattel slavery and the Middle Passage, to Jim Crow and lynching picnics, to housing codes and religious segregation, to a new middle passage from the inner city to the prison industrial complex and the new lynching tree of uncontrolled police violence on black bodies. The materials change but the goals, structures, and sins remain the same—just more difficult to perceive, confront, and conquer.

The assumption that Baldwin observed in *Notes of a Native Son*—that for black people to become truly human and acceptable they must assimilate to whiteness—has taken another form.[56] In this age of professed colorblindness, African Americans are not "reduced to anonymity" unless they begin to look and act like whites. Rather, their identities, concerns, and bodies, their personalities and experiences have been rendered invisible by a whitewashed lens that professes to "not see color." This is not a condition of assimilation, but a supposed toleration of differences as long as it does not require those in power to change their lifestyle.

White supremacy doesn't require intentional racism, but only the willingness of those in power to benefit from the privilege afforded them by it. Colorblindness assumes that racism is an individual and intentional act, and attributes structural racial inequality to nonracial factors.[57] It has the advantage of appearing innocuous, even virtuous. It convinces us that the election of Obama initiated a "postracial" era and people of all colors now have equal access, protection, and privilege. Yet, as Kelly Brown Douglas observes, "The only thing postracial about this time in the nation's history is the refusal to talk about race."[58] Such refusals mask colorblindness's true identity as the universe-maintaining machinery that renders unseen the structural and systemic controls that reproduce racial oppression. This involves "invisible" mechanisms like the continual segregation of American schools, which were more segregated in the year 2000 than in 1970; political gerrymandering that keeps minorities underrepresented in legislative bodies and with limited potential to impact policies that might change this; and the criminal justice system that imposes black people with longer sentences and more death sentences than whites for the same crimes.[59] Because whites have not been trained to think complexly about race in school, in mainstream discourse, or in social institutions, and because it benefits them not to, "Many whites believe their financial and professional successes are the result of their own efforts while ignoring the fact of white privilege."[60] They form a false belief in meritocracy, that everyone has equal opportunity to succeed and those who do not succeed obviously failed due to their own fault—laziness, licentiousness, and so on—a belief perpetuated by the "American Dream." Inequality is explained by many factors other than systemic racism. Colorblindness fails to account for residual and renewed effects of racism in the United States, including the persistence of wage and wealth inequality and the lack of upward mobility within African American communities.[61] Yet the power of these mechanisms is their ability to operate while keeping white supremacy cloaked and empowered. "White America is largely unconscious and mute, unable to address the question of its identity as white," observes white theologian James Perkinson. "Power normally does not have to give an account of its own basis of operation."[62]

How does colorblindness operate? How do such blindnesses occur? One philosophical answer comes from H. Richard Niebuhr, who suggested that the Self only encounters others through the interpretive equipment of its personal and social past. It interprets others—and their experience, intentions, and reactions—through the lens of its own historical community, "a society which has taught it a language with names and explicit or implicit metaphors and with an implicit logic."[63] This hermeneutical lens binds the Self to the heritage of its particular social past (in the case of whites, a past of unquestioned privilege and belief in meritocratic freedom).

Sociologist Eduardo Bonilla-Silva provides the classic theory of colorblind-ness in his book *Racism without Racists*, and identifies the ways this interpretative lens enables "colorblind" white folks to interpret, explain, and ultimately justify the racial structure of society in a manner that protects white privilege. He iden-tifies four main racial frames through which white people interpret racial data, emerging out of our racial history and formation—even if we do not recognize we are using these frames. First, whites perceive that racial matters and differences are a natural phenomenon rather than a product of history—a process he calls *naturalization*. Through the cultural racism frame, white people avoid the essen-tializing dynamic of attributing racial inequality to biological inferiority, but now consider it a consequence of "cultural" characteristics, such as lack of family struc-ture or conditioned laziness. The frame of minimization simply discounts the role discrimination still plays in hiring practices or neighborhood segregation.[64]

The most significant frame, according to Bonilla-Silva, and the one most important for this study, is abstract liberalism. By employing the core ideas of liberalism in an abstract manner to explain racial matters, whites appear reason-able and even moral while simultaneously opposing practical approaches to racial inequality. The two core tenets of abstract liberalism are the strongly held convic-tions of equal opportunity and individual freedom. The belief in equal opportu-nity allows whites to urge equality while opposing affirmative action because it grants special treatment to a group. It upholds a belief in meritocracy that consid-ers everyone to have equal access and opportunity—and thus equal, individual responsibility to "make it on their own."[65] Yet, the belief in equal opportunity is abstract because it ignores the history and conditions that created the inequality. A commitment to individual choice, often expressed as "freedom" in the United States, permits whites to send children to segregated schools, live in segregated neighborhoods, or oppose group-based solutions to inequality. It is abstract because it neglects the policies that create power differences between races. "If minority groups face group-based discrimination and whites have group-based advantages," argues Bonilla-Silva, "demanding individual treatment for all can only benefit the advantaged group."[66]

These frames help explain white belief in racism as individual prejudice and our blindness to its structural machinery. But how are these racial frames passed on to new generations? Two factors function to shape racial imaginations of com-munities across time. First, environmental cues, according to cognitive scientists, literally shape the brain development of future generations along racialized lines, as early as preschool.[67] Human cognition is extended across time, almost like liv-ing memories, through which the accumulated knowledge of previous genera-tions is passed on to new ones. This happens in the form of linguistic signifiers or environmental cues, what cognitive scientists call "designer environments," which offload cognition into the world—for example, how to use certain tools or inter-pret environmental stimuli—and then shape the brain development of future generations. In the case of white supremacy, for example, the phenomenon of (mostly white) gated communities with nice homes and (mostly black) impover-ished inner cities—both the environmental products of racist knowledge—now shape the racial imaginations of children, imposing a frame, or in George Yancey's words, a "constitutive imaginary background," by which they begin to see and understand the world.[68] The environments, the structures of the world around us, shape our cognition—our patterns of thinking and social imaginations—in a way that, observes Erin Kidd, "one need never vocalize a belief in white supremacy to operate according to its logic and patterns."[69]

Second, racial imaginations are shaped, and the designer environments are interpreted, through the use of stories. Stories form a centerpiece of human com-munication because of their persuasive power. They are the "oldest primordial meeting ground in human experience," Richard Delgado claims. "Their allure will often provide the most effective means of overcoming otherness, of forming a new collectivity based on the shared story."[70] They have this power because they teach us about social structures and prepare us for social situations implicitly and subconsciously. They naturalize our perspectives, or as Bonilla-Silva puts it, they "seem to lie in the realm of the given."[71] Storytelling is powerful because it helps us make sense of the world but, despite its natural and neutral veneer, does so by "serving particular interests without appearing to do so."[72] Dominant groups create stories to construct and reinforce their identity in relation to oppressed groups, and provide them with a forum for "shared reality in which its own supe-rior position is seen as natural."[73]

Thus, stories have a mutually reinforcing effect: we make them as they, in turn, make us.[74] They build consensus, a common culture of shared understandings, and even the character and ethics of a community.[75] Narrative is the most power-ful universe-maintaining machinery of whiteness: it constructs social reality and justifies the world as it is, with white people at the top. Narrative is what Delgado and other Critical Race Theorists understand to be the principal instrument of subordination.[76] The theme of narrative in constructing white supremacy, and its power to deconstruct it, are major themes of this volume going forward. For now, recognizing the role that stories play in shaping the white racial imagination and passing it along is crucial.

Through racial frames, environmental cues, and narrative, the violence of racial oppression implicates even the most well-meaning white people and keeps them oblivious to this reality. It prevents them from seeing the ways in which, as philosopher Charles Mills notes, even poor whites were and are able to affirm the whiteness (or at least receive the benefits it bequeaths) that distinguish them from "the subpersons on the other side of the color line."[77] White people are ferociously barricaded inside a sanitized version of this history (and often gated neighborhoods). Colorblindness, in the words of Baldwin, is founded on white people's "necessity to find a lie more palatable than the truth,"[78] and therefore leaves uninterrogated the assumptions and histories that have caused us to arrive at the current situation.

Colorblindness is therefore the problem of whiteness. Definitions of *whiteness* abound, but for my purposes it is helpfully described by Robin DiAngelo as a constellation of processes and practices that "include basic rights, values, beliefs, perspectives, and experiences purported to be commonly shared by all but which are actually only consistently afforded to white people."[79] "Dynamic, relational, and operating at all times on myriad levels," DiAngelo argues that whiteness simultaneously trades in pretensions to universality while also othering those who are seen as not white. Ruth Frankenburg further delineates whiteness into three registers.[80] First, whiteness "is a location of structural advantage, of race privilege"—the reality of white privilege. Second, "it is a 'standpoint,' a place from which White people look at ourselves, at others, and society." This reflective dimension of whiteness drives the deceptiveness of colorblindness for white people. As Emilie Townes notes, colorblindness has made whiteness an "abstraction . . . distanced from our immediate concerns and material experience."[81] It allows white people the privilege of abstracting from skin color—not seeing color, even our own—and assuming that our access and opportunity pervade universally. White people seem unable to perceive whiteness as a racial category.[82] Third, it refers to a set of cultural practices, though due to its universalizing tendencies, these practices are usually unmarked and unnamed. All three of the registers emerge in the account of white evasion and racial harm I analyze in this book.

The Problem of Whiteness Unseen

Yet an even more insidious dimension to colorblindness often goes untreated in public discourse on the subject. Most often, colorblindness is considered to be the presumption to not see the color of minority others. But colorblindness also names the inability (or refusal) of whites to see their own color. In other words, colorblindness allows whiteness to camouflage itself. Even perceptive whites who acknowledge the existence of systemic social injustice often have difficulty connecting this explicitly to the sordid history of race, rather than simply class or some other social category, and acknowledging that all white people benefit from the systems set in place by antiblack racism. African Americans who suffer the structural effects of racism know this is not true. "What is invisible to white

Christians and their theologians is inescapable to black people," James Cone says.[83] Yet because whites have a dominant hold on the narrative, whites define the terms of the conversation and limit the horizon of vision. "Most whites do not see the problem of race in America as a white problem," write sociologists Joe Feagin and Eileen O'Brien,[84] because racial privilege is lived, unconsciously experienced, rather than seen. Once it became interwoven into the fabric of American culture and institutions, white supremacy could disappear and operate in a clandestine fashion. But this elusiveness had the effect of hiding whiteness from the very people benefiting from the privileges it conveys. Colorblindness, therefore, shields white people from seeing that we too have a color, and seeing the ways in which that color shapes our vision of the world and of others. It is blindness to our own racial formation—that is, the ways we have been conditioned as whites to accept, unquestioningly, the benefits of our whiteness.

More specifically, this is fundamentally a problem of particularity versus universalizing: projecting the particularity of whiteness universally onto the particularity of others because that particularity of whiteness is invisible within our own epistemology. This allows whites to think of ourselves as universal humans who represent all of human experience.[85] As Cone charges, white people "do not recognize the narrowness of their experience and the particularity of their theological expressions. They like to think of themselves as universal people."[86] Our universal, neutral, and natural pretensions make it difficult to discern, much less uncover, talk about, and confront. As the self-appointed universal surveyor and judge, enabled to see and categorize all, the one thing whiteness cannot see is itself.[87]

With this in mind, Emilie Townes more precisely names colorblindness as uninterrogated whiteness. She describes this as the avoidance of asking "how whiteness has been constructed and how it is maintained as a largely uninterrogated phenomenon of alleged neutrality, or worse of being the norm."[88] In short, it is an "evasion of color": a failure to examine the ways that whiteness determines the issues we address, the questions we ask, and the answers we derive from those questions.[89] It is the privilege of ignorance that allows white people to avoid addressing the ways that the particular opportunities, experiences, challenges, and successes afforded to people have been largely determined by one's racial location, and in the case of white folks, likely a privileged racial location. This is what Baldwin was able to perceive over fifty years ago: that "White America remains unable to believe that black America's grievances are real; they are unable to believe this because they cannot face what this fact says about themselves and their country."[90]

These reactions not only reveal the limited abilities of the privileged to empathize but also suggest deeper political implications as well. White Christians' refusal to reckon with our own racial formation restricts our ability to see its effects, and Townes identifies the ways this limited epistemology contributes to the formation of harmful public policies.[91] Angelina Castagno accurately calls this *powerblindness*: white people's avoidance of race is "linked to power and the distribution of resources in the United States."[92] Again, this is an issue of particularity and universalism: when decision-makers do not realize that they have a socially and racially conditioned lens that allows them to see only a small portion of the world based on their experience and context—what Townes calls "unexamined particularity"[93]—and then project this unseen particularism universally upon everyone's experience, then they make policies that do not account for the contexts, struggles, and obstacles that others face.

One example of this attitude can be found in former senator John Danforth's book, *The Relevance of Religion*. Living near St. Louis and reflecting on the events in Ferguson, this white, Episcopal priest, politician, and philanthropist laments the involvement of churches and faith-based groups in the protests outside police stations. Instead, he wishes churches would have taken a more "pastoral approach" rather than the "confrontational demand that individual police officers repent."[94] Only in situations of grave injustice, he says, are such tactics warranted. With this he reveals his epistemological limits as someone—a policymaker—who fails to see the connection between individual actions and systemic injustice, and therefore misunderstands the urgency of those protesting. Examples abound, and such perspectives embed colorblindness within all forms of policy: like housing systems through practices of redlining, or educational resource distribution, or, as Michelle Alexander observes, the criminal justice system.

While many factors contribute to this lack of reflexivity among whites, several of which I have identified above, Townes also addresses two deeper factors. The first is the impact of the Enlightenment focus on the autonomous individual. Our enlightened rationality perceives of the Self as self-asserting and self-determining. Therefore, whites tend to see ourselves as individuals rather than part of a racially socialized collective and accent personal responsibility over against an assessment of structural forces. Second, on a theological level, Townes notes how our soteriological focus on the salvation of the individual soul reinforces this sociological attention to individualism and personal responsibility—the individualist worldview and individualistic conception of sin and salvation noted above.[95] Together, these factors blind us to systemic conditions, as well as corporate culpability for enabling those systemic issues. They compound the privilege of white people to avoid seeing the effects of their whiteness, far from understanding ourselves as agents responsible to contest it.

White Fragility

The most significant consequence of this element of colorblindness—the unin-terrogated character of whiteness—is what Robin DiAngelo calls *white fragility*. White people in North America live in an environment that insulates us from race-based stress, and this privileged insulation builds white expectations for racial comfort while lowering our ability to tolerate racial stress. Whites experi-ence racial comfort in nearly every situation or context, and maintain unchal-lenged expectations to experience this comfort. When it is challenged, we often mistake comfort for safety—because we have never had to develop the nuance to know the difference—and claim that we don't feel safe when confronted with our own racial bias, or given information that challenges our racial assumptions. This is especially true when whites are confronted with accusations of racism in ways that do not conform to their expectations of polite, rational, and unemotional dialogue. Lynn Itagaki calls this "civil racism," the idea that discussions of rac-ism are inherently uncivil, so that decorum prevails over interrogation of white supremacy.[96] Whites have not been conditioned to adequately reason or converse about matters of race and racism because we have been shielded from doing so by the social factors of segregation and perception.

DiAngelo identifies the resulting resistance to racial stress, to any interruption to what is racially familiar, as white fragility.[97] She defines it formally as "a state in which even a minimum amount of racial stress becomes intolerable, trigger-ing a range of defensive moves." These moves can include emotions such as fear, anger, and guilt, as well as behaviors such as argumentation, silence, and leaving the stress-inducing situation. This concept reflects the insight of James Cone that "it is not easy for whites to listen to a radical analysis of race because blackness is truly Other to them—creating a horrible, unspeakable fear."[98]

This phenomenon occurs, DiAngelo says, primarily among those who claim not to be racists, including many white liberals, and especially among those who proclaim some sort of colorblindness. Because whites have the privileged posi-tion of being able to choose when, how, and how much to address racism, when we are confronted with it, or when our advantage to make these choices is identi-fied, it triggers confusion, defensiveness, fear, or just silence. This is often accom-panied by claims of victimization, and these behaviors, in turn, simply reinstate white racial privilege. DiAngelo identifies white fragility as a product of habitus, "a response or 'condition' produced and reproduced by the continual social and material advantages of the white structural position."[99] Triggers of white fragility can include not only direct challenges that one's behavior had a negative racial impact, but also include challenges to objectivity (that one's viewpoint is shaped by their whiteness), challenges to perceived equality (that access to a good is unequal between races), or challenges to white comfort (when people of color choose not to protect the racial feelings of white people). In these situations, and others, white people do not know how to respond in constructive ways because "whites have not had to build the cognitive or affective skills or develop the stamina that would allow for constructive engagement across racial divides."[100]

And herein lies the paradox of the problem: as white objection to racism increases (racism is bad), so does white resistance to acknowledging our own complicity in racism (but I am not racist). Thus, "At the same time that it is ubiquitous," DiAngelo argues, "white superiority also remains unnamed and explicitly denied by most whites."[101] This is the belief that "race" exists in people of color, so whites never have to envision ourselves as racialized subjects. We are free from carrying the burden of race. This allows whites to spend time and energy on other issues, and enervates the stamina to give sustained attention to an issue as charged and uncomfortable as race.[102] This "racism without racists" paradox further evidences colorblindness and whiteness as wicked problems.[103]

5. Conclusion: The Wicked Problem of Whiteness

Yet another level to the problem of whiteness is its uncanny ability to morph, shapeshift, adapt, and mask its violence. Recall William Barber's insight that white power employs strategies of abstraction in order to commit its colorblind violence.[104] This makes it an especially difficult monster to catch, much less to eradicate.[105] As M. Shawn Copeland observes, "Racism is no mere problem to be solved; it is a way in which we define our reality, live the most intimate moments of our lives. Racism is not something out-there for us to solve or fix; racism is in us, sedimented in our consciousness" and institutions.[106] One of the most significant symptoms of white supremacy is the need to deny that problems exist because of white supremacy. As someone once said of the devil, the greatest trick white supremacy ever pulled was convincing white people that it doesn't exist. Melvin Rogers contends that we must consider "the possibility that white supremacy generates far too many psychological, libidinal, cultural, political, and economic goods to be sufficiently destabilized or decentered." He continues,

> The goods, although not few in number, that seemingly come from a racially inclusive society that affirm the equal dignity of persons appear far too weak to create an ethical society that can find institutional and cultural support. Overcoming this impasse suggests, at a minimum, that tinkering within the existing structures of the United States or imagining that those structures would permit a radical transformation of values would simply not match the gravity of the problem.[107]

This analysis suggests that racism, or more specifically white supremacy, in an age of colorblindness has reached the status of a "wicked problem"—and perhaps it always has been. Religious ethicist Willis Jenkins develops this term, first coined by Horst W. J. Rittel and M. M. Webber, and describes a *wicked problem* as one so complex that it allows for no determinate solution. Responses assuming that some definite solution exists only obscure the fundamental character of the problem.[108] Jenkins uses the term to describe and encapsulate the gravity and shiftiness of climate change, as a problem that outstrips our capacities to determine an adequate solution. And I believe that the current climate of racism, with its invisible and colorblind nature—which leads to a paralyzing fragility on the part of white people—evinces a similar character. It is not a problem for which we have arrived at a practical solution, for example, like we have now achieved for eradicating global poverty (if we just had the willingness to do so). Rather it is a problem more akin to climate change, for which we can only see incremental solutions to slow its progress, not its resolution.

Jenkins further describes wicked problems in the context of moral and religious traditions' attempts to address such problems. When new problems appear to outstrip the competence of a tradition or religion, he writes, "The meaning carried by a tradition's way of life is jeopardized until its participants create a way to extend its interpretation to a new domain." Only when a tradition recognizes its own incompetence can it begin to produce "reform projects capable of generating new possibilities of action that can be recognized by its members as legitimate interpretations."[109] In such grave circumstances, we must recognize that religious traditions and communities may at times find themselves incapable of identifying a solution to a particular contextual problem. They may not yet have developed the conceptual resources with which to even properly describe the problem, much less address it. In such circumstances the first need is an acknowledgment of moral uncertainty, even moral incompetence, to address an issue as a tradition is currently configured. At those times, greater attention to the concrete reality of the problem, the concrete realities of those who are suffering in light of the problem, will help a tradition in its deliberations about what sort of problem this is, and what types of responses may be legitimate, necessary, or faithful.

Visible explosions of white supremacy like I witnessed in Charlottesville—and we have since seen in a Pittsburgh synagogue or an El Paso Walmart—are only the symptoms of a deeper, wicked problem. White supremacy not only describes individual actors: Dylann Roof or the Charlottesville ralliers. It is a system that implicates all white people. The danger doesn't only carry a Nazi flag but sits in our pews, stands in our pulpits, and occasionally tells racist jokes, talks of immigrant "invasions," cites "cultural differences," or identifies problems "on many sides." The more pressing problem is everyday white supremacy masquerading as colorblindness. The casual disinterest, appeals to unity and sameness, and premature calls for reconciliation by many white Christians leave us no better than those the prophet Jeremiah admonished for "superficially healing the brokenness of my people by saying, 'Peace, peace,' when there is no peace" (Jeremiah 6:14).

This chapter has attempted to address what is going on—what racism looks like at the end of white Christian America. It runs deeper and is more tightly entangled than imagined, yet often hidden from the sight of white people. This makes what's happening now even more difficult to confront. To have any chance of challenging this wicked problem of whiteness, white fragility, and colorblindness, we need to take a deeper look at the role of Christianity in the development and deployment of white supremacy. While in this chapter I have examined the symptoms and analyzed the immediate reactions to whiteness, the next task is to uncover its roots and diagnose its causes, even if they reside much closer to home than we want to admit. White Christians must begin to see that white supremacy is our invention. I turn to that task in chapter 2.

2

The Theological Origins
of White Supremacy

1. The Polluted Waters of Baptism

In graduate school I planned to write a dissertation on James Cone, the founder of black theology—a dissertation that did not concern race. My research interests were in political theology and the American church, and I wanted to compare the ecclesiology of Cone to that of Stanley Hauerwas, one of the most influential contemporary theologians writing about the church. I considered Cone and Hauerwas to be the most prominent representatives of the two dominant strands of Christian ethics today. Yet, in my two-thousand-word dissertation proposal featuring the architect of black liberation theology I did not include the word *race*. I did not even mention *racism, blackness,* or *whiteness*. To me, Cone was an obvious choice for a study in church and politics. But at the time, like many other white theologians, I didn't consider racial justice to be a significant theological factor in my work or a major problem for the politics of the American church.

Ten days later a grand jury in Ferguson, Missouri, failed to indict white police officer Darren Wilson in the shooting death of black teenager Michael Brown. This sparked a nationwide controversy and protests that only grew in intensity following the high-profile deaths of many other unarmed African Americans. A national movement grew, taking the name Black Lives Matter and developing a new racial consciousness, yet white theologians were slow and floundered in their responses to a fraught situation.

I found it increasingly difficult to think of church and politics in the abstract terms I had outlined. Far too slowly I came to realize that the story of the church in America is also the story of race. I had evaded the issue of race for years, failing to see the integral role white supremacy played in any account of ecclesiology in the American context, which simply highlights the power of white supremacy to

Witnessing Whiteness. Kristopher Norris, Oxford University Press (2020). © Oxford University Press.
DOI: 10.1093/oso/9780190055813.001.0001

blind white Christians from seeing the depths and history of our implication in
its oppression.

In her landmark book *The New Jim Crow*, Michelle Alexander contends that
white supremacy "became a religion of sorts." By this she means that it operates
"as a deeply held belief system based on 'truths' beyond question or doubt."[1] In
our current moment it may be even more instructive to say that white supremacy
is a theological innovation—an invention, specifically, of the Christian church.
My contention is that beyond white fragility, blindness to systemic racism, and
a universalized (white) ethic, the deepest obstacle to racial justice for Christians
is a failure to acknowledge the Christian theological origins of white supremacy.

Theologian and pastor Brad Braxton writes of a visit to the slave castles of
Ghana, the last stop and holding place for millions of Africans before they were
prodded onto ships bound for the Americas. Many were forcibly baptized, stripped
of their communal and familial identities and bound sacramentally to their new
white, Christian masters.[2] In Cape Coast, he reports, a slave dungeon sat directly
beneath the chapel in which the European Christians held their worship services.
At another castle in Elmina, a slave fort constructed by the Portuguese ten years
before Columbus's arrival in the New World, Braxton observed that "the slave
auction block was literally beneath the chapel used for worship."[3] Reflecting on
these spectacles, Braxton says, the church was literally "propped up by the backs
and bones of enslaved Africans." This is not only true regarding Christian slave
traders in Africa but in America as well. Enslaved people were not only responsible for building governmental structures like the White House and Capitol,
but religious institutions like Georgetown and Yale Universities. In fact, by 1767
the Jesuit order owned the greatest number of Africans of any institution in the
Western Hemisphere.[4]

Like the dark waters of the Atlantic, the white church's baptismal waters are
not pure, Braxton concludes; they are polluted with the blood and dead bodies of enslaved Africans. If churches do not begin to reckon with the reality of
these toxic waters and start taking responsibility for our collective history—and
present—we must ask ourselves if we are simply baptizing one another into a
church of white supremacy.[5]

It is simply too hard to deny the white church's silence during the black freedom movement of the 1950s and 1960s, its support of Jim Crow laws and lynchings, and its justification of slavery and proclamation of a slaveholder gospel that
taught enslaved people to maintain fidelity to their masters as Christian obedience. Yet most white theologians neglect this dark side of Christianity in their
work. The few white theologians who do address the legacy of white supremacy, structural racism, or colorblindness generally identify them as external

problems: they are evils in which the church is only complicit, sins that are "brought to church," and ways we have been "shaped by 'the world.'"[6]

My contention in this chapter is that the problem is stronger than mere complicity and runs deeper than most white theologians want to admit. Theologian Willie Jennings indicts Christianity in the development of white supremacy through its collusion with what he calls a "diseased social imagination" of colonialism and European superiority.[7] Consequently, white supremacy is the product of what we might call Christianity's diseased theological imagination. Attributing white supremacy to the world outside the church obscures our role in its development. White supremacy is not something in which the white Christian church is merely complicit—as if it is something "out there" that we let escape into our churches or something to which the church simply lent theological justification. White supremacy is not a result of the church assimilating to the world or being co-opted by external worldly liturgies or practices. Rather, it is a result of liturgies and practices inherent to the church itself—of malformative liturgies and practices that the church actually gave to the world. White supremacy was not simply justified by Christian theology but invented by it.

Sociologist Joe Feagin shows how this "white racial frame"—by which he means the racist narratives, ideologies, imagery, and attitudes that shape our discriminatory actions and systems—began developing during colonialism. Yet he concludes that "after developing an extensive colonial system," Christian colonizers developed the ideology of whiteness to "rationalize, explain, and structure" how they could commit such atrocities. For him, white supremacy was merely "dressed up in religious language" and "religiously sanctioned."[8] While this analysis moves us deeper into the problem, I am arguing that the origins of white supremacy reside in theology itself.[9] Thus, I believe the white church will never fully confront and contest the depth of the problem—nor our responsibility for it—if we do not begin to see it as a failure of our theology itself. Again, as Kelly Brown Douglas pointedly asks, if Christianity has been used for centuries to oppress black people, "Was there not something wrong with Christianity itself?"[10]

In this chapter I analyze Douglas's question. My task is to assess how white supremacy developed out of the church and its theology, but also to uncover the impact that development had reflectively upon and within the church—contorting and distorting its theology. The relationship between Christian theology and white supremacy is a mutually reinforcing, symbiotic one, suggesting the important task of identifying the ways white Christian theology is responsible for the diseased imagination and concrete practices of white supremacy, and responsible to do something about it.

My argument proceeds in three steps. First, I give a brief historical account of the theological roots of white supremacy, identifying several key episodes in its theological development. Next, from this account I draw out four theological elements that contributed to the development of white supremacy and were, in turn, distorted and continue to be malformative aspects of white Christian theology. These elements demonstrate the way that this corrosive relationship between theology and white supremacy persists. Finally, to further demonstrate these claims I investigate the ways these elements of white supremacy show up in the work of two of America's most influential theologians, Walter Rauschenbusch and Reinhold Niebuhr. Their cases illuminate the power of white supremacy to corrupt theological personalities and systems despite their best efforts and intentions to resist it. This chapter, therefore, illustrates why I believe the white church in America should take responsibility for white supremacy by demonstrating its theological origins and continuing presence in inflecting and corrupting even the most well-meaning white theology.

2. The Theological Invention of White Supremacy

In 1554, three ships bearing the names of Trinity, John the Evangelist, and Bartholomew set sail for the coast of Guinea from England. These voyages undertaken by Christian enterprisers—on ships bearing theological names, hoping to mine the abundant resources of this "dark" continent—returned with five Africans, the first black enslaved people to set foot in England (though the Portuguese and Spanish had been enslaving Africans for the past century). As Joseph Washington comments, "Extracted from Africa and transported to England on waves of symbolism, these first black slaves were far from repulsive to Englishmen of Puritan pride and piety."[11] In just over half a century the next generation of English entrepreneurs would bring the first African enslaved people to the shores of the American colonies. Beginning with the arrival of twenty-something enslaved people from the Ndongo region of West Africa, stolen by an English privateer from a Portuguese ship, these first enslaved people were sold to residents of Jamestown in 1619. By 1700 the slave population of the colony of Virginia would reach eight thousand.

By 1594, 47.9 percent of ships arriving in the Americas were already part of the Atlantic slave trade, and by the turn of the nineteenth century, ships had brought three times as many African enslaved people to the British colonies as white Europeans.[12] The Atlantic became a "conveyer belt to early death in the fields of an immense swath of plantations that stretched from Baltimore to Rio de Janeiro and beyond."[13] Before it was all over, between 10 million and 15 million Africans would be ripped from their land and imported to the New World, not counting those who perished in the Middle Passage or in slave castles on African shores.

But what led European Christians to such depths of depravity? As the names of the slave ships sailing on that "wave of symbolism" suggest, the white supremacy that animated the institution of slavery was rooted in Christian theology and promoted by Christian churches. Tracing the theological development of white supremacy requires gaining perspective on several historical episodes before and after this moment. These moments suggest a thread that runs through early efforts to distinguish Christianity from Judaism, church-funded anti-Semitism transitioning to supersessionism, colonial conquest resulting in slave trade, and the uniquely American form of racism. The thread woven through them is one of European Christians attempting to make sense of alterity and bodily encounter with the theological tools at their disposal—of religious difference morphing into racial difference. The story that follows traces these particular moments and identifies the theological ingredients that began mixing at an early stage to form white supremacy.

The "Enlightenment Construction of Race"

First we must address many scholars' claims of later and more secular origins for race and racism. Journalist Jamelle Bouie summarizes one popular belief: "Race as we understand it—a biological taxonomy that turns physical difference into relations of domination—is a product of the Enlightenment."[14] Similarly, postcolonial philosopher Emmanuel Chuckwudi Eze concludes that Enlightenment philosophy was instrumental in generating and institutionalizing European ideas about race.[15] Though primitive forms of the modern conception of race began taking shape in the fifteenth and sixteenth centuries, it took the scientific thought of the Enlightenment to construct a biological racial taxonomy, so the argument goes. Only then did beliefs in a natural superiority of whiteness capture the Western imagination and begin structuring its political and economic institutions. For scholars including Cornel West and historian Ivan Hannaford, it was in fact the displacement of theology as queen of the sciences created the conditions for racism to develop. West pins the origin of modern conceptions of race and practices of racism to "the classificatory categories and the descriptive, representational, order-imposing aims of natural history" that emerged during the Enlightenment. He tells the story as an "Enlightenment revolt against the authority of the church."[16] Hannaford argues that the concepts of race and racial superiority were necessarily achieved by "the setting aside of the metaphysical and theological scheme of things for a more logical description and classification."[17] In this portrayal, the *loss* of theology fostered the rise of white supremacy.

This scholarly focus on the Enlightenment as the origin of racism, however, overlooks the role of Christianity in developing white supremacy before the

Enlightenment period, and in nurturing its maturation during the Enlightenment. Historian Terence Keel, in his book *Divine Variations*, argues that the European "stories" that surface in the Enlightenment about the origins and diversity of human life, while pretending to encompass universal, scientific objectivity, have a particular origin that frames their attempts to explain race: Christianity.[18] Christian intellectual history shaped later Enlightenment scientific efforts to construct theories about ethnic and racial variations in humanity.[19] West and others too easily discount the impact of the church, not only in promulgating biblical accounts of racism but also in producing white supremacy before, independent of, and in collusion with these Enlightenment developments. Even by the time of the Enlightenment, the persistent role of theology in shaping cultural, scientific, and political thought is apparent. Enlightenment liberalism and theology are not so easily untethered.[20]

Take John Locke, himself an investor in a slave-trading company. He wrote into the Fundamental Constitutions of Carolina a provision declaring that enslaved people could be "of what opinion or Religion soever. . . . But yet, no Slave shall hereby be exempted from that civil dominion his Master has over him, but be in all other things in the State and condition he was in before."[21] In fact, most colonial legislation codified this thought, declaring that baptism was not a reason for emancipation.[22] Here, in declaring that conversion does not alter the status of the slave, Locke is making a theological claim. This legal provision is based in liberalism, but one predicated upon a prior, even age-old theological distinction between body and soul: salvation of the soul does not demand liberation of the body. If Christian theology presented a problem for slavery, then Christian theology was needed in order to develop an adequate resolution.

In a world still dominated by Christianity, theology was necessary to make sense of new encounter and bodily difference, and ultimately to legitimate the subjugation of other human beings. In this way, theology offered a theory of white supremacy that would draw on the pseudoscientific "evidence" of the Enlightenment to weave a theological rationale of black physical, moral, and spiritual inferiority.

Blood and Conquest

Though the modern, scientific concept of race may not have emerged until the Enlightenment, one can detect the tentacles of white supremacy spreading from the moment that bodily difference—especially regarding skin tone—converged with and eventually superseded religious difference in delineating insiders and outsiders.[23] The strange cocktail of theological elements that would combine to invent white supremacy began mixing well before Enlightenment, even in the earliest moments of Christianity itself. Crucially, then, white supremacy was not the result of setting theology aside, but was precisely a theological and ecclesial invention.[24]

The theological origins of white supremacy lie at the point at which religious difference morphed into racial difference, especially around the status of Jewishness. That is, before European explorers and slave traders set foot in Africa or America, white supremacy appears to develop out of Christian attempts to identify Jewishness as a race, prior to a well-established account or definition of race. A few historical episodes mark this transition. One of the clearest and earliest pieces of evidence of Jewishness becoming racialized comes from the controversy over the "Jewish Pope" in 1130. When Pope Anacletus II, whose great-grandfather had been Jewish, contended for the seat, theologians as venerable as Bernard of Clairvaux clamored to oppose him. Four generations after conversion, the descendant of a once-Jew was still a Jew, portending already the impotence of baptism upon racial difference.[25] As historian Robert Stacey contends, "There was clearly an irreducible element to Jewish identity in the eyes of many Christians, which no amount of baptismal water could entirely eradicate."[26] Jewish conversion, in this way, projected an early instance of hybrid identity, whereby the convert passed as Christian interiorly—as a matter of soul—but not bodily, where a person's appearance and lineage betrayed one's true racial identity. Race became marked upon the body. As medievalist Geraldine Heng puts it, "Jewish bodies were always giving themselves away."[27]

Heng focuses on the story of Jews in England in the twelfth and thirteenth centuries to demonstrate how medieval Europe had already begun understanding Jewishness in racial terms. She argues that what appeared to be contentious financial and religious relationships between Jews and Christians betrayed a more significant difference. Considerable Christian debt to Jewish lenders led to an identification of Jews with usury,[28] resulting in mass executions of Jews for violating financial law. In 1189–1190, 10 percent of English Jews were slaughtered and documents of debt to Jews were destroyed.[29] She suggests that because these executions were actually orchestrated not by lower-class subjects indebted to Jewish lenders but by members of the powerful gentry, they were not motivated by economics alone. Additionally, medieval stories of host desecration (tales of Jewish people attempting to destroy the Eucharistic wafer), shaped the religious imaginations of Christians toward their Jewish neighbors and led to further executions.[30]

The church seemed almost obsessed with marking and ensuring Jewish difference.[31] A series of decrees from the Fourth Lateran Council in 1215 began imposing regulations on the activities of European Jews. The most significant and foreboding imposition was the requirement in Spain and England that Jews wear

a badge of identification.[32] This ruling was motivated, in part, by the fear that
"through error Christians have relations with the women of Jews and Saracens."[33]
A Statute of Jewry issued by the English Crown in coordination with the church
segregated Jews into their own towns and declared, "no Christian shall go to bed
nor rise up among them," as well as demanded that any Jewish person age seven
or older must wear a yellow badge.[34] This not only evinces a fear of intimacy but
constructs appearance as a way to distinguish and categorize Jews as a people.
That is, concern over the mixing of blood suggests a shifting ambiguity among the
categories of religious and ethnic identity. In fact, Heng concludes that Canon
68, the rule in the council requiring Jewish badges, "thus in effect instantiates
racial regime, and racial governance, in the Latin West through the force of law."[35]

   Though Jews had been persecuted across Europe for centuries, mass executions and ritual murders of Jewish people increased after the ruling in 1215, and
many Jews began converting—not always by choice—to Christianity. This new
ecclesiastical class of people, known in Spain (where persecution was the strongest) as *conversos*, gradually became known as *marranos*—or swine—because
church officials viewed them as religious frauds.[36] The first tribunal of the Spanish
Inquisition in 1480 further infused racial meaning into theological categories by
instituting a test of blood purity, which "had the effect of turning the search for
heresy within the faith into a search for the defilement of blood wherever it might
be found."[37] This test targeted the formerly Jewish marranos, who were obviously
unable to prove purity of Christian blood. While the idea of blood purity was
not a full-fledged concept of race, it blurred theological categories with those
that began approximating race and added a new identity marker to the ecclesiastical orders that had previously divided groups of people.[38] Before the invention
of a systematic and biological racial taxonomy, this innovation marked a significant shift in the development of white supremacy. These religious and political
events suggest public and ecclesiastical practices of supersessionism, functioning
to assign Jewishness a racial designation and then replace it through badge or
execution with a white, Christian center.

   This shifting notion of Jewishness as a race and focus upon blood purity as a
marker of religious identity set the stage for a "racially" charged colonial encounter with another form of otherness. Twelve years after the first tribunal of the
Spanish Inquisition, in the same year Columbus set sail for his ultimately genocidal "discovery" of the Americas, the Catholic monarchies of Ferdinand and
Isabella expelled all Jews and Muslims from the territory of Spain. This spiritual victory over its enemies linked Christian faith and European genealogy at
the very moment European Christians began encountering ethnic others in the
Americas.[39] This allowed the Spanish colonizers, and the church that supported
them, to claim divine favor on their missions as they encountered differently

bodied people in the New World. The theological foundation for racial difference began in blood and, with colonialism, transferred to skin.

Upon Columbus's triumphant return, Pope Alexander VI issued two papal bulls in 1493, now known as the founding documents of the "Doctrine of Discovery." *Inter caetera* and *Dudum siquidem* gave the Spanish monarchs authority to expropriate any new land that was not owned by a Christian lord.[40] Earlier papal decrees had already provided legitimacy for the slave trade of Africans by Portuguese explorers. These statements reasoned that Africans were religious enemies and granted explorers full authority "to invade, search out, capture, vanquish, and subdue all Saracens and pagans whatsoever, and other enemies of Christ wheresoever placed, and reduce their persons to perpetual servitude."[41] Behind the missiological veneer of evangelism resided an imperial effort to conquer infidels, now marked as such by skin tone.

In this context, white identity was taking shape as a theological identity born out of European attempts to make sense of their encounter with people who did not fit into their preestablished Christian taxonomy of insiders and pagans.[42] Physical characteristics and blood lineage now signaled important anthropological distinctions between superior and inferior humans. Theologian Willie Jennings and historian Anthony Pagden both point to the story of Gomes Eanes de Zurara as the beginning of modern, race-based slavery, a colonial product of theological white supremacy. Zurara was the royal chronicler for Prince Henry of Portugal who recorded the day in August 1444 when the first human cargo from Africa set foot on European soil for the prince's inspection.[43] After recording Prince Henry's pleasure at all the "souls that before were lost," Zurara attended to their bodies. He divided the Africans into categories—some "white enough, fair to look upon" and others that were "black as Ethiops, and so ugly, both in features and in body, as almost to appear the images of a lower hemisphere."[44] Drawing on the writings of Zurara and countless others who also began categorizing people according to skin tone in this period, Jennings claims that the ordering of existence from white to black signifies the beginnings of racial formation on a global scale. Out of this developed the conceptual frame of whiteness, often invisible, always juxtaposed with blackness in such a way that "black bodies are the ever-visible counterweight of a usually invisible white identity."[45]

In European Christians' attempts to evaluate the new people it encountered in Africa and America, the question of one's ability to be saved became indexed to skin color. The dark-skinned humans encountered in colonial missions were spiritually questionable, making white skin the marker of soteriological security. In fact, it was because the peoples of the New World and Africa were not under God's salvific grace that they could be ruled.[46] "Dark skin came to symbolize, both in Africa and America, the voluntary and stubborn abandonment of a race in sin," writes Roger Bastide.[47] The original missional mandate to convert and save evolved into an obsession not only to "civilize" for the sake of salvation, but also to classify humans, as white superiority subtly replaced salvation within the same structure of theological comparison. Theologian James Perkinson observes that the question "Are you savable within the economy of salvation, determined by Christ?" became "Are you orderable within a taxonomy of civilized humanity, determined by whiteness?"[48] Whiteness indicated a high probability of salvation at the top and then moved along a sliding scale of darkness, with black bodies being the least likely to be saved—except perhaps through force or slavery.

In this way, theological hierarchy became a tool for colonialist evaluation, assessing bodies socially, politically, physically, and spiritually.[49] Jennings argues that from the first moment of colonial discovery, whiteness "evolved into a method of understanding the world"—ordering judgments regarding who was capable or incapable of rationality, morality, and religion.[50] Being white placed one at the symbolic center of an expanding world, and whiteness became "a way of organizing bodies by proximity to and approximation of white bodies."[51] Blackness was "more than skin deep"; it penetrated to the person's character and soul.[52] In short, salvation became white. As the Reconstruction-era hymn proclaims, being saved was simply a matter of being "whiter than snow."[53]

According to Jennings, racial agency was fundamentally a "theologically articulated way" for Europeans to understand their white bodies in relation to the new territories and peoples they encountered. "Before this agency would yield 'the idea of race,' 'the scientific concept of race,' the 'social principle of race,' or even a fully formed 'racial optic' on the world," he argues, "it was a theological form."[54] Put simply, white supremacy emerged before and out of colonialism in its development of race as a theological tool of evaluation and later justification for slavery.

Jennings's claim is that Western Christianity lives within a "diseased social imagination": "the Christian theological imagination was woven into a process of colonial dominance. Other peoples and their ways of life had to adapt, become fluid, even morph into the colonial order of things, and such a situation drew Christianity and its theologians inside habits of mind and life that internalized and normalized that order of things."[55] The church established the framework through which Europeans would make sense of the differently bodied others they encountered through exploration and conquest.[56] And these violent encounters at the bows of ships christened with divine and apostolic titles not only spawned one of the most devastating institutions the world has ever seen, but reflexively altered the shape and integrity of Christian theology in ways the church has yet to fully address.

Slavery created such a distance from a subject position that the enslaved body became, in a real sense, simply "real estate"—a commodity.[57] Slave merchants and traders "transformed African bodies into perishable goods and fragile services."[58] At the auction block, slave prices could be based on particular bodily features or characteristics, or enslaved people were simply sold by the pound. Orlando Patterson writes, "Hands were opened and shut and looked at inside and out. Arms and legs were felt to decide whether slaves were muscular and regular. Backs and buttocks were scrutinized for the welts that heavy blows with a whip usually left. Necks were rubbed or pinched to detect any soreness or lumps. Jaws were grasped, fingers were run into . . . the teeth and gums could be seen."[59] As Toni Morrison describes, a black person was reduced to "the dollar value of his weight, his strength, his heart, his brain, his penis, and his future."[60] As the auctioneers and slaveholders touched, manipulated, controlled, and punished black flesh in a liturgy of domination, black bodies lost their humanity and became objects.

Epidermal logic captivated most European—and later, American—theology, both Roman Catholic and the emerging Protestant strands. Colonial theology placed white Christians at the top of the human scale of being, and now their mandate was to subdue the earth. Those whose skin tone deviated from this white norm were religious, moral, and intellectual degenerates. The institution of slavery and the terror of the auction block were constructed to reinforce this normalization, deconstructing particular human beings into functional bodies that were useful and available for manipulation, economic exploitation, and sordid pleasure.

From the first moments of their encounter with nonwhite others, colonists created the conditions for their sustained social superiority through exploitation and violent control. They did so with the support of a church and its theology that had sold its soul to provide legitimation for the exploitation, possession, and dehumanization of dark bodies—predicated upon a centuries-long process of developing racial difference out of religious difference. Theological concepts like creation, election, and sovereignty were baptized into the colonial agenda of comparing these newly discovered bodies: sorting them into insiders and outsiders, those who had been created further from and closer to the "elected" Christian norm of the white European Whiteness had become the marker of true Christianity—God's chosen people. All others—those in need of conversion, often through the catechetical method of slavery—were organized around this racial center. Thus, systematic theology began to develop around this racial center as well. As Jeannine Hill Fletcher contends, "Rather than an anomaly in the theological discipline," whiteness came to express "a dominant theological outlook by which non-White, non-Christian persons have been assessed along a hierarchy of humanity."[61] The Christian evangelistic impulse became systematically wedded to a "sliding scale of humanity [that] could be seen in God's favor on [white] Christians and God's curse on [non-white] Christians."[62] These proclamations and practices clearly cannot be dismissed as simple misuses of theology, but theologically generated convictions themselves.

3. Malforming Theology

In her account of the Atlantic slave trade and personal journey along a Ghanian slave route, *Lose Your Mother*, Saidiya Hartman claims, "The stories we tell about what happened then, the correspondences we discern between today and times past, and the ethical and political stakes of these stories redound in the present."[63] The story told in the previous section sets the stakes for Christianity by suggesting a symbiotic relationship between Christian theology and white supremacy. Theology did not simply invent white supremacy, but this invention reflected back upon the church to reshape its theology in the image of its newly invented whiteness. The Christian tradition funded a collective theological consciousness that sanctioned a racial hierarchy and provided resources for the oppression of human beings that fell on the underside of this taxonomy. As theologian Kelly Brown Douglas puts it, Christianity provided a "sacred canopy" for racism, and thus found its own tradition malformed and continually malforming in the wake of this alliance.[64]

Since the relationship is symbiotic, parsing the contributing factors from the corrupted effects is less urgent. The crucial task is collectively identifying the ways Christian theology is responsible for and responsive to this diseased imagination. In this section I draw from the earlier historical account to identify four key theological elements that contributed to the development of white supremacy and that, in turn, continue to be malforming aspects of white Christian theology. Some were present at the beginning of Christian faith.

Emerging Dualisms

Christianity emerged with three sets of dualisms structuring the thought of early writers and thinkers on materiality. First, as it developed within a Hellenized context, Christianity quickly adopted elements of Platonic thought, especially the dualisms of spiritual and material, soul and body. Womanist theologian Kelly Brown Douglas claims that Platonism provided the definitive dualistic paradigm that was built into Christian thinking.[65] It privileged soul over body in a relation of opposition, demonizing the body as the source of sensuality and lust. As Douglas notes, we can see how this dualism shaped the early Christian imagination in the Apostle Paul's frequent denigration of flesh as the site of sin and in the works of Saint Augustine.[66]

Another, related contributor to this dualism was Docetism, a general name for theological teachings in the first centuries of Christian history, including Gnosticism, that denied Christ's embodiment. Docetists could not stomach the idea that God would assume carnal human flesh and claimed that, despite appearance, the body of Jesus was composed of exclusively spiritual matter.[67] Like Platonism, this movement denigrated materiality in general and bodies in particular. The body is bound to its sinful form, but the soul—and the rational mind— can aspire toward divine transcendence. In fact, salvation was understood to be the final escape from the fleshly prison of our material world. Some Docetic sects believed that not all human beings contain spirit; some are purely carnal and "thus irreparably condemned to destruction."[68] While the church rejected Docetism as heresy and combated it in early confessions such as the Apostles' Creed, Docetism's sharp dualism between the spiritual and material left an indelible mark on the Christian tradition. By divinizing the soul and demonizing the body, even identifying some humans as purely "carnal" and "condemned to destruction," this tradition provided "a foundation for easily disregarding certain bodies."[69]

A third source of dualism emerged from the use of color labels in early Christian texts, even biblical ones that delineated whiteness and blackness. Blackness, within the biblical and social imagination of the early church, and later of European Christians, symbolized sin and evil. Historian Jean Devisse suggests that, before substantial encounters with people with black skin, "blackness as a hermeneutic was able to grow and thrive in Western Europe"—evolving from a theological, even biblical association of dark and black with sinfulness, and white with purity.[70] Before their colonial travels to Africa, European Christians encountered black-skinned African Muslims on the Crusade battlefields in the eleventh and twelfth centuries. Black skin was thus already registered as an enemy to Christianity; paganness and barbarianism were indexed to blackness. "Within Christianity the color black accrued a slate of negative significations that yoked the 'abstraction' of blackness," Heng notes, "to sin, ignorance, shame, error, and the state of unredemption."[71] Consequently, when European Christians encountered Africans with black skin during their exploitative explorations to the western coast of the continent, this hermeneutic shaped their perceptions of the inhabitants. As Jennings puts it, the Christian tradition "falter[ed] in the face of new materiality."[72]

Likewise, because European Christians "had been coming in contact in large numbers with brown infidels, and with [black] sub-Saharan Africans," these European Christians first began regarding themselves as white by 1250, argues Madeline Caviness.[73] Thus, a sliding scale of humanity developed with superiority indexed to whiteness and inferiority indexed to blackness (with the racial classifications of red, brown, etc., later filling in the normative spectrum). Whereas the white race was capable of achieving a universal existence because of its capacity for rationality and spirituality, black flesh was, in J. Kameron Carter's words, "trapped in its particularity"[74] in a way that would not be true for universal white flesh. Black people could never obtain the transcendent and universal status of white flesh; in fact, their blackness posed a danger to the soul of white folks.[75] All three of these dualisms converged in Christian thought to create a "dualistically defined theo-ideological foundation" that created hierarchical dichotomies of material/immaterial and blackness/whiteness. These dualisms would provide sacred symbolic justification for racial hierarchies and contribute to the Christian denigration of black bodies.[76]

Christian Superiority

On a theological register, the intrinsic soteriological exclusiveness of Christianity—based on scriptural claims that Jesus is "the way, the truth, and the life" and no one approaches God except through him (John 14:6)—birthed a social antagonism toward religious difference.[77] That is, this belief projected a polarized universe in which anyone who did not adhere to these faith claims was deemed evil, or at least inferior. It created a dualistic world of "us versus them" where nonbelievers are not only outside the truth but automatically enemies of it.[78]

The belief that Christians understood and represented God's will for humanity better than any other religion further codified this emerging sliding scale of humanity. Again, since Europeans understood themselves to be the center of Christianity, and Europeans were almost exclusively white-skinned, their sliding scale placed whiteness at the top, making this theological hierarchy also a racial one.[79] White supremacy emerged within this polarized world, as religious difference and superiority transformed into racial difference and superiority. God's creative design for humanity and therefore God's favor were reflected in skin tone.[80] This became an interpretive lens through which to see and evaluate other peoples, as closer to or further from this salvific center of whiteness.[81] As Jeanine Hill Fletcher summarizes, "Christian supremacy" underwrote white supremacy.[82]

Supersessionism

The impact of Christian superiority was most evident in the relationship between Christianity and Jewishness, as the just-rendered historical account suggests. The borders of European/Christian identity were clarified by Jewish otherness, even before the first explorers set sail. "The troubling instability of Jewish difference,"

Daniel Boyarin writes, "shaped both Christian Europeans' self-image and their reactions to those they encountered in the course of exploration and conquest."[83] The seeds of supersessionism were planted in the Christian faith at its outset, nurtured through church fathers including Justin Martyr and made explicit in Reformation texts like Martin Luther's, which enabled the earliest Spanish explorers to begin to conceive of the newfound peoples as racially other.[84] Rather than recognizing Paul's caution to Gentile Christians to remember they have been "grafted in" to the root of Israel—"it is not you that support the root, but the root that supports you"—so that they should not boast (Romans 11:17–18), Christians came to believe themselves to be the first fruits, the elect.

This was funded, perhaps paradoxically, by the way early Christians understood what it meant to be part of their community in ethnic terms. We can see this in the early church debates about gentile inclusion at the Council of Jerusalem (Acts 15:2–35) and in their use of the language of citizenship: conversion was "transformation from one descent group, tribe, people, or citizenship to a new and better one."[85] This was especially salient, historian Denise Kimber Buell contends, in the ways they contrasted the universalism of Christianity—in its availability to all and its teleological goal for all humanity—with ethnic or quasiracial affiliation, like Jewishness.[86] Without making a direct link to modern racism, she argues that early Christianity provided conceptual tools for racist discourse by designating Jewishness as a rival.[87] With this we see the early codification of supersessionism, drawn from New Testament texts that vilify Jews, especially in Jesus's death (Matthew 27:25) and passages that seem to identify the church as the new Israel (1 Peter 2:4–10). Through a history of gradually displacing Israel from the soteriological and identity-making center of Christian formation, European theologians created a conceptual vacuum that was easily filled by those who had done the displacing: white Europeans. During the colonial and Enlightenment periods, Europe became conceptually mapped onto Israel's journey and special relationship with God, and Israel's history and covenant disappeared. European Christianity took Israel's story as its own.

Regarding this history of supersessionist practice, J. Kameron Carter focuses on the work of Immanuel Kant. There is ample evidence for Kant institutionalizing the modern use of a concept of race, defining it as a "class distinction between animals of one and the same line of descent, which is unfailingly transmitted by inheritance."[88] There is also, in the words of Robert Bernasconi, "no shortage among Kant's writings of remarks that would today unquestionably be characterized as racist"—not the least of which is his claim that black skin was proof of one's stupidity.[89] Yet Carter provides an argument that it was his treatment of Judaism and its supersession by Christianity that generated his lasting contribution to white supremacy, an argument worth revisiting briefly here specifically because it reflects the racializing of Jewishness in medieval Europe.

Carter contends that Kant draws on the racial logics of colonialism to contrast Jews not only as a religious group but also as an inferior race group due to the soteriological centerpiece of white, European Christianity.[90] Jewishness became a race alien to Western civilization and culture—even if it lived within it—and thus made all nonwhite races also alien to Western civilization and unseen in Western Christianity. With this racializing move accomplished, Kant next contrasts Judaism with the "rational religion" of Christianity, which he unconsciously ties to "the stock of the races of whites in whom the species will realize its destiny."[91] This shift again draws upon a Docetic Christology. As Jonathan Hess argues, for Kant, Judaism is bound to the empirical details of history and must be overcome by Christianity's universality, that is, its ability to transcend history.[92] Kant's contrast between Jewish empiricalism and Christian transcendentalism results in a dualism of Christian rationality with material life and, again, a rejection of the body. Without discounting the incarnation as do the earlier Docetists, Kant legitimates this account with a Christology that still severs Christ from his Jewish flesh.[93] As Carter comments, Christ's divinity "inaugurates a discontinuity, at the level of his humanity or his flesh, with Israel."[94] After Kant, Christ loses his particularity and ceases to be Jewish, and now "represents the wisdom of Europe."[95] Like blackness, Jewishness is too bound up in its own particularity. Thus, Christianity finds its teleology in a rational and universal white European transcendence—even mastery—over all of life, while Judaism is a religion that finds its teleology, ominously according to Kant, in its "euthanasia."[96]

Finally, people who exhibit whiteness, because of its universality, supplant Israel as God's elect. Carter argues that with Kant, Christianity is "reimagined as 'racially' severed from and ethnographically triumphant over its oriental Jewish roots."[97] With the refashioning of Jewishness as a racial identity and Christianity as a religion of universal rationality, theological reasoning and Christian formation became reconfigured around the European body as the true marker of divine election. The result of all of this is that now racial discourse becomes the primary grammar for understanding the relationship between Christianity and Judaism—and between Christians and colonized, dark-fleshed others as well.

European recalibration to the pinnacle of salvation history theologically justified them to judge civilizations as well as individual humans—eventually transforming them into goods and services. Walter Mignolo indicts the "theological foundation of knowledge"—that is, the privileging of soul over body—as leading directly to imperialism, colonialism, and white supremacy. Theology produced the colonial mission endeavors that quite literally redrew the maps of the globe in the sixteenth century. When the pope granted Spain and Portugal dominion over the New World, maps identified Europe as the center of the globe and, thus, the "zero point" of knowledge; Europe and Christianity assumed an epistemological hegemony over all other geographies and people. The "zero point," Mignolo says, "is the site of observation from which the epistemic colonial differences . . . are mapped out." Yet this zero point, he claims, "hides its own local knowledge universally projected." While the zero point configures theology and geography around differences in bodies, it simultaneously denies that bodily differences are relevant to knowledge, foreshadowing the colorblindness we witness today. Thus, the zero point veils its own contextuality, its geo-historical location, "assuming to be universal and thus managing the universality to which everyone has to submit."[98] Theology spawned not only racial discourse through its supersessionist supplanting of Israel, but specifically a culture and practice of white supremacy that views itself as universal, triumphal, and elect. And theology itself morphed into a form now bound to its spawn.

These three factors of dualism, superiority, and supersessionism distorted the way Europeans began envisioning God's work of creation and redemption, viewing humanity on a sliding racial scale in which white people were more capable of salvation—because of the way God created them—and darker people were further from salvation. Salvation for the nonwhite may require physical coercion and the spiritual guidance only available in the form of slavery. Linked with their zeal for evangelism and conquest, Europeans shipped these theological innovations to the American colonies along with the human cargo in their hulls. The church in America, fleeing persecution itself, was founded on the persecution of dark bodies, justified theologically in order to secure their salvation.

In the American colonial context, one can see this logic explicitly in the national seals proposed by both Thomas Jefferson and Benjamin Franklin. The latter identified the new nation with Israel by depicting Moses dividing the Red Sea, Pharaoh overwhelmed in the waters, and the motto: "Rebellion to Tyrants Is Obedience to God." Jefferson's proposal included, "The Children of Israel in the Wilderness, led by a Cloud by day, and a Pillar of fire by night, and on the other Side Hengist and Horsa, the Saxon Chiefs, from whom We claim the Honour of being descended and whose Political Principles and Form of Government We have assumed."[99] Jefferson explicitly projected America's whiteness and its presumed Saxon heritage (a favorite defining racial and political myth) as indicative of the new Israel—God's new, chosen white people. As Kelly Brown Douglas comments, for these founding fathers, "America was the New Israel and Americans the New Israelites," and "Anglo-Saxonism was their religion."[100]

Political Power and the Nation-State

With this white supremacist corrosion of Christian theology complete, the last factor links Christianity with the political power of the nation-state, as evident

in the national seal example. The theological developments that led to antagonistic dualisms between body and soul, Christian and non-Christian beliefs,
and white and nonwhite bodies theologically predisposed Christians to become
oppressors.[101] When this disposition was united with political authority, specifically a colonial power, it was given the force to effect this oppression all over the
globe. This power only expanded when the political landscape shifted with the
rise of modern nation-states. As wars between religious groups exploded across
Europe during this same period of colonialism, the rivalries between nation-states
mixed with the holy-war mentality remaining from the Crusades to transform
Christians' notions of love into group loyalty and justification of violence toward
anyone outside of one's group. That is, the crusading mentality significantly corrupted visions of Christian social responsibility that simultaneously developed
into an ethnonationalist identity of the nation-state.[102] Viewing those outside of
one's state as a degenerate "other" was a culmination of the transformation of
religious enemy to racial outsider.

Additionally, Carter argues that the same modern discourse that molded
racial discourse and white supremacy also gave rise to the modern state and its
apparatus of power—often disguised in the form of liberal democracy, or sovereignty as the will of the people. Referencing the insights of Michel Foucault,
Carter notes the way a people produces, defines, reproduces, and redefines itself
continually as a people over and against other people. As a group begins to see
itself as a nation-state, an identity arises between that people and the state, but
quickly takes on a bellicosity that can only conceive of itself in agonistic relation to other nation-states, and thus to other peoples. The nation, in this way,
incorporates itself through a nationalism that racializes other peoples and can
only imagine them as enemies.[103] The state presumes to save its people from violent human division through the creation of an exclusive social body, identified
in antagonistic relation to other peoples.[104] As William Cavanaugh explains,
"The nation-state tends to develop its own . . . worldview and a discipline which
aspires to train us in certain virtues, to mold our thoughts and our actions."[105] The
modern arrangement was that the church was charged with care for soul and the
nation-state with care for (or control of) the body, but as it turns out, the state
is not satisfied with just the body; it wants to colonize the soul as well. The state
derives its power from and legitimates that power with theological language, and
requires ultimate allegiance from its subjects-citizens.

Race and nation-state formed twin products of modern discourse shaped
by the racial anxiety of a world that now included contact with ethnic others.
Douglas claims that the state often implicitly draws upon an implicit natural-law
theology that risks the moral collapse of *is* into *ought*: "The world, the way that it
is, is viewed as the way it ought to be."[106] If those with political authority—those

with the power to create law—"rationally" discern the good and proper within a world that they believe was divinely created with levels of inferiority and superiority, then this entanglement of theology and state "serves to justify unjust structures, and thus it sanctifies an oppressive status quo."[107] Morality becomes naturalized; specifically in this case, once dark-skinned people are evaluated and classified as naturally inferior, this quickly becomes a theological truth that justifies their mistreatment. The linking of a dualistic theology to political power, and the desire to maintain the social and cultural status quo that preserves this power, resulted in the diseased theological imagination that interpreted black bodies as subject to slavery and death.

The four factors identified here are not the only contributors to the emergence of white supremacy. One might discover other resources within particular atonement theories, interpretations of Scripture, or elsewhere. Still, these factors illuminate a contiguous line between early dualism and modern racism. White supremacy did not emerge as an isolated tumor in the tradition or an external factor; it emerged from within Christianity. In more popular terminology, white supremacy was not a bug but a feature. When a dangerous constellation of theological factors was exposed to the new situation of colonial encounter with the dark-skinned other, and Europeans had to make sense of human otherness within their Christian social imagination, these elements converged to birth white supremacy. This malformed theology—infused from its earliest years with the resources to support white supremacy—is now malforming, continuing to shape the world according to its imagination.

4. The Legacy of White Supremacy in the Theologies of Rauschenbusch and Niebuhr

Recognizing the ways these corrupted theological impulses have generated and abetted the practices of slavery, Jim Crow, and racial segregation in U.S. history, as well as the white American church's justification and support of them, is not difficult. These theological impulses have granted legitimacy to America's racial caste system, founded upon a theologically invented doctrine of white supremacy. One could easily discern these theological corruptions in the sermons of antebellum southern pastors or theologians who defend of segregation. Yet, in order to fully observe their power and identify the ways they have persisted into the twentieth century to infect and inflect white theology in the United States, I turn now to two of America's most prominent and influential theologians, both respected as progressive social voices in their time. Walter Rauschenbusch and Reinhold Niebuhr serve as important test cases not only because they were the key figures of two of America's most important theological movements since the Civil War: the social gospel and Christian realism. Rauschenbusch and Niebuhr also illuminate the power of white supremacy to corrupt theological personalities and systems that perceived themselves to be contributors to racial equality and justice. In order to see the power of the four corrupting theological elements of whiteness identified earlier as well as the "colorblind" elements of individualism and projected universalism (analyzed in the previous chapter), we should investigate if they persist, and in what forms, in the theologies of the most formative progressive figures of the previous century.

Rauschenbusch and Niebuhr were both aware of racial injustice in the United States, and unlike many theologians and pastors of their days, they determined to use the resources of their theological perspectives to address the issue. But each serves as an example of the ways white supremacy exists as a sinister canopy casting a wicked shadow over even the best-intended efforts. Both theologians exhibited a general blindness to the complexities of the issue. While eventually addressing the "race problem," Rauschenbusch viewed it primarily as an issue for the American South. Serving as a pastor and theologian in Hell's Kitchen in New York City in the first decades of the twentieth century, Rauschenbusch never collaborated with black leaders to develop social goals or expand his vision of social evil to include racism.[108] New York City was still primarily white at this time, and his lack of encounter with the reality of black suffering led to a belief that it was the South's problem to solve.[109] Niebuhr, on the other hand, lived in Detroit in the 1910s and 1920s during the "great migration" of black people from the South, and in Harlem during its renaissance of the 1930s and 1940s. Niebuhr could not avoid seeing the reality of black life in America. While a pastor in Detroit he served as chair of the Mayor's Committee on Race Relations and on the board of a farming co-op in the Mississippi Delta.[110] Reflecting on these experiences he observed the situation of African Americans as a "really desperate one" and claimed that most people do not understand "the misery and pain which exists among these people."[111] He called white racial pride a "form of original sin" and advocated for nonviolent coercive strategies like boycotts.[112] Yet, as Traci West argues, despite living in Harlem, he was blind to black women activists like Ella Baker, right outside the window of his Union Seminary office, who were already carrying out the nonviolent strategies of boycotts that he proposed. West suggests that Niebuhr evinces the "erasure of the significance of what people of color were doing and thinking within history."[113]

Rauschenbusch and Niebuhr serve not only as examples of the way well-intentioned Christians are embedded within an expansive repertoire of white supremacist theological concepts that inflect their theological perspectives. These theologians also serve as a bridge between the formative factors in Christianity's development of white supremacy (see chapters 1 and 2 in this volume) and the way similar elements frame the discussion of race and racism in contemporary theology (chapters 3–4). That is, as I mentioned in the introduction, Rauschenbusch and Niebuhr cultivated the theological ground that produced Hauerwas and Cone. It is difficult to understand the emergence of postliberalism and black theology without accounting for the theological innovations and shortcomings of the social gospel and Christian realism. Therefore, I show here, for both Rauschenbusch and Niebuhr, how one or more of the factors described in this chapter shape the way they approach the question of race. These same elements presage the comparative account I offer of Hauerwas and Cone in part II of this book.

Rauschenbusch and the Social Gospel

In a 1914 essay, "The Problem of the Black Man," Walter Rauschenbusch expressed regret for not addressing the race problem. Yet even his meager late-career attempts never completely remedied this oversight. The social gospel emerged at the turn of the twentieth century, proposing to "Christianize the social order" in the face of growing economic and social crises. It may seem surprising, then, that Rauschenbusch had little to say about race in spite of the fact that the social gospel reached its apex during the United States' worst years for lynching. In fact, Preston Williams contends that the social gospel's "astigmatism" regarding race was no simple oversight, but an embedded feature of its mode of analysis.[114]

But racial oppression was not simply a blind spot for Rauschenbusch. His failure to address racial justice was a larger symptom of his methodology and the broader perspective and aims of the social gospel. In his messages about love and social progress he enjoined Christians to love without distinction for race. Yet, because the situation of African Americans "seemed to me so tragic, so insoluble," Rauschenbusch seldom found a way to speak beyond such platitudes and address the reality of racial injustice.[115] Since the social gospel developed out of a European context that was dealing with issues of labor and poverty, and collaborated almost exclusively with white churches, Rauschenbusch "analyzed America in terms of class alone with no reference to race."[116] He considered racial injustice a problem limited to the American South that would gradually be resolved through economic reform.[117] He did dedicate a few lines to lynching but mostly noted the economic "slavery" of the industrial system and mob violence as elements of "the present crisis" in Christianity and the social gospel failing to make a connection to lynching or the legacies of racial slavery. He frequently called on those suffering to wait patiently for God's coming kingdom of justice.[118]

This gradualism and "superficial optimism" were characteristics of the social gospel that Martin Luther King Jr. would later suggest contributed to its failure to comprehend the systemic nature of racism and depths of suffering caused by it.[119] Rauschenbusch's optimistic account of human moral agency led him to support gradual change in achieving social justice. He employed the idyllic example of fruit trees blossoming to describe the gradual moral growth of society—"the culmination of a long process."[120] God's kingdom advances slowly, meaning that Christians "can afford to wait" while working for moderate social changes. All of this resulted in calls for patience in the struggle against racism. Rauschenbusch's insistence that we "give it time" strikes a bold contrast with King's later assertion of "Why we can't wait."[121] Regarding the issue of race, then, Glenn Bucher claims that "the social gospel was less an effort to Christianize the social order and more a Christianing of the status quo."[122]

On a deeper level, Rauschenbusch and the social gospel reveal the persistence of Christian superiority and the remnants of the racial hierarchy that it constructed. Rauschenbusch wrote an extended version of his "The Problem of the Black Man" essay that focused on aiding the "belated race" and "backward people," which include "the Negroes of the Black Belt."[123] He recognized the devastating effects of colonialism and Christian missionary activity upon these communities but perceived their only hope for social progress in the work of white Christians. Rauschenbusch identified the real problem of race as "how to get a really quickening and uplifting religion implanted" in these backward communities—a claim that suggests two aspects of the Christian superiority described earlier: (1) the acceptance of a racial taxonomy that placed whites as intellectually and morally higher than blacks, and (2) the belief in Christian exceptionalism—that Christianity was not the culprit but, in fact, the only solution to the race problem.[124]

First, while encouraging the black community to engage in nonviolent civil disobedience in order to achieve greater self-determination, Rauschenbusch simultaneously addressed black people paternalistically as culturally "backward" and as among the "belated" races. "The Christian way out," he proclaimed, "is to take our belated black brother by the hand and urge him along the road of steady and intelligent labor, of property rights, of family fidelity, of hope and self-confidence."[125] In other words, African Americans were a backward group that needed to be "urge[d]" along by the "hand" of white leaders to self-determination by instilling Christian values like family commitment and "stead[iness]."

This vision of white racial superiority was fueled by an embrace of the "new science" of social Darwinism, which led social gospel leaders to uncritically accept the assumptions of the racial pseudoscience of their day.[126] The social gospel, in its eagerness to distance itself from the anti-intellectual tone of fundamentalist and conventional Christianity, embraced cultural and scientific ideas like evolution. But in this cultural period, accepting evolution also meant accepting theories of racial stages of development—superior and inferior races. Rauschenbusch too easily promoted the racist presuppositions of the period with too little criticism and resistance. For him and the other social gospelers, Preston Williams claims, "Evolutionary theory provided an explanation for the visible difference between blacks and whites and suggested a new understanding of God's creative act" in which different races matured at different rates.[127] These "belated races," as Rauschenbusch would call them—those who trailed behind the white race in civil evolution—needed the assistance of the more advanced races for social progress.

This led not only to a cultural accommodation in Rauschenbusch's theology but also to a white Christian exceptionalism: the conviction that only when (white) church members reach out to these belated communities can they "can expand the intellectual horizon of these people, awaken their intellectual appetites, elevate their music and art, create a new architecture, set new standards for their marriage customs and the comforts of their homes, and in one generation lead them farther in social progress than they would have moved unaided for centuries."[128] The white Christian church, according to Rauschenbusch, is the only institution capable of bringing the belated races to social salvation.[129] According to Daryl Trimiew, this conviction was based on an assumption that "only Anglo-American males were moral agents fit to make changes in society."[130] Rauschenbusch's outlook suggests a second aspect of Christian superiority: an ecclesial exceptionalism that perceived as external to Christianity the factors that oppress the belated races. The social gospel was concerned with reforming society through ecclesial means rather than uncovering problems internal to the church, thus rendering its theologians blind to the ways that the church perpetuated or even caused evils like white supremacy.

Niebuhr and Christian Realism

The optimism and sentimental hope of the social gospel began to dismantle in the trenches of World War I. Taking as his starting point for theological reflection "the facts of experience,"[131] Reinhold Niebuhr became the key figure in the emergence of Christian realism, a theological movement cognizant of the sinful self-interest of society and concerned with creating tolerable forms of order and justice through rational analysis of a given situation.[132] Niebuhr's realism in some ways allowed him to see the depth and complexity of the issue. By assessing the facts of experience and all the factors that contribute to it, especially self-interest and power, Niebuhr gained a fuller understanding of the race situation.

Perceiving the structural nature of racism, the theologian knew that interpersonal strategies—for example, race commissions or relying on the goodwill and philanthropy of well-meaning white citizens—were limited because "they operate within a given system of injustice" and do not address political and economic factors.[133] Niebuhr famously admitted that "the white race in America will not admit the Negro to equal rights if it is not forced to do so."[134] Such sober reflections made him less confident of various panaceas proposed to resolve racism. In fact, he lamented, "There is no absolute solution to this problem."[135]

These prescient observations did not, however, render Niebuhr immune to the universalizing tendencies of whiteness, or other ways of evading the depth of the problem, and his own complicity in it. While his realism allowed him to perceive the reality of racial injustice in ways obscured for Rauschenbusch, such realism is also to blame for Niebuhr's failures.[136] Niebuhr perceived the reasons black people were impatient with calls for patience, but he still believed that "prudence is what is demanded in such critical situations as this one";[137] Niebuhr suggested that "on the side of minority groups a little more Christian realism [and compromise] would also have its advantages."[138] These concerns are revealed by his worry that his former Detroit church would integrate too quickly,[139] or his claim that the *Plessy v. Ferguson* ruling mandating the separate-but-equal policy was "a very good doctrine for its day." His reasoning was that anything more radical would have prompted revolt.[140] Christian realists maintain a clear sense of human sinfulness and therefore tend to seek the most "realistic" solution available in a fallen world. Niebuhr's ethical pragmatism led him to promote a "gradual and evolutionary process" of social change. He condoned applying pressure through coercive measures like bank boycotts and nonviolent resistance, but insisted that such pressure must be "gradually applied."[141] He recognized why African Americans were impatient with calls for patience, but still considered patience "the course of wisdom in overcoming historic injustices."[142] As Robert Bellah contends, a danger of Christian realism is that it may blind us to the desperate realities in which we live. Bellah continues, with realism "one may be forced into the defense of established interests on the grounds that after all, human nature being what it is, this is the best we can expect."[143] Also indicting the pragmatism of Niebuhr's realist theology, James Cone concludes, "Niebuhr had 'eyes to see' black suffering, but I believe he lacked the 'heart to feel' it as his own."[144]

Like Rauschenbusch, these failures betray the persistence of the racial taxonomy forged from white supremacist theology. Niebuhr frequently used the term *cultural backwardness* to describe African Americans without ever fully defining what he meant.[145] For example, he insisted that the black race in the United States suffers partly because of its "cultural backwardness [which is] only transcended by the most gifted members of the race."[146] So, even while advocating for the "peculiar spiritual gifts of the Negro," he simultaneously essentialized the race as one of "vindictiveness" and "lethargy."[147] Such beliefs would lead him to express sympathy for white southerners who had "honest scruples" about "common education for races with different cultural inheritances."[148] Thus, Niebuhr would grant that "cultural differences between the two races are still great enough to warrant a certain amount of disquiet on the part of the [white] parents."[149] Therefore patience and prudence were necessary measures to appease these anxious parents.[150]

One piece of evidence for Niebuhr's implicit racial taxonomy lies in his confutations of communism, in which he addresses why some people—specifically Russians (whom he distinguishes racially from Europeans)—may be susceptible to its allures. He writes that rather than economic or political reasons, the real explanation is "the soul of an Asiatic rather than a European nation" and its "very lack of intellectual sophistication.[151] The reason Russians were susceptible to communist manipulation lies in their racial inferiority. Niebuhr never says this explicitly, of course. Rather, he engages in the colorblind language game of naming "culture" as the marker of inferiority—an increasingly transparent stand-in for race from the time of the U.S. Republican Party's Southern Strategy (see chapter 1) to present-day debates over entitlement programs. For Niebuhr, the "primitive culture" of the Russians rendered them unsophisticated by the "influences of intellectualism." As Traci West observes, "It seems for him, when measured against the European soul, the 'Asiatic soul' [of the Russian] was lacking. To Niebuhr, this racial deficit explains why the Russian people were so available for manipulation."[152] Perhaps this same taxonomy of racial superiority and inferiority, with Europeans placed at the top, explains the need for white liberals' paternalism in their dealings with and advocacy for African Americans. All of this simply highlights the "white superiority inherent in Niebuhr's audacity" to locate flaws in the struggle in terms of "Negro character flaws" as well as "liberal, white self-interest in maintaining paternalistic superiority over the Negro."[153] In Cone's words, it is another case of white people, who, whether "for us or against us . . . [,] seem to think that they know what is best for our struggle."[154]

In his attempts at an unvarnished realism regarding racism, Niebuhr frequently invoked "racial pride." Yet, for him, this was "a general human shortcoming,"[155] an inevitable and ubiquitous symptom of what he calls "the ethnic will to live" that exists within every racial group. Here Niebuhr displays the universalizing tendency of whiteness that I addressed in chapter 1, as well as the antagonistic dualisms that emerged from Christian theology and the European church's encounter with other races. Niebuhr believes that whenever one racial group encounters another, this integration generates a collective "survival impulse."[156] Thus, all racial groups "tend to preserve their self-respect by adopting contemptuous attitudes toward other groups and to express their appreciation of their own characteristic culture by depreciating that of others."[157] He suggested that black and white leaders not analyze racism as primarily white supremacy but as a "universal characteristic of Homo sapiens." As evidence he cites northern black men who contribute to racial injustice as much as their white counterparts. These are the effect of "man's incapacity to comprehend his own finiteness," or as he believes, the root of all sin.[158]

Niebuhr understands that the source of human sin is to be found in humanity's willful refusal to acknowledge the finite and determinate character of our existence. "Man seeks to overcome his insecurity by a will-to-power to overreach limits of creatureliness," he says.[159] In light of this reality of universal racial prejudice, Niebuhr proposes "mutual repentance and forgiveness" on the part of all groups.[160] According to Cornel West, however, Niebuhr's theological definition of sin as existential anxiety followed by pride, and promotion of that as a universal reality, "presumes that one is uncertain about the sources of one's suffering and the basis of hope for redemption."[161] This may be true for white liberals like Niebuhr, but not for black people in America. By invoking the universal nature of sin, including the sin of racism, and the universal need for forgiveness and repair, Niebuhr flattens the sins and prejudice of all racial groups into a false equivalence.[162] He, like Rauschenbusch a few decades before, exemplifies the lingering impact of Christianity's long legacy of white supremacy—from its early antagonistic dualisms to modern colorblindness.

James Cone observes, "Whether we speak of Jonathan Edwards, Walter Rauschenbusch, or Reinhold Niebuhr as America's greatest theologian, none of them made the rejection of white supremacy central to their understanding of the gospel." He adds, "It takes a lot of theological blindness to do that."[163] This blindness is a symptom of a larger legacy of white supremacy that was both invented by and corrosive for Christian theology. The problem does not lie elsewhere as something that the Christian church can resolve. Rather, it continues to inflect and corrupt white Christian theology, even among those who consider ourselves working to eradicate it.

5. Conclusion: Thus Have We Made the World

The pollution of our baptismal waters is ubiquitous. At stake here is not just a matter of white Europeans using Christianity, among a number of options, to justify white supremacy. Rather, these white Europeans were white supremacists because they were Christian. I am not claiming that Christianity was the only oppressive religion or ideology that resourced dehumanization, slavery, or genocide. My assertion in this chapter is that the particular form of oppression that is white supremacy was a symptom of their Christianity. This legacy of Western Christianity is now our responsibility.

Whiteness originated within our tradition; it stewed in our sanctuaries, was proclaimed from our pulpits and with our pens, and spread with our slave ships. It shapes the work of some of our most revered and progressive theologians. This legacy continues to hold captive the modern, white Christian imagination, now abetted by a colorblindness that refuses to reckon with this inheritance. Whether memorialized in a twisted or burning cross or a painting of a porcelain Jesus hanging in the church narthex, we have unleashed this invention on the world in white nationalist rallies and quotidian microaggressions.

There is a chilling scene at the conclusion of the film *The Mission*, about missionary activity in the South American colonies. As the Jesuit priests prove unable to prevent the slaughter and enslavement of the natives by their own church partnership with the colonial state, the Portuguese governor attempts to reassure the cardinal who is now lamenting his support. He tells the cardinal, "We must work in the world, and the world is thus." But staring at the devastation his church had just wrought, the astute cardinal corrects him: "No, thus we have made the world."[164] White Christians provided the logic, worldview, rationalizations, and stories that have shifted the weight of the world onto the backs of nonwhites. For our crucial roles in producing and maintaining this system of white supremacy, Jeannine Hill Fletcher contends, "Theologians are not only responsible for the past construction of ideologies of White supremacy and conditions of dispossession for people of color. Those past constructions of White supremacy created the conditions of the racialized disparity we experience in the United States today."[165]

Our diseased theological imagination has infected the world and re-created it in the image of the masked white supremacy that holds us captive. Put simply, white supremacy is an infection we gave to the world; it is our responsibility to do something about it. This means, first, heeding the Apostle Paul's words, to take care of our own house (1 Timothy 3:4–5). We cannot propose to help with the world's redemption while our own house is out of order with a contagion of racism that continues to infect all our global neighbors. In the same way that most American theology portrays the character of whiteness, whiteness itself has an inherent theological quality. Because of the way the two are tethered, as I hope to have shown in this chapter, in the next I provide a deeper analysis of white theology in its most popular and influential form. We must first more deeply and painfully examine our own theology in order to uncover and uproot the products and causes of white supremacy that have extended throughout our theology. The problem is worse than we thought, and the effort to undo this harm will be more difficult than we expect. We must exorcise our own demons.

PART II

"Who Is Christ for Us Today?"

3

Witnessing White Theology

1. The Church of the Colorblind

Fresh out of seminary I took a job as senior pastor of a fledgling Baptist congregation on the outskirts of Raleigh, North Carolina. The church got its start after splitting from a larger congregation (as Baptists are prone to do) over some issue not serious enough to recall. We met in a local, nondescript Woodsman of the World lodge (think Masons, but in the woods) amid the tall pines of the Tar Heel State. Each Sunday morning, my drive would take me through the wealthy suburbs into an area that seemed to sit on the borderlands of lower-middle-class suburbia and rural farmland.

The local neighborhood that housed the WOW lodge (as I liked to call it) was a typical blue-collar area that had become increasingly diverse in recent years, as many white families moved to more prosperous corners of the city. Simply due to our location, several African American families had begun attending regularly before my arrival. They participated in the weekly Bible study as well as the praise and worship band. The church leadership had made a decision, around the time I began serving as pastor, to reach out to young professionals in the growing Research Triangle area. The church's leaders were willing to devote the congregation's resources, even dip into our endowment, to relocate closer to the area that housed numerous technology firms and global businesses. Our contemporary worship style, nimble leadership team, and tentative relationship to our neighborhood reflected this desire and primed us to become a church of young professionals, they thought.

At the same time, we were unintentionally growing into a multiethnic congregation, a rare feat for a rural southern congregation. Yet no one ever brought attention to this fact. No one left the church because of its changing color, but no one seemed to mark it as a gift either. We saw no particular value in multiethnic community—social, pedagogical, or spiritual—and viewed the integration of

Witnessing Whiteness. Kristopher Norris, Oxford University Press (2020). © Oxford University Press.
DOI: 10.1093/oso/9780190055813.001.0001

black families into the church body as no reason to make changes to the structures, practices, or leadership of the congregation. No one mentioned the possibility of singing gospel music, reading Scripture commentaries by black authors, or changing the leadership team to more accurately reflect the congregation's demographics. The gospel is colorblind, the leadership believed, and at the time I possessed no resources to challenge this claim. Grace is universally available; God is no respecter of persons (Acts 10:34). So I agreed that the racial demographics of the congregation need not alter our practices or leadership structure.

I never questioned why the church was so eager to draw in young professionals from the local technology and business park. The unspoken—likely even unperceived—desire was to fill the pews with young, upwardly mobile white families. These were the types of people who would help "grow" the congregation—in numbers, prestige, and budget. I don't think this was an intentionally racist desire. Rather, it was unreflective. Nevertheless, both this desire and the failure to recognize an inherent value to racial diversity were based on a theology of colorblindness, one that had its roots firmly planted in the legacy of white supremacy outlined in the previous chapter. And I, as pastor, was blind to that.

The witness of this congregation, proclaiming the good news of colorblindness to a world divided by race, is echoed in the work of contemporary white theology. That is, white churches and white theologians have drunk deeply from this same gospel. We are children of the inheritance described in the previous chapter—a theology employed to construct a racial hierarchy that promoted whiteness to the pinnacle of human existence and to justify the enslavement and oppression of those at the bottom. Now that theological inheritance blinds us to its lingering reality, repeated on segregated Sunday mornings and in theologians' silence on race.

Strikingly one of the most important Christian theologians of the past half-century, and certainly one of the most prolific, has failed to engage one of the most consequential theological issues of that time. Stanley Hauerwas's first published essay was a defense of Black Power. Yet he has only directly addressed the issue of race in three subsequent essays, and did not do so at all until twenty-five years after this first publication. Put simply, Hauerwas does not write about race, and he is certainly not unique in this respect. In response to the legacy described in chapter 2, and perhaps for many, due to this legacy, white theology today generally avoids altogether the issues of race, racism, white supremacy, and whiteness.[1] Hauerwas, as one of the most pivotal and formative influences in contemporary Christian theological ethics,[2] is representative of a great cloud of white theologians similarly limited by their own colorblindness.

James Cone claims that theology's "great sin" is its "silence in the face of white supremacy."[3] The same could be said for most white theorists of modernity as well, upon whose critiques many white and postliberal theologians draw.[4] For the few white theologians who have begun to address racism, the problem is identified as one of complicity to the worldly sin of racism. Two recent works of ecclesiology that include explicit treatments of race serve as examples, one from an evangelical Reformed perspective, the other from a Baptist/Anabaptist perspective. I highlight these texts specifically because of their explicit postliberal inheritance from Hauerwas and the progress they each demonstrate by writing theologically about race in the first place. In his book *Awaiting the King*, James K. A. Smith argues that white supremacy is the result of a "worldly liturgy," or a rival tradition, that has infected and deformed the church.[5] In other words, it is not inherent to the church's tradition itself. Likewise, for Ryan Andrew Newson, in his book *Inhabiting the World*, Christian practices are "corrupted" and "perverted" so that they "reinforce" racism; "white superiority will be brought to church by its members." In short, he writes, "the world comes to church."[6] Revealingly, Smith's answer to this corrupting worldly liturgy of racism is threefold: (1) even distorted practices like baptism can still be sources of "counter-formation" if practiced properly, (2) pastors ought to become better "ethnographers" capable of more clearly diagnosing "the ways churchgoers are shaped by 'the world,'" and (3) Christians must commit to a more immersive catechesis and "liturgical way of life."[7] Simply, the answer is more church, and while we should praise such reflections on worldly practices and the sin of racism as a welcome departure from most works of white theology, especially white ecclesiology, that simply ignore or avoid racism, these reflections are still not enough.[8]

More pointedly, beyond their own failure to reflect on the church's shortcomings, white theologians have neglected to reckon with the ways their own racial formation has influenced their work. White theology has never had to consider itself a contextual theology. It has always presumed the ability to speak universal truth without the need for racial self-awareness,[9] because white theologians have never seen race as necessary or integral to their own theological work and experience. According to Cone, "White theologians, because of their identity with the dominant power structure, are largely boxed within their own cultural history."[10] This history of cultural and social privilege, as H. Richard Niebuhr says, shapes the "interpretive equipment" we use to perceive reality—and blinds us to the experiences of those whom white privilege oppresses.[11]

While Rauschenbusch and Reinhold Niebuhr created the white Christian American milieu that produced Hauerwas, Hauerwas's traditionalist (some would say "neo-traditionalist") white theology both reflects that inheritance and offers an important contrast to them. He saw Rauschenbusch and Niebuhr as erring on the side of cultural accommodation. We see this in Rauschenbusch's acceptance of the racial pseudoscience that was culturally prevalent at the time and Niebuhr in his ethical pragmatism that limited itself to politically efficient options. In both instances, they made their theology susceptible to the fourth factor I identified in chapter 2, aligning their theology with political or cultural power in a way that only maintains the status quo. Hauerwas rejects that for various reasons, and in so doing rejected some of the elements of whiteness that had infused their theology—such as accommodation to power structures, or emphasis on rationality and universality. But in doing so, his alternative only reified other elements of white supremacy. That is, in Hauerwas's rejection of their cultural or political accommodation, we can already diagnose a problem: this positions racism as a sin outside of church. By rejecting the sins of the world (racism is a problem of liberalism for Hauerwas) and turning inward to the tradition and practices of the church for moral formation, Hauerwas believes Christians can avoid racism. Yet, as I demonstrated in the previous chapter, this traditionalist theology neglects the specifically Christian character and origins of white supremacy.

Much of the theology produced by white scholars today is indebted to traditionalism—a commitment to historical resources of the Christian tradition as a means for addressing new challenges to the church. In this chapter I focus on the ways that traditionalism, as a dominant theological force for white scholars, has influenced the ways white theologians approach race and white supremacy. Jeffrey Stout labels this same reclamation movement "New Traditionalism" and places Hauerwas squarely in its theological center. The label of New Traditionalist indicates a debt to the philosophical work of Alasdair MacIntyre on the concept of "tradition."[12] Sociologist James Hunter also analyzes Hauerwas as the centerpiece of a theological movement, but from a slightly different angle. He identifies Hauerwas's theological community as neo-Anabaptists, signaling a focus on the distinctive "witness" of the church and an understanding of the church's radical separation from the world.[13]

These two categories of tradition and witness come together to shape a broad arc of white theologians, influenced by one or both of these movements. This is true in much of the white theology produced in recent years, but is, helpfully, most clearly exemplified in Hauerwas's thought. For him, the commitments to tradition and distinctive witness converge to establish a strong boundary between church and world. This does not result in sectarianism as some argue, but it does refuse to consider the ways external and cultural influences and "narratives" affect the church as a distinctive culture founded and guided by a more or less singular Christian narrative. The church influences the world through its witness—not through political activism or other means that may compromise this witness—but the world, ideally, does not influence the church. The centripetal attention and focus on a unifying story holding the community together often ignores bodily difference and the ways that racial formation impacts the character of the church community, its witness, and the theological sources that shape it.

In this chapter I focus on Hauerwas as the ideal representative of these movements in white theology and their obliviousness or willful resistance toward engaging with race. I do this for several reasons. First, Hauerwas offers specific reasons for his silence, and these specific reasons along with the tendencies of whiteness he evinces when he does engage the issue helpfully illuminate this general trend among white theologians and ethicists. He provides a model by which we can address this broader pattern of evasion. Second, inexplicitly and unintentionally, some aspects of Hauerwas's constructive work—again not insights exclusive to him but most clearly emphasized in his work—resonate with the methods and proposals of theologians like James Cone who do place racial justice and liberation at the center of their work. By focusing on Hauerwas in this chapter and Cone in the next, I draw out some of these critical contrasts and resonances between the broad threads of (white) traditionalist theology and black liberation theology. These contrasts and resonances are most pronounced in matters that bear upon their ecclesiologies, and so much of the theological work in this part of the book focuses specifically upon the church's identity and mission in regard to racial justice. This comparison can then help to illuminate the foundations of an ethic of responsibility that takes seriously the wicked problem of whiteness and offers substantive and practical resources for confronting it.

2. Hauerwas on Race

Hauerwas confesses that he grew up embedded in practices of segregation. "I have no idea how deeply the habits of racism are written into my life," he admits, "but I know that they are not the kind of habits you simply 'outgrow' or 'get over.'"[14] This confession of racism marks Hauerwas's treatment of race through the years as well as his reasons for generally avoiding the topic. However, this confession does not penetrate his work to the level of reflecting on how his racism—or mere standpoint as a white theologian—influences his work. Here I outline his infrequent engagement with race and racism, highlighting the ways he employs race for other theological agendas, abstracts it into broader theological concerns, and avoids it as not his "story."

Hauerwas wrote his first published article for the campus newspaper at Augustana College, the site of his first teaching job, on the occasion of a campus symposium on Black Power in February 1969.[15] Writing on Black Power the same year James Cone published his groundbreaking *Black Theology and Black Power*, and in language that reads more like the Christian realism of Reinhold Niebuhr than the Stanley Hauerwas we have come to expect, he calls Black Power an appropriate democratic strategy to secure social equality. Further, this "morally healthy development" robbed white liberals of their ability to assuage their own guilt. He writes,

> The phrase "black power" and what it represents has come as a severe shock to many Christians who liked to think of themselves as liberal on the question of race. They feel as if the starved dog they tried to feed has suddenly bitten the hand of his benefactor. Moreover, it has made sentiments such as "All men are loved by God and should therefore be brothers" seem rather shallow, platitudinous, and logically doubtful.[16]

Deploying his usual criticism of Protestant liberalism, Hauerwas demonstrates an awareness that the equality and integration that white liberals advocated was, in practice, a call for blacks to accommodate to white values and culture. Any achievement of an actual equal and common social life cannot be founded on the terms of those in power who think equality means assimilation. Rather, in words resembling the co-temporary social analysis of James Cone, it is found in the particularity of black identity, in liberating self-sufficiency: Black Power is simply "a call from one black to another that the goods of this society are his not as he becomes what the white man wishes him to be, but only as he becomes a black man."[17]

Hauerwas claims that the Black Power movement is morally sound for two reasons. First, "It perceives with greater clarity and honesty the role of power in group relations" by asserting that African Americans no longer depend on the "good will" of whites. As such, Black Power was a necessary response to the idealism of Martin Luther King Jr. Second, "The black has had a special experience in America that he is intent on bringing with him into the future. This experience leaves him dissatisfied with the quality of life he sees in the wider society, and he is determined not to mimic it."[18] This, in fact, holds promise, he says uncritically, to enhance the "American experience."

Turning to white liberals, Hauerwas notes that they must now reckon with the fact that black people have given up on relying on the guilt of whites as motivation to act ethically. Though Hauerwas worries about a movement predicated on a refusal to form coalitions with others to achieve its goals, he believes this offers white people an "opportunity to seriously rethink [their] own position." He writes that it is only in this new reality in which "all the avenues which could relieve the guilt of being white have been cut off by the very people with which he wished to identify" that "we may someday find ourselves able to meet the black as a brother, in a far more profound way than is now possible."[19]

These insights were short-lived. Even when the Christian realism of this piece would fall away at the words of Alasdair MacIntyre and John Howard Yoder, there is no necessary reason this endorsement of Black Power and concerns about the effects of colorblindness could not be sustained.[20] Yet Hauerwas went twenty-five years before ever again broaching the subject.

When he does take it up again, Hauerwas identifies racism as a murky, shape-shifting issue: "The problem of race, it seems, is that it is by no means easy to say what the problem of race is."[21] This resonates with much of his analysis in the first 1969 essay, and identifies what is certainly an accurate and important claim. Yet, in this later form, it signals a breakdown in Hauerwas's treatment of race by turning his attention to white people's refusal to accept the forgiveness necessary to be free from their sin of racism.[22] This obfuscation of the most pressing issues of racism, and focus on the liberation of white people from their guilt, follows the tendency of white thinkers to prioritize the experience and feelings of whites, even in conversations about racial oppression and privilege—a symptom of white fragility.

In some of his best moments, Hauerwas focuses on the role of memory in white supremacy. In an article on Martin Luther King Jr. he argues, "The crucial question remains whether Americans can ever acknowledge what it means to be a slave nation."[23] America does not want to remember its history of slavery. "Rather, we want to assume that if everyone has 'civil rights,' if everyone is free to be an 'individual,' if everyone is moderately well off," he says, "then we can say to those who are still upset about past wrongs, 'Oh come on, what's a little slavery between friends?'"[24] To his credit, here Hauerwas uncovers an important insight about the new form of racism that infects a "postracial" society after the civil rights movement has "won," when whites presume equality for all. Prefiguring the growing number of scholars who would later write about the temptations of "colorblindness" and postracial racism, Hauerwas identifies the source of contemporary racism as a national amnesia regarding its long history of racial injustice. The loss of even traumatic or horrific memories forestalls any movement toward reconciliation, even when there is no easy way to right the situation.[25] Liberal civil society has an amnesic proclivity, and this is nowhere more true than when it comes to racial memory: "The member of the dominant race—failing to know how to speak of our wound—knows it only grows more painful the more deeply it is hidden within ourselves."[26] He contends that, as a society, we literally lack the language required to sufficiently recognize ourselves across the divisions our history has created. Despite liberalism's claims that we can be masters of our own story, we are bereft of any means of objectively narrating or interpreting our own experience outside of our community. This leaves us all in silence, lacking the tools to even articulate what we are now recognizing.

He adds, significantly, "As a result, blacks and whites can find no common story that will enable them to heal the wound."[27] Hauerwas then challenges proposals by C. Eric Lincoln and Miroslav Volf that reconciliation is actually predicated on the ability to forget. Hauerwas objects to both with the claim that atrocities remain locked in an inescapable "eternal present."[28] Our sins are made part of an economy of salvation and, thus, part of God's new community and our new story.[29] But this new story of God's faithfulness and salvation makes possible the truthful remembering of our past and its sins (presumably, those both perpetuated and suffered): "God does not forget our sins but rather redeems our sins in Eucharistic transformation."[30]

In nearly every occasion, however—even when waxing eschatological—Hauerwas chooses to direct these insights on forgetting into a critique of liberalism, and in doing so, neglects the parallel history of racism and amnesia within the church. Many white churches do not want to remember that slavery is part of their own history, but Hauerwas does not reflect on this. This is likely due to Hauerwas's partitioning of church and world and his frequent failure to acknowledge that the same "liberal" temptations that pervade the world emerge within and shape churches as well. The ecclesial origins of race and white supremacy in Western missionary and colonial ventures ought to place a primary challenge to the church's racism before society's, yet Hauerwas fails to acknowledge the church's role in inventing, spreading, and sustaining white supremacy.

He begins a 2008 essay by acknowledging criticisms of his insufficient dealings with race—attributed to his failure to "adequately support calls for justice or democracy."[31] Against these charges he levies his typical defense: that the church fails to be the church when it attempts to demonstrate its relevance by adopting humanistic strategies to make the world more free or just or democratic. This is not the work of the church, even if these may be worthy goals. And with one swift move the issue of racism is abstracted as a peripheral issue (one among a number of humanistic and democratic matters that ought to factor minimally in theology).

Hauerwas argues that liberalism may have actually impeded the process of racial reconciliation by placing humanity at the center of theological thought; it "confused humanism with the gospel" and deluded Christians into thinking that race can be solved through political machinations and maneuvers.[32] Civil rights discourse also relied too heavily on liberal rhetoric—"the freedom of the individual and all"—and that continues to inflect too much theological writing on racism today, he contends.[33] Instead, race must be first and foremost understood as a theological problem.[34] And here, Hauerwas identifies where he sees the conceptual location of the problem:

The sin therefore is that the whole issue of race is an effort to deny the sovereignty of God, to negate the absolute supremacy of God. Once a person has truly seen this truth, that person can no longer be a racist, and can no longer grovel in the agonies of self-pity. [Once she accepts the sovereignty of God] the racist is now afraid to call anyone unclean, to discriminate against anyone, to stand in judgment over any group or individual, or to set himself above any of God's human creatures.[35]

For Hauerwas, better theological descriptions can help us to understand racism as a matter of sin and reconciliation. Yet he appears to make the same move for which he criticizes other theologians and church leaders: spiritualizing or doctrinalizing an ethical issue in a way that abstracts it from the concrete suffering of actual people and the practice of actual churches. In a theological maneuver like this, he dismisses the insights of black theologians like James Cone that theology must be coupled with social analysis to have any concrete effect.[36]

Various criticisms of Hauerwas's evasion of race have emerged in the last few years. Derek Woodard-Lehman calls Hauerwas to account for his lack of sustained attention to the issue of race. Woodard-Lehman, a white scholar, claims that Hauerwas needs to demonstrate how his radical pacifistic ecclesiological ethic could offer a political form of resistance to the "dominative power" of racism. Because systemic and institutional racism does not qualify as a form of the narrow, physical violence on which he focuses, Hauerwas "leaves intact nonviolent forms of dominative power residually present in the everyday lives of Christians."[37] A society and theology that consider themselves "raceless" blind themselves to these deeper, more subtle forms of racist violence and fail to grasp social structures and arrangements that close off institutional and social access to particular groups. "In short, racially correlated lived inequalities are actual violence," asserts Woodard-Lehman and, thus, implicate "the white church itself [as] a structure of nonviolent violence."[38] James Logan, a black scholar, offers a similar critique, pondering, "Why Hauerwas refuses to risk writing constructively about 'the struggle,' and why he views the potential for unity and peace regarding the issue as hopelessly 'eschatological,' given his insights into the politics of ontological intimacy, is a real puzzle."[39]

Vietnamese American scholar Jonathan Tran argues in contrast that Hauerwas has already said too much on the issue of race. In fact, Hauerwas's self-confessed racism "absolves him of the need to say much of anything about the church's racism." Silence and the proleptic patience his silence conveys are more interesting options in the shadow of the church's racism, Tran contends.[40] He asks: Why does Hauerwas, particularly, need to say something about the church's racism? Couldn't others perhaps say it better? Not every white guy with influence needs to talk about race—and some may contribute more by actually remaining silent. By having the patience to remain silent, Hauerwas best confesses his racism within the structures of colorblindness that shield him from recognizing the effects of his own racial formation in whiteness. "Stanley can't see his racism because he is not supposed to," Tran argues. "This means that while he struggles against that which he sees as racist, he also misses a lot and in turn benefits from that rela- tive blindness. Much to his credit, Hauerwas doesn't pretend to get it, doesn't play that game in its personal or professional versions."[41] Often, Tran observes, Hauerwas's occasional excursions into the topic suggest that silence may be a bet- ter option for him! The vagueness that accompanies his treatments of race—like the discussion of sovereignty above—is "often what happens when white guys feel compelled to say something about a racism they can hardly see, and so cannot help but make inferences that the racism they created isn't so bad."[42] And if this is the alternative, silence is golden.

Beyond the insights of these criticisms, perhaps the most revealing line by Hauerwas is a confession that, due to the inescapable racism of his upbringing, "I have therefore refrained from pontificating on 'race' because I feared that that is what it would be—pontification."[43] He continues with an example: "For me to 'use' Martin Luther King Jr., and the church that made him possible, to advance my understanding of Christian ethics seems wrong." And then he adds, signifi- cantly, "That is not my story, though I pray that God will make that story my story, for I hope to enjoy the fellowship of the communion of saints."[44] He clari- fies in a footnote that his hesitancy in writing about race is "not that white people should not write about black people. . . . The issue is not whether we can under- stand one another's experience, but rather what one is trying to do in appropriat- ing another's story."[45] Hauerwas worries that speaking beyond one's own story risks inevitably instrumentalizing the other for the sake of one's own purpose or agenda.

This contradicts Hauerwas's claims elsewhere that avoiding speaking to oth- ers' stories risks a "kind of fatal abstractness" that floats above the lived realities of everyday existence and "makes no difference for how we live."[46] Thus, in this exchange (with himself) Hauerwas demonstrates the tension between the real- ity of one's epistemological limits and the perpetual need to reach beyond one's own story to connect with others. Yet, with this, Hauerwas does raise important and difficult questions about white subjectivity in relation to blackness. That is, he properly worries about the possibility of white engagement with black experi- ences or theology without also recolonizing or exploiting them. James Perkinson, a white theologian who often engages in theological treatments of race, frames the difficulty this way: "The world of black experience . . . must necessarily be comprehended as irremediably 'other' if it is not (yet one more time) to be reductively annexed to white experience and distorted by white theory." Yet "dismissal of Black Theology as a 'closed hermeneutical circle' of difference offering no point of contact or entry for white Christians obviously halts exchange before it can even begin."[47] The fraught task for white theologians and Christians is to avoid the twin poles of colonizing another's story, or simply evading it. To put this task constructively, white theology must begin to give an account of itself first and foremost, a witness of white theology "that is itself contextual and thus accountable to the situation of race."[48]

3. *Analyzing Hauerwas's Silence*

In light of this tension, two aspects of Hauerwas's treatment of race deserve further analysis for their broader implications for white theology. First is his tendency, when writing about "the black story," to either weaponize race as a tool against liberalism or theologize it away from its concrete empirical realities. These are both tendencies—perhaps even strategies—of the abstraction of whiteness. Identifying race as a theological problem is not itself an error; white supremacy is an invention of the Christian church, so race and racism cannot be untethered from their theological roots. However, when the act of naming race as a theological problem draws the theologian away from concrete matters of oppression and into broader concerns like the issues of God's sovereignty, theology becomes detached from the "concreteness of Christ's continued presence today"[49] as well as the practices and lived experiences of congregations. This reflects the habit of many white theologians to abide on the level of abstraction in order to avoid the complexity of concrete engagement—engagement that might reveal their own complicity in structures of injustice or compel them into costly action. In some ways this is simply a product of Hauerwas's anticonsequentialist and antiliberal ethical project: it is not the church's job to manage the world or make it turn out all right. He generally avoids talking about most marginalized communities or engaging with feminist, queer, or womanist theology. But on a practical level, Hauerwas's abstraction of race reinforces the dangerous colorblindness of our contemporary "postracial" culture. It is a strategy of evading the concrete realities of racism, white privilege, and white supremacy within actual churches, and fails to challenge the visible forms of racism that are now all too apparent in videos of police violence, voter restrictions, and data on structural inequality.

Second, he further, and personally, distances himself from the realities of race and the consequences of racism by claiming that the black story is not his story.[50] He acknowledges that this epistemological distance contradicts his claim that one risks an abstractness that floats above the lived realities of everyday existence when one avoids others' stories. Yet this reflects Charles Long's observation that for whites "to make this memory concrete and public would be to plunge the community into a radically contingent state."[51] In my interview with him, Hauerwas admitted that maybe this was not the most appropriate way to articulate his hesitancy. "To say it's not my story I mean there really is white privilege and I've enjoyed it even though I came from working-class people," he responded. "The story of civil rights, I always worried that there is such a desperate need for whites to have a moral identity and you could show that by siding with those in the struggle." He worried that any attempt to write about it risked instrumentalizing their struggle. "I didn't come to terms with the agony of not being able to know how to be on the right side without using the right side," he admits. "When whites are part of a black movement we take over!"[52]

This illuminates a concern that seems to paralyze his work: how might white theologians address or engage with the stories—including the suffering, hopes, resistance, flourishing, and modes of reasoning—of those oppressed by whiteness without colonizing and instrumentalizing them? He has not yet been able to reconcile this tension, but instead diagnoses that, as a society, Americans lack the language required to sufficiently recognize ourselves across the racial divisions that our own history has created. Such reasoning, then, can only leave most white theologians in silence. "I guess I haven't done more with [race] because I didn't see how," he laments.[53]

In the end, these two criticisms of Hauerwas's engagement with race reflect and illuminate the tendencies of white theology. They highlight the types of abstraction that are encouraged by the universalizing tendencies of whiteness that I outlined in chapters 1 and 2. And they press the question that Toni Morrison asked of white literary discourse, now in a theological register: "What are the strategies of escape from knowledge? Of willful oblivion?"[54] In his attempt to avoid universalizing his own story, Hauerwas simply disconnects his story from the experience of African Americans. However, in claiming that the black story is not his story, he only perpetuates the problem of white alienation from the struggles of African Americans.[55] Such a move effectively releases whites from accepting culpability and responsibility for black oppression in a time of colorblindness. James Baldwin identified this tendency sixty years ago among white Americans "who evade, so far as possible, all genuine experience, [and] have therefore no way of assessing the experience of others and no way of establishing themselves in relation to any way of life which is not their own."[56] Baldwin would later register a more pointed observation that this detachment is often intentional; whites do not accept the grievances of black America because they cannot face what this reality says about themselves.[57] Thus, Hauerwas's reasoning reflects that of many other white theologians who fail to address race because of thoughts of inadequacy, colorblindness, denials of reality, or other detachments

from the story—the lived experience—of persons of color. In an attempt to analyze these reasons at a deeper level, I now turn to the ways in which white witness
theologians' reliance on the concepts of narrative and tradition employed by philosopher Alasdair MacIntyre impact their theological approach to race.

4. *White Theology's Captivity to Tradition*

That Hauerwas is indebted to Alasdair MacIntyre is no secret. Hauerwas has
absorbed MacIntyre's concepts of tradition and narrative, and these have guided
and shaped his theological and ecclesiological work for the past forty years. I argue
that Hauerwas's commitment to MacIntyre's concepts also frames his views of
race—racial communities themselves are traditions—and therefore underlies his
reluctance to address the issue, a perspective not unique to Hauerwas. The concept of tradition, as defined by or at least filtered through MacIntyre, has not
only informed the conceptual imaginations of traditionalist theologians but also
shaped much of Western theology over the past thirty years.[58] It has given philosophical scaffolding to the notions of community, story, and pluralism as well
as to questions of what to do with inherited traditions and how to think about
the contested boundaries of those traditions—questions that theologians have
wrestled with for many years, but especially in this time of growing plurality.

Tradition and Evaluation

For MacIntyre, the concepts of tradition and narrative are inextricably intertwined; the coherence and explanatory power of a tradition's story is what
constitutes that tradition.[59] A tradition "not only embodies the narrative of an
argument, but it is only to be recovered by an argumentative retelling of that
narrative which will itself be in conflict with other argumentative retellings"—a
kind of "tournament of narratives."[60] Since all moral questions and judgments are
bound within a tradition of moral inquiry, for MacIntyre, every tradition maintains its own conception of the good, inherent to its own modes of reasoning,
with no common reason or universal rationality to adjudicate claims between
traditions; thus, most traditions will hold rival and incommensurable conceptions of the good. When one tradition encounters another, they must adjudicate their divergent conceptions of the good through a process of immanent
critique—evaluating and challenging the alternative tradition on its own terms,
discovering flaws in its own logic or narrative. In this process, it is "possible for
one such tradition to defeat another in respect of the adequacy of its claims to
truth and to rational justification," whether adherents of that other tradition ever

realize it or not.[61] Significantly, in this mode of adjudicating rival, incommensurable truth or moral claims, one system of thought and practice—one tradition—emerges as rationally superior by revealing that a counter-standpoint fails by its own standards.[62]

One observes in this description the hypercompetitive language and goal of rational superiority inherent to this form of "traditioned" reasoning. One tradition or community must attend to the rival tradition's strongest claims and present its own claims with full transparency in order to be vindicated—and vindication or victory is the goal. At his most agonistic, MacIntyre describes in these terms the competitive encounter between rival traditions: "that narrative prevails over its rivals which is able to include its rivals within it, not only to retell their stories as episodes within its story, but to tell the story of the telling of their stories as such episodes."[63] In other words, in addition to its competitive agonism, there is a hegemonic, imperialist impulse at work here. There will be winners and losers.

This account of tradition has received direct criticism from liberation theology and black theology. For example, Willie Jennings argues that the notion of tradition already exhibits racially coded language. In *The Christian Imagination*, Jennings analyzes MacIntyre's concept of tradition in light of the theologically-infused New World colonialism that triggered white supremacy. As he puts it, "The inner coherence of traditioned Christian inquiry was grafted onto the inner coherence of colonialism."[64] Jennings's critique points to the failure of the Christian tradition to recognize its captivity to a colonialist and racist logic and reform itself in light of its racist vestments.[65] According to Jennings, MacIntyre's (and presumably Hauerwas's) unreflectiveness about the colonialist origins of this fusion of theology and tradition masks the dangerous evaluative power of the concept. Jennings observes that for MacIntyre, tradition "carries within itself the apparatus of judgment," that is, the ability to judge the practices, practitioners, and tools of evaluation of its own and other traditions. Once European theology adopted the evaluative, colonialist impulse and lens I described in chapter 2, its apparatus of judgment became defined by this racist moment: tradition served as a tool for evaluating and sorting groups of people based on bodily characteristics like skin color. The ability to judge turned European Christianity's evaluative gaze comprehensively onto the bodies of the new, native, and darker bodies it encountered in the New World.[66] According to Jennings, deployments of tradition in theology functioned as a technology of racial formation by enabling a coherent vision of evaluation (of people, their cultural goods, and their rationalities and spiritualities) and provided a means to sort people into insiders and outsiders—and still do.[67] This desire to sort and evaluate that continues to pervade white theology is predicated on racially charged notions of comparison that developed alongside the modern capitalist market economy during colonialism. In the way that theologians like Hauerwas have adopted and even amplified MacIntyre's comparative and competitive model of tradition, they enter into the performance of white, masculine hegemonic subjectivity, since this modern concept developed alongside the notion of race. I suspect that Jennings has the hypercompetitive, agonistic methodology of MacIntyre's concept of tradition in mind when he makes his critiques. In this worldview, communities necessarily exist as rivals, continually evaluating the other with the ultimate aim of defeating or conquering one another.[68]

Identifying Hauerwas's debt to MacIntyre, Jeffrey Stout observes that, for Hauerwas, "rational discourse must proceed within a framework that accords [his] own point of view legitimacy over against its competitors." This is true, he indicates, both in Hauerwas's polemical rhetoric, but also in the content of that rhetoric. That is, according to Stout, for Hauerwas there is no possibility of a noncompetitive intertraditional discourse, or what Stout calls a "loosely structured democratic conversation in which variously situated selves tell their own stories on their own terms."[69] Such a practice is impossible on Hauerwas's terms due to his skepticism of models of "democratic" conversations. Hauerwas does not possess a framework for engaging this type of dialogue that would not lean on some foundational universal rationality. In fact, he admits that a common criticism of his work is that he "can give no account of how tribal groups can ever come to share a language."[70]

This influences his account of the church and its relationship with the world—certainly two rival traditions—and, I argue, seems to do the same with his treatment of race. While other white theologians may not follow Hauerwas in his sharp delineation between church and world, this framework of tradition, and specifically of the rivalry and incommensurability inherent to it, is implicated in the racial logics of white theologians more broadly. That is, in their avoidance, defensiveness, or oblivion to issues of race and racism as well as the ways their social location of whiteness impacts their work, many white theologians implicitly or explicitly replicate MacIntyre's notion of tradition in their approach to race. As Hauerwas frequently claims, "You can only act in the world you can see and you can only see what you have learned to say."[71] It seems that once you have learned to say "tradition" you begin to see it everywhere.

Rival Racial Traditions

There are two further implications of this traditioned framework for thinking about race. First, Hauerwas's claim that the black story is not his own appears to be influenced by this MacIntyrean disposition: Hauerwas sees the two stories of white America and black America (or the white church/theology and black church/theology) as two "rival traditions." That is, in claiming that blackness and whiteness represent two separate "worlds" or "stories," Hauerwas treats them as two rival traditions of moral inquiry: each contains its own internal logic that is incommensurable and untranslatable to those outside the community.[72] This is illustrated by a story Hauerwas told from his graduate school days of attending a lecture by Malcolm X. Hauerwas remembers Malcolm chastising his largely black audience to stop black-on-black urban violence, secure employment, and stay faithful to their families. "He was saying all the things to his black audience that we were taught by racists to say about African Americans," Hauerwas observed. "And what do you do as a white man in that?"[73] Malcolm X deployed what appeared to be the same language as white racists to goad his mostly black audience toward self-sufficiency. The same words operated in different and incommensurable registers, or according to different grammars, because of the community from and to which he spoke. Thus, the white story and black story remain closed systems, comprehended only within their own incommensurable grammars in the competitive and agonistic manner MacIntyre charts. In this situation of inescapable rivalry between these stories, Hauerwas is concerned that whites will take over, at worst, and use the black story for their own agenda, at best. His eschewing any language that smells of liberalism prevents appeal to mediating concepts like justice or democracy and only adds to this constrained imagination.

But this account of race relations is simply too agonistic. Hauerwas's MacIntyrean captivity limits his ability to imagine the possibility of listening across cultural and racial divides, and in response, amending one's own narrative. His sense of tradition and narrative renders white theology and the white church too closed and too bounded, and also renders any encounter with another community an agonistic threat—amplifying the antagonism to other traditions (religions) that helped generate white supremacy in the first place (see chapter 2, this volume). In Hauerwas's case, this understanding of tradition leads only to two responses: (1) a theological abstraction that threatens to reinforce colorblindness and overlook the effects of whiteness, or (2) complete avoidance of the other in order to prevent a clash of cultures.[74] We have seen already the ways Hauerwas deploys both of these options—abstraction and detachment. If white theologians continue to employ this notion of tradition, and its implicit agonistics, we are vulnerable to seeing the stories of any other, such as liberation, black, and womanist theologies, as necessarily rival to our own. Understanding the black story and white story as two independent, intersecting, and overlapping stories—predicated on the competitive and evaluative concept of *tradition*—places the white story as normative hegemon in a fearful, defensive posture rather than in a relationship of mutual exchange and self-correction.[75] This understanding obscures the ways these stories—if they are distinct stories at all—can be porous, embedded in one another, and malleable through the encounter.[76] Such reasoning reinforces white theology's blindness to the reality that "the oppressed and the oppressor are bound together within the same society; they accept the same criteria, they share the same beliefs, they both alike depend on the same reality."[77]

Second, the defensiveness of a theology framed by this account of tradition and the closed ecclesiology it projects obscure the ability of these theologians to understand their own formative narratives. Specifically, understanding the white story as a tradition prevents white theologians and the churchgoers they influence from understanding the formative role whiteness plays in that story—that is, how it limits the horizon of vision, rendering some objects, concepts, and people invisible. A tradition certainly adapts, as an internal argument, in light of changing circumstances, but it rarely questions the naturalness of the resources upon which it draws to construct that argument—in this case, whiteness. In other words, embedded within the witness of this theology is a blindness to its own whiteness.

Uncovering this blindness would involve understanding the MacIntyrean model, as Jennings insists, to be a product of whiteness. The captivity of traditionalist theologians like Hauerwas to this model is a consequence of what Emilie Townes calls uninterrogated whiteness: a failure to examine the ways that whiteness determines the issues we address, the questions we ask, and the answers we find for those questions.[78] This traditioned mentality that results in a view of the church as a faithful colony of "resident aliens" in the midst of sinful world invites Hauerwas's readers to inhabit a state of self-righteousness at best, and victimhood at worst—to embody the ressentiment addressed in chapter 1. I don't think he intends this consequence, but his church/world dualism does nothing to prevent this thread of white theology from legitimating what Katie Grimes calls a "batten down the hatches" approach to changing demographic realities and the need for interrogating its own racism.[79]

Specifically, while Hauerwas maintains that it is not the responsibility of Christians to manage the world, he fails to see the ways churches have already participated in managing the world wrongly. James Logan observes that Hauerwas fails to understand racism as a "distortion in the grammar of the Christian faith" itself.[80] Hauerwas himself has not learned to see the ways the church itself is a community shaped by racial formation because, in Hauerwas's own terms, he has not learned how to say that. Put another way, his church—the white church—has not provided the habits of speech that enable him, and other white theologians to properly see and make sense of a racially formed world and church. It has not engaged in the sorts of practices that open up new ways of seeing and saying. The particularities of whiteness that shape white theology and churches are eclipsed. As Townes recognizes, "unexamined particularities" render theologians a dangerous bunch when we then attempt to shape ideas and social realities based on those particularities.[81] As representative of white traditionalist theologians, Hauerwas's predisposition toward MacIntyre's model commits him to a language and structural mechanism that help to justify this eclipse. In doing so, he illuminates the tendencies of many white theologians to avoid, abstract, or remain blind to our own racial formation. By speaking of the white Christian story as a tradition, he falls into or even promotes white fragility. Any proposals to engage, co-narrate, or amend that tradition can only be perceived as threats that must be combated or evaded.

5. Conclusion: Postliberal Resources for Confronting Whiteness?

The silence of white theologians like Hauerwas reveals the blindnesses and biases of those committed to defending the Christian "tradition," even—perhaps unwittingly—at the expense of concrete racial justice. Yet even morally compromised figures may be instructive in the ways they are compromised. Hauerwas's particular shortcomings may be theologically insightful and productive in combating the silence that whiteness—and his witness—engenders. While Niebuhr may have been the most attentive to racism—at least among the three white theologians I have analyzed here—Hauerwas most clearly names the reasons for his own evasion. While they promote a posture of evasion, the reasons he provides for his silence, in the distinctive forms developed by witness theology, may be useful in directing white theologians to address a topic as complex and shifty as whiteness—even if he does not.

Thus, my argument is not a generic plea for white theologians to "write about" race. What Tran says is true: not every theologian must engage every issue. In doing so, some may, in fact, do more harm than good. Yet because the tentacles of white supremacy touch every social issue, and every white person and white scholar participate in it, the more precise and urgent work of white theologians is uncovering the ways whiteness already configures our work.[82] We must expose the ways our work has been inflected by whiteness, but also look for the forms of resistance that may inhabit it. This may well result in writing about it, especially in the mode of repentance, but will hopefully more broadly result in generating resources for and commitments to an ethic of responsibility that addresses the complex history, theology, and injustice produced by whiteness.

In addition, I am suggesting that Hauerwas may be particularly useful in this task. The way race figures within his theological model illuminates three conceptual resources that align with James Cone's proposal for white Christians' response to racism; the three concepts of memory, particularity, and concreteness that feature somewhat prominently in Hauerwas's work also constitute the building blocks of Cone's vision of white solidarity with oppressed black people. Yet while Hauerwas engages them—a promising development for resistance to white supremacy—these same theological resources also help to undergird his white supremacy because of the shortcomings I have already identified in this chapter. I analyze and develop these resources more fully over the final three chapters—most immediately in the next chapter, taking a look at the ways they are critically redirected in Cone's theology—as they animate my argument for an ethics of responsibility to confront white supremacy that composes the remainder of this book. However, I want to briefly identify these three resources at the conclusion of this chapter in order to demonstrate the ways they are indicated, and misdirected, within white theology—and specifically within Hauerwas's thought—while still holding out promise for their redemption.

Memory

The focus on narrative intrinsic to traditionalist and witness theology helps to identify racism as fundamentally a problem with memory. In one essay Hauerwas notes, "The member of the dominant race—failing to know how to speak of our wound—knows it only grows more painful the more deeply it is hidden within ourselves."[83] I contend that memory of our own sins and oppression of others is not only a key to Christian witness but also the first, and necessary, step toward responsibility. This forms the first move in combating the amnesic tendencies of a society that prides itself on being postracial and colorblind. Hauerwas insists on the importance of memory in order to tell our story correctly. There is even a promising moment in an extended reflection on friendship in his most recent book, *The Character of Virtue* (published in 2018 but this chapter written in 2005), Hauerwas admits, "For what is friendship but the discovery that I don't want to tell my story—can't tell my story—without your story?"[84] This reference to narrative falls out of the discussion quickly, but this moment suggests that Hauerwas recognizes the ability to see, even the necessity of seeing, the interconnectedness of stories, and of attempting to narrate our own story as entangled with another's. Yet his account of incommensurable racial stories cripples any engagement with theologians of color and produces his silence in regard to race. This results in a tapered memory that neglects the racist history of the church. While he highlights the importance of memory, his memory of racism focuses on "the world" and ignores the theological significance of lynching, for example, or the role of the church in developing and supporting race-based slavery.

In his description of theology as a work of *practical wisdom*, Hauerwas defines this wisdom as "a habit of attentiveness that makes past experiences a resource" to "unconceal" the significance of the present.[85] The next step will be to move past Hauerwas in order to attend to the past in such a way that it unconceals the latent racism veiled in our present pretensions to colorblindness. This step begins with acknowledging the sordid theological history outlined in chapter 2 in a way that leads white Christians to take responsibility for white supremacy.

Particularity

Hauerwas begins his treatment of race in his first published essay (1969) by suggesting that white liberals' calls for integration and reconciliation only mask their hidden desire for African Americans to assimilate to white values and culture. As I noted earlier, the early Hauerwas recognizes "a call from one black to another that the goods of this society are his not as he becomes what the white man wishes him to be, but only as he becomes a black man."[86] This astute claim about self-determination points to his deeper concern for particularity.

Yet this attention to particularity is manifest most prominently and provocatively in his staunch defense of the distinctiveness of the church from the world and the particularity of Christian witness. For Hauerwas, the church has a particular communal identity because of its commitment to a particular narrative. This narrative gives the church its identity, which is what makes Christians distinct from the world—whether they live up to it or not. Communities train members in the virtues necessary to embody the truths that their stories make meaningful, offering members a teleological vision of their life together. For Hauerwas, then, truth is knowable only within the context of particular traditions and communities. His claim that a universally valid objective model of morality does not exist is perhaps his most fundamental claim. Truth must correspond to the vision of reality of the tradition-bearing community that proclaims that truth. He contends that the modern epistemological assumptions of a least-common-denominator universal truth (and postmodern, atomized, individual "truth") sever persons from the communities and stories that order their lives. In contrast, he claims that people need these stories to make their lives intelligible, and these stories are discovered within the communities in which we locate ourselves. "All ethical reflection occurs relative to a particular time and place," he claims, "[and] the very nature and structure of ethics is determined by the particularities of a community's history and convictions."[87]

This demonstrates that Hauerwas is concerned for multiple social and cultural particularities and opposes many forms of universalism more generally. This emphasis on particularity could be applied to the dangers of abstracting from the realities of our racial pasts and presents—even Hauerwas's own. And while he seems to do this in the conclusion to his 1969 essay, in which Hauerwas calls whites to critically question the character of whiteness—in Hauerwas's words, "what kind of men we wish to be, and in what kind of society we wish to live"— this self-interrogation is short-lived. After this point, the invisible witness of Hauerwas's whiteness is a theological ethics that occasionally addresses racism (and admits his own racism) as a symptom of liberalism, or a consequence of an insufficient accounting of God's sovereignty, but is reflexively unable to illuminate the ways its embeddedness within whiteness has sculpted the story he tells.

In his claims that the black church story is not his to tell, Hauerwas seems to be concerned about Christianity's fundamental deformity of colonialism, even supersessionism: taking over another people's story as its own and insisting that the appropriated people do not understand that story as well as we do. Hauerwas is concerned with colonizing the black church's story. But his worry about a very real and sinful tendency in Christianity, and specifically here in white Christianity, leads him to avoid engagement with that story—and its storytellers—altogether. The particularity of Hauerwas's witness becomes a whitewashed universal ecclesiology incapable of digging deep enough to uncover the points at which that whiteness takes over and blinds him—and most white theologians—to the particularity of our privilege. This is one of the lessons of black theologians like James Cone: white theologians cannot escape the pretension to universality that plagues much of white theology, despite our best efforts, and often because of no effort.[88]

Concreteness

Finally, Hauerwas's (limited) commitment to particularity leads to an ethics that attempts to deal with concrete reality. Again, in his first published essay, he claims that Christians must critically evaluate all of our values in light of the "concrete situation." Here he has the resources to argue that attention to the concrete and fleshly realities faced by persons of color, as well as concrete realities of our own whiteness, will enable white theologians to see past the blindnesses and amnesia that our abstract values and thinking perpetuate. This approach would mean attending to the way we perceive bodies and flesh, to structural evils in the criminal justice system and voting laws, to empirical churches and the plethora of social analysis on the racial damages they continue to inflict, and to the ways our white flesh directs and constricts our vision.

Yet, this early attention to concrete reality, again, falls out of his concern. Hauerwas's church floats above the concrete and lived reality of people in the pews. The empirical reality of churches is much more textured than Hauerwas often allows, as Kathryn Tanner contends, and admits of an internal pluralism—the intersection of many formative stories interacting in various ways to shape a particular community.[89] This account of the church, Willis Jenkins notes, leads Hauerwas to conclude that "concrete responsiveness to social context does not matter for the church's performance of itself."[90] The result is an inadequate reflection on the concrete lives of congregations, an abstraction that he himself would criticize if he had eyes to perceive it.[91]

While each of these theological concepts highlights the unexplored commonalities between traditionalist and liberationist theologies, Hauerwas fails to understand them as resources capable of contesting white supremacy. For that, we need to analyze the ways that James Cone employs them to this end. I turn to Cone and black liberation theology in the next chapter.

4

Narrating Black Theology

1. A Story-Shaped Ebenezer

Dr. Raphael Warnock stood behind the pulpit at historic Ebenezer Baptist Church in Atlanta. Small in stature, his voice booming, he was bringing the morning's sermon to a climax. I was one of a sizeable number of white visitors (and several white members) scattered throughout the packed sanctuary. It was the Sunday before the 2008 presidential election.

I frequently visited Ebenezer during my short tenure in Atlanta. Portraits of Martin Luther Kings Jr. and Sr. hung on the narthex wall. The Southern Christian Leadership Conference (SCLC) was established in one of its basement rooms; King Jr. inspired marchers and freedom riders from its pulpit. The legacies of King and the civil rights movement are still thick in the air. That story continues to shape the identity of this church. In fact, portraits of the elder and younger Kings hang in nearly every room, as if watching over the congregation. The vision inspired by these two leaders guides the work and mission of this church, a reminder that this church is accountable to the groundwork laid by the sweat and blood of those struggling for black freedom. "We must always remember that this is the church he came from," one pastor said. "We are built on the bones of King."[1] Two days later the church would host an Election Night Watch Service, turning into a celebration at the election of the first African American president of the United States. Associate Pastor Shanan Jones would tell me that Watch Nights have been an ingredient of black religion since the days of slavery as a way to commemorate the story of black faith.[2] The retelling of this history, of slavery and Jim Crow lynching, of marches and dreams of freedom, of contemporary police brutality and stand-your-ground laws, permeates Ebenezer's worship and community outreach. Stories of struggle and liberation emanate from their hymns, emerge in testimonies during worship, and merge with scriptural accounts of God's providence and deliverance.

Witnessing Whiteness. Kristopher Norris, Oxford University Press (2020). © Oxford University Press.
DOI: 10.1093/oso/9780190055813.001.0001

This Sunday, Warnock was preaching about the Israelites, standing on the verge of the Promised Land. When all the other spies came back and said crossing into Canaan was too dangerous, Warnock placed the words of Obama's campaign theme into the mouths of Joshua and Caleb—"Yes, we can!" The congregation joined the refrain, chanting, singing, and rejoicing in the story that was now theirs. According to Warnock, central to the black church's mission is the proclamation of a liberationist faith rooted in the stories of Scripture and the black church's history.[3] As preacher, Warnock self-consciously serves as the storyteller of the community, the one charged with recalling and interpreting these stories of liberation in Scripture readings, prayer, song, and sermon.

Warnock studied under James Cone, the founder of black liberation theology, who claimed, "In black churches, the one who preaches the Word is primarily a *storyteller*. . . . The story was both the medium through which truth was communicated and also a constituent of truth itself."[4] Warnock does this by preaching with the Bible in one hand and the newspaper in the other; he recounts writing a brand-new sermon late one Saturday night after the Trayvon Martin shooting verdict was announced. Ebenezer is shaped by stories of Scripture as they are woven into and alongside the stories of black suffering and victory and the history of this particular congregation. In this way, Cone's black theology permeates this congregation, connecting liturgy, history, and current reality within the mission and story of the church.

Another of Cone's students, James Evans, writes that the black religious experience has been "story-shaped" from its beginning. In fact, it arises from the intersection of two stories: the canonical story of God's liberation of the Hebrews and continuing liberation through the ministry of Jesus, and the folk story of African American hope amid oppression.[5] It becomes the job of both theologian and church to relate these two stories in the people's life and worship. Evans appeals to his mentor, who argues that the black church originated as a storytelling community during the time of slavery. Enslaved people "had to devise a language commensurate with their social situation," Cone writes. "That was why they told stories. Through the medium of stories, black slaves created concrete and vivid pictures of their past and present existence, using historical images of God's dealings with his people and thus breaking open a future for the oppressed not known to ordinary historical observation."[6] Drawing on these claims, Evans observes that the practices of the black church, from preaching to protest, express a story that relates the hope of the biblical message with the reality of black experience.[7]

Building on Evans's claim, I argue that the black liberation theology James Cone founded and proclaimed is a story-shaped theology, because Cone is a story-shaped theologian. He began his career in 1969 with his *Black Theology and Black Power*, written in the aftermath of King's assassination. He is credited with founding the field of black liberation theology, which he defines as "a theology that is unreservedly identified with the goals of the oppressed community and seeking to interpret the divine character of their struggle for liberation."[8] By identifying the forces of liberation as the essence of the gospel—that is, the person and work of Jesus Christ—Cone discovers this theology in anyone working for the liberation of the oppressed, identified in his first book as residing in the Black Power movement.

Thus, while he is not often referenced as an ecclesially minded theologian, he is often eager to note his debt to the spiritual and theological influence of his rearing in Macedonia AME Church in Bearden, Arkansas. Cone was formed in a spiritual environment where story was key. "The Christian life is not identified with doctrine but with story," he writes, "with the story of Jesus."[9] In fact, as much as Cone criticizes the church, white and black, he knew that he had to return to the formative story of the black church in order to write his theology. In his posthumously published memoir, he recalls, "I had to go back home to Arkansas to write my first book." Cone writes that he would immerse himself in black church worship, "reminding me what I was writing about and for whom I was writing."[10] He did the same thing when he realized that he needed to make a sharper turn away from the white, European theology of the academy and toward the organic theology of the black community. So he returned to Bearden. "Without going back to Macedonia and re-experiencing what I felt as a child, I couldn't have written *The Spirituals and the Blues*," he confesses.[11] Returning home and experiencing the story of black faith once again, proclaimed in sermon, testified in song, "I felt as if black folk in Bearden were talking to me, telling me to speak the truth."[12]

Cone explains that growing up in Macedonia AME, he was "given a faith that sustained my personhood and dignity in spite of white people's brutality."[13] He continually claims that the church was and still is formative for his life and work: "It was the world I grew up in. My identity as a human being comes out of the church."[14] In an earlier memoir he asserted,

> After being treated as things for six days of the week, black folk went to church on Sunday in order to affirm and experience another definition of their humanity. In the eyes of the Almighty, they were children of God whose future was not defined by the white structures that humiliated them. . . . Everybody became somebody and there were no second-class people at Macedonia.[15]

In these passages, Cone recognizes the power and significance of the black church experience during his childhood for shaping his theological development; this acknowledgment helps to fuel his theological attention to the particularity of theological claims and sources. While Cone's debt to the church is often over-looked in light of his criticism of it, such passages reveal the way he tethers black theology to the story the church tells.

My argument in this chapter is that black theology is a narrative theology, founded in the story of the black church and shaped by that community's par-ticular history, faith, and struggle for liberation. This is to affirm, as Cone claims, that black theology "is expressed in the style of story."[16] The intent is not to sub-sume black liberation theology into the conventional modes of white, postliberal narrative theology but to look at it as a narrative theology that not only offers an alternative to the narrative of white theology but also illuminates the racist aspects of white theology and church practice. I draw here upon the resources of the black experience and black culture to construct a path forward for liberation and flourishing for all by clinging to the belief that the white and black stories share a common life and end.

In this chapter I demonstrate the ways Cone's story-shaped theology, and specifically ecclesiology, present a direct challenge to the unexamined whiteness within white theologies, such as that of Stanley Hauerwas. Thus, I identify Cone as a narrative theologian, not in the conventional sense, rather, but through the genre of counternarrative.[17] By drawing his theology out of the twin stories of the gospel and black experience, Cone breaks open the discipline of narrative theology into a broader category inclusive of narrative models that disrupt the normative stories shaped by those in power. As the founder of black theology, Cone offers an urgent correction to white theology and white churches by dem-onstrating the ways its story and practice are bound up in whiteness—sometimes directly, often indirectly. Hauerwas's narrative leads to incommensurability—Cone's, ultimately, to invitation and conversion.

In order to analyze these challenges I offer an account of Cone's narrative theology, issuing first in sharp criticisms of the church, which display their loss of foundational stories and seduction by white theology. I then argue for reading Cone as a narrative theologian in the sense just described, one who provides a particular concept of story, emerging in his writings on "blackness," that refines and challenges the concepts of story, community, and church found in white wit-ness theology. In the chapter's conclusion, I identify how Cone's story-shaped theology offers resources to construct an ethic of responsibility for resisting white supremacy.

2. Cone's Church Criticism

Most of Cone's constructive ecclesiological work can be gleaned from the specific criticisms he levies against the church. The church, for him, is the community that participates in God's liberating work in history.[18] He defines *the church* in his early work: "The church is that people called into being by the power and love of God to share in [God's] revolutionary activity for the liberation of man," constituted by the marks of proclamation of the gospel, service to others, and fellowship in community (*kerygma, diakonia,* and *koinonia*).[19] As such, the church, through its preaching, proclaims the reality of divine liberation; through its service actively shares in the liberation struggle; and through its life together becomes a visible manifestation—or witness—to the reality of the gospel.[20] In a later writing he also explicitly frames the church Christologically as "that people who have been called into being by the life, death, and resurrection of Jesus so that they can bear witness to Jesus' Lordship by participating with him in the struggle of freedom."[21] The church tells the story of Christ's victory and invites people to live as if God has already won the battle over racism—that is, to live into this gospel reality.[22] He goes on, however, to suggest that this Christological basis privileges the church's human and political role over its spiritual task: "This means that the primary definition of the church is not its confessional affirmations but rather its political commitment on behalf of the poor."[23] Cone is more likely to find the church wherever one discerns that God is moving (such as the Black Power and Black Lives Matter movements), even if participants do not presume to know that they are advancing the cause of God. These parables of the kingdom, to employ Karl Barth's term, then chastise and instruct the institutional church in faithfulness. Cone's vision of the church is intentionally more ambiguous than Hauerwas's, though it is never far from Macedonia.

Criticism of White Churches

Cone actually spends little time criticizing white churches relative to the attention he gives his own black church tradition. While the sins of the white church are certainly more egregious, Cone devotes most of his critical attention toward his own community. In fact, his underlying critique of the black church concerns the ways that it mimics the pitfalls of the white church. Consequently, a few significant elements of his assessment of the white church are directly related to criticisms I have identified in previous chapters.

First, Cone claims that the white church operates with a truncated view of the gospel. He simultaneously describes this failure as a circumscription of the gospel narrative and its abstraction into an exclusive focus on spirituality with little to say to the empirical social or political conditions of the oppressed.[24] White Christians embrace a gospel vision that eclipses the political demand for the liberation of victims that Cone finds in both the black church's history and the scriptural narrative. Like the history of Christian superiority that supported racial oppression, this narrow view of the gospel is due both to the position of privilege held by the white church (its lack of material need blinds it to the material elements of the gospel message) and, in a more sinister manner, to the white church's position of oppressor (white churches present religion as an opium for the oppressed so that they will not challenge the unjust conditions of society).[25]

The second element of this critique is the way in which white theology has become an agent of the state and its racist policies, reflecting the coupling of theology and nation-state and the church's use of state power to inflict its oppression. "At least since the time of the Emperor Constantine and his making of Christianity the official religion of the Roman State," Cone writes, "the chief interpreters of the Christian tradition have advocated a spiritual view of the gospel that separated the confession of faith from the practice of political justice."[26] As this Constantinian theology became translated into Reformation theology and then European colonialist theology, white American theology followed suit and became subservient to the state—which for Cone means blindly patriotic in a way that perpetuates the structural racist inclinations of the state.[27]

Third, white churches fail to see how their theology is inseparable from their oppressor mentality, which shapes everything they say about God.[28] In other words, white theologians and churches are blind to the contextually dependent nature of all theology, especially discourse about the community of God. Cone understands this to be, in fact, a Docetic denial of the incarnation.[29] Racism that is supported by a theology blind to its own contextuality displays as a simple failure to understand how God chose to enter into a particular context with a particular ethnicity and particular sociopolitical location—as an oppressed Jew in Roman-colonized Palestine—rendering all theology particular. The problem of universalizing results in the white church's blindness to the ways its own racial formation shapes the narrative it tells itself.

In light of these critiques, Cone still offers a proposal for white churches and theology. I return to this proposal in more detail later, but he contends, in short, white churches must recognize the manner in which their own racial formation has shaped their theological perspective, acknowledge the ways in which their story has become heretical and harmful, and shed their white being and submit to be created anew in black being in order to have any chance of becoming reconciled with the black community.[30]

Criticism of the Black Church

Cone directs most of his attention and criticism to the black church. "There can be no genuine Christian theology," he says, "without prophetic self-criticism of the Christian community that gives birth to it."[31] In my interview with him,

Cone soberly claimed, "If there is any Christian religious identity, it is coming out of African Americans."[32] The power of the black church lies in its long history of being the "single most important institution in the black community."[33] The black church's antebellum origins reside in people whose daily existence was scripted by their encounter with the reality of white power. For enslaved people the black church provided a strengthening source of identity and community. The historical and social context of the black community formed the church into a public communal space set apart from the hegemonic force of white society and control, a necessarily more expansive public—and political—role than their white counterparts performed. Affirming the church's intersectional public role, Cone writes that "the black church was born in protest,"[34] and as the sole source of community, it became the home base of revolutionary activity. Enslaved people used the church as a platform to proclaim freedom and equality, and occasionally plan uprisings. This activist antebellum church became involved in activities like aiding the Underground Railroad and coordinating insurrections.[35] Such action was possible because the community refused to accept white interpretations of Christianity that focused on otherworldly salvation.

Black churches experienced a significant shift after the Civil War, however. As former enslaved people were expelled from white churches during Reconstruction, these sociopolitical developments led to two changes: the expansion of black congregations and development of independent black denominations, and a shift from revolutionary social activism to therapeutic social escape.[36] The church became a sanctuary where African Americans could shake free from the white reality that demeaned and humiliated them.[37]

Cone views this time as a loss of the church's origin and identity—an accommodation to the oppressor's worldview and wishes. "The injustices of the present were minimized" as black churches adopted the theology of white preachers and theologians, their congregations to look only to eschatological redemption.[38] He insists that congregations became "perversions of the gospel of Christ and places for accommodating the oppressed plight of black people."[39] Though some black churches participated in the black freedom struggle, most have remained retreatist, focused on spiritual concerns over the liberation of black people in their communities.[40] Even in this current period of visible white supremacy and black resistance, he believes, the black church remains an obstacle to black liberation.

Cone diagnoses the reason for this failure of black churches: they abandoned their formative narrative and adopted the story that white theology tells. "The black church," he says, "has not responded to the needs of its people. It has, rather, drained the community, seeking to be more and more like the white church. Its ministers have condemned the helpless and have mimicked the values of whites."[41] In his memoir Cone tells of his debates with Charles Long, who dismissed theology as a "western concept created by Europeans."[42] Yet, despite his many critiques, Cone did not give up on the black church and black theology.

For Cone, the particularity of a community's own story shapes its identity and mission. But when churches turn elsewhere, outside of their own story, they lose their way. When the black church's story began to identify with a passive Jesus concerned exclusively with saving souls, this narrative shaped the social outlook of the black church as well as the story it told about itself. It allowed the white church's alien narrative to become its own. The postbellum black church "fell into the white trick of interpreting salvation in terms similar to those of the white oppressors. Salvation became white: an objective act of Christ in which God 'washes' away our sins in order to prepare us for a new life in heaven."[43] This adoption meant that black congregations became agents in their own oppression, perpetuating the very systems that kept them underfoot. He writes, "By failing to connect the gospel with the bodily liberation of the poor, black churches forgot about their unique historical and theological identity and began to preach a gospel no different from that of white churches."[44] When the black church's formative particularities were lost, "they [had] no other alternative but to assume the identity of the group that conquers them."[45] Instead of turning to its own sources to develop its own creeds and liturgy, the black church adopted the resources of the dominant white theological culture and incorporated them into its practice. This signaled not only a failure of mission but a failure of hermeneutics—that is, a failure to properly understand the gospel story and the story of its own heritage.

In no way does Cone perceive the story of the black church to be untethered from or incommensurable with the story of the white church, as Hauerwas claims. Cone recognizes the ways the two communities exist in a symbiotic relationship of oppressed and oppressor. They share two versions of the same story, two sides of the same experience. But the black church must draw on its own particular interpretive sources to tell that story, rather than allow a white theological hermeneutic to define its identity. The problem for the black church is, "They do not know the rock from which they were hewn," Cone laments. "They and their people do not know who they are and the inheritance that was passed on to them."[46]

3. Narrative and Particularity

The discussion so far reveals the importance of narrative and particularity in Cone's black theology. This section and the next demonstrate the role these themes play in his methodology and concept of blackness. I suggest that Cone is a narrative theologian who provides an account of story that refines and corrects the ideals of story and community that allow white theologians to avoid engaging the issues of race and white supremacy.

The Style of Story

In an article on story and black theology Cone observes, "The form of black religious thought is expressed in the style of story.... White theologians built logical systems; black folks told tales."[47] The obstacles to black liberation—that is, the history of the auction block and lynch mob—could not be resolved through philosophical debate; these problems were more urgent and had to be addressed at the level of concrete history. Cone describes how enslaved people spoke through the language of story because that was the form commensurate with their social situation. "Through the medium of stories," he writes, "black slaves created concrete and vivid pictures of their past and present existence, using historical images of God's dealings with his people and thus breaking open a future for the oppressed not known to ordinary historical observation."[48]

But appeal to story was not only out of necessity. It was also itself a form of subversion because it allowed enslaved people to "defy conceptual definitions that justif[ied] their existence in servitude" by forming counternarratives that humanized them and deceived "those who stand outside the community where it was created."[49] This is sometimes called "signifying" in the African American tradition because it expressed truth through innuendo or indirection while identifying a symbolic historical marker with a present reality. For example, Cone observes that biblical locations like heaven or the Jordan River in slave songs served as references to specific earthly places like Canada, the Ohio River, or locations on the Underground Railroad, where enslaved people might physically escape.[50] Andrew Prevot argues that the slave spirituals are integral to Cone's theology, "foundational to his overarching perspective and inseparable from his sense of his own identity." The doxology of the spirituals is constitutive of his theology—a narrative doxology. The spirituals not only sustained the self-narration of African American history through the trauma of slavery but also helped create that narrative in very concrete ways, Cone argues, by upholding particular stories of redemption. These are not texts from the past, but a "form of living memory" that make up the story of which he is part.[51]

Story formed the medium through which truth was communicated and became part of the truth itself. Similar to Hauerwas, Cone claims that the reality of the story is revealed in its telling, and the truth of the story is dependent on the transformative effect it has on the community that hears it.[52] Stories aim at transformation and character formation, argues James Evans. "The stories in which one lives," he says, "do not only reflect what kind of individual one is, but also shape one's identity and sense of values."[53] This is why the storyteller is so important in black faith: the preacher in black churches must be able to recite God's historical dealings with God's people and relate these biblical stories to

contemporary black stories. In the sermon, "The past and present are joined dia-
lectically, creating a black vision of the future"[54]—as in the example of Warnock
collapsing Obama's hopeful campaign theme into the story of Israel at the verge
of the Promised Land. The story-formed character of Cone's theology leads to his
most striking criticisms of the church. The church fails when it leaves behind the
story that gave it shape.

The Particularity of Community

For Cone, every story emerges from a community and gives shape to that community's identity, hopes, and practices. Cone constructs a cohesive methodological model to suggest the importance of particularity as a corrective to abstracting
and universalizing tendencies in white theology. I outline here in four steps this
commitment to particularity.

   1. *Cone identifies the contextual nature of all theology.* There is no objective theology; theological speech is always a product of its social environment, limited by
history, time, and community. Cone appeals to the intellectual heritage of philosophers including Ludwig Feuerbach and Karl Marx to argue for the contextuality
of intellectual thought. "Theology is subjective speech about God," he writes, "a
speech that tells us far more about the hopes and dreams of certain God-talkers
than about the Maker and Creator of heaven and earth."[55] Ideas do not have independent existence but are a social product of theologians' reflections about divine
things—and are always intertwined with manifestations of actual life. He appeals
to Gustavo Gutiérrez's claim, "Theology is done by persons who, whether they
know it or not, are caught up in particular social processes. Consequently, all
theology is in part a reflection of this or that concrete process. Theology is not
something disembodied or atemporal."[56]

   This concept of theology as a social product challenges white theology's
claims to universalism. The trend in the academy of identifying black, feminist,
queer, or liberation theologies as "contextual theologies" reinforces the notion
that classic European (white) theology is universal and normative. But white
theologians' insistence upon their universality only arises from their own particular political and social interests. Thus, "they do not recognize the narrowness
of their experience and the particularity of their theological expressions," Cone
argues. "They like to think of themselves as universal people."[57] White theology
is not only contingent like any other theology, but its situatedness in regimes of
white supremacy and oppression reveals its complicity in these regimes as well as
the ways such complicity distorts its aims and claims. "To understand Christian
identity from a white dominant point of view," he says, "is like trying to understand Jesus from a dominant Roman point of view."[58]

2. As a corrective to its adoption of white theology, *Cone proposes that African American Christians must allow their theological reflection and practice to emerge from the experience of black people.*[59] "Theology is not a rational concept to be explained," according to Cone, but is "a story about God's presence in Jesus' solidarity with the oppressed."[60] As a result, theology is about, and must continually engage with, the material. Even white theology's pretension to universalism is grounded in some concrete reality—a particular community's story about itself. Theology must arise from the experience of a particular people; indeed, it cannot help but do so.

This stance led Cone to search for African American sources for theological reflection. In fact, after writing *The Spirituals and the Blues* in 1973, Cone understood himself to shift almost exclusively to sources from within the black community and experience.[61] Black theology must follow the form and style of the community that gave birth to and continues to shape it: slave stories, folk tales, spirituals, even the blues. "Using Barth, Tillich, Niebuhr as my theological authorities would never liberate my mind and black people from white supremacy," he writes. "I had to look back and recover the black heritage that gave birth to me."[62] The textual sources of intellectual thought as well as the categories of interpretation themselves must arise out of black experience, which takes priority as a critical hermeneutical element in black theology.[63] With these methodological moves, according to Kelly Brown Douglas, Cone "made clear that the Black story of suffering and struggle was God's story, and this was a story necessary to tell."[64] While some may question whether Cone ever successfully departed from white theology (especially the dialectical intellectual framework he inherited from Barth),[65] his final reflections urge theologians to immerse themselves—critically and constructively—in the story of their faith, the particularities of the Christian witness of the community that gave them life. Cone reflects, "I soaked myself in 'the world I came from'—the world of the spirituals and the blues, folklore, and slave narratives and found the language of freedom and liberation black slaves and ex-slaves sang and talked about."[66] Cone insists he had to come "back home" in order to write black theology—literally to Macedonia AME—and this home is the black church and the story it tells.

3. *Theology is never neutral, but must always take the side of the oppressed.* The content of black theology is liberation for the oppressed. "When I turned away from white theology and back to scripture and the black religious experience," he reflected toward the end of his life, "the connection between Black Power and the gospel of Jesus became crystal clear. Both were concerned about the liberation of the oppressed."[67] In ways similar to the postliberalism of Hauerwas, the theme of particularity limits who is able to participate in the theological practices of a community. About the project of black theology, Cone says a deeper experience

is only available to those who "participate in the faith of the people who created these songs."[68] Black being is possible only in community, he says. The social and cultural environment of a people determines not only the answers a people come to but also the questions they ask.

4. *Every theology should aspire to move beyond its own particularity, while still staying rooted firmly within it, to the concrete experiences of others.* "In our efforts to accent our particularities," he says, "we must be careful not to limit God to them or to remain enclosed in them ourselves. The encountering of the God of biblical faith draws us beyond ourselves to the poor of the world."[69] He challenges the black church to develop a theology that emerges from its own particularity but seeks connection to the stories of others told within their own particularity. This particularity relates to its own ethnic history and also is accountable to the experiences of other Christians who are suffering too.[70] Later in his career, Cone began connecting the struggle of African Americans to Latin American and African liberation theologies, learning not only from one another's shared experience of suffering but also attending to womanist theology's insistence on the intersectionality of oppression.

With his emphases on narrative and particularity, Cone developed a theological method that corrected for the evasive and universalizing tendencies of dominant white theology and spoke to the reality of the black experience in America. This method directly contests the theological method of the white theologians I analyzed in the previous two chapters. White theology begins with a theological system that diagnoses social problems from an unreflective—often supposedly objective—position and proposes abstract antidotes. Its model assumes that our divine ideas will make us well, that we can contest sins like racism by thinking rightly about God or rightly about society without first engaging with people who are suffering from these sins. White theology's model ends up proposing that we can unmake our racism by patiently waiting on God, calculating the most realistic step, or properly understanding God's sovereignty. Cone calls us to refuse this way of thinking about the theological task. His model reveals that we cannot properly discern the work of God in the world without first taking hold of our reality, beginning on the underside of history, and asking "what is going on" and, as I address in the next section, "who is Christ for us today."

4. Christology and Blackness

So far I have analyzed the communal point of departure and particular social conditioning of theology. For Cone, black theology, however, must strike a balance between the centrality of Christ and the experience of the community that interprets that center within its own hermeneutical resources. Cone provides an alternative model to the universalist overtones of white theologies by holding in tension both the Christological center of theological thought as well as its particular communal point of departure. He asserts that theology's task is to analyze the changeless gospel in a way so that it can relate to changing situations.[71] In words that reflect the work of German theologian and martyr Dietrich Bonhoeffer, it must express the "concreteness of Christ's continued presence today."[72]

While the themes of narrative and particularity shape Cone's description of the task (and limits) of theology, they likewise lead to one of Cone's more controversial and often misunderstood Christological claims: Christ is black. Cone's assertion means that Christ identifies himself with the oppressed of society, and in an American context, the oppressed are black.[73] Just as theology is not neutral but compels theologians and communities of faith to choose a side, Christ is not neutral and universal, but identifies in life and death with the oppressed of the earth. Like Bonhoeffer, Cone recognizes that Christ is not some universal symbol but he meets each person and community in their own particularity and form. Cone answers Bonhoeffer's question "Who is Christ for us today?"[74] Christ is black today. Any American Christian theology, Cone says, must begin with attending to the "crucified people in American history," and those people are black.[75] Since Jesus identified with the oppressed during his historical life, and black people are the oppressed ones in a white racist society, Christ is black today.

The Black Christ

By claiming that "Christ is black," Cone explains, blackness serves both as an ontological symbol and a visible reality that best describes the situation of oppression in America—but blackness stands for all victims of oppression.[76] "God has made the oppressed condition his own condition" through the actions of electing the oppressed people of Israel as God's people and becoming the Oppressed One in Jesus Christ. Cone observes, "Jesus and the whole story of the Christian message is about God's solidarity with the poor and oppressed anywhere in the world."[77] The gospel reveals that Jesus is the man "for others . . . disclosing to them what is necessary for their liberation from oppression. If this is true, then Christ must be black with black people so they can know that their liberation is his liberation."[78]

For Cone, the idea of the black Christ cannot be understood solely in a symbolic nor literal sense. Rather, it is a theological claim. Cone's Christology begins with humanity, even the particular humanity of the historical Jesus.[79] Thus Christ's blackness, his identification with the oppressed of the world, is based in Jesus's Jewishness, his embodiment as a member of an oppressed religious and ethnic community in Roman-occupied Palestine. "He was not a 'universal' man," Cone asserts, "but a particular Jew who came to fulfill God's will to liberate the oppressed."[80] The black Christ, then, identifies Jesus's ethnic identity as part of his existential condition. "The particularity of Jesus' person as disclosed in his Jewishness is indispensible for Christological analysis," Cone suggests. The historical particularity of his Jewishness means that theology must affirm the Christological significance of Christ's present blackness: "Thinking of Christ as non-black in the twentieth century is as theologically impossible as thinking of him as non-Jewish in the first century."[81] Put simply, "He is black because he was a Jew."[82]

James Evans argues that the black Christ functions in four ways in Cone's black theology. First, it expresses both Jesus's victimization and his victory—constitutive of his work of liberation. Second, it serves as the bridge between the historical Jewish Jesus and Christ proclaimed today. Third, it proclaims a theological truth about Christ's relationship with the oppressed: that Christ chooses to side with them. And fourth, it points toward the future and requires all to choose with Christ the side of the oppressed.[83] Thus, Cone integrates Christology and concrete communal experience. The two are the same reality, and one cannot become secondary to the other.[84]

Cone's Captivity to Whiteness? Ontological Blackness and Womanist Criticisms

Cone's black Christology is also not without its critics. Certainly many white theologians object to identifying Christ—a universal agent of salvation—with a particular racial community. Such objections reflect the abstracting and universalizing tendencies of whiteness I outlined in chapter 3. Yet Cone's most interesting criticisms have come from other black scholars. In order to better understand how Cone's concepts of blackness and the black Christ shape his narrative theology and refutation of white theology, I briefly address two of these critiques: first, Victor Anderson and J. Kameron Carter criticisms of Cone's promotion of an "ontological blackness," and then womanist criticisms of the patriarchy and binary production of black theology.

Ontological blackness, Anderson claims, "is a covering term that connotes categorical, essentialist, and representational languages depicting black life and experience."[85] Anderson believes this approach treats race as if it exists independently of "historically contingent factors and subjective intentions."[86] While Anderson commends Cone's understanding of black collective consciousness as revolutionary and liberatory, Anderson worries that Cone's concept of blackness is identified exclusively with black experience, and black experience is defined as the experience of suffering and resistance. Black theology, then, becomes a theology of crisis: fully encapsulated within struggle, overriding internal distinctions, and neglecting the flourishing elements of black culture.[87] It spirals, in Brian Bantum's words, into "a perpetual space of self-preservation."[88] Black suffering and survival became its substantive content, and any notion of transcendence fades to the background.

On a deeper level, Anderson argues, Cone's expression of blackness relies on a dialectical matrix—positing blackness and whiteness in an antagonistic opposition. This dialectical sensibility results in racial reification and succumbs to the objectivist sense of blackness that white supremacy nurtured. Anderson writes, "Black existence is without the possibility of transcendence from the blackness that whiteness created," and therefore fails to provide the tools for transcendence over white supremacy.[89] The outcome is black theology's dependence upon whiteness, white supremacy, and white theology for its own legitimacy.[90] Anderson argues,

> When black life is fundamentally determined by the totality of a binary racial dialectic that admits no possibility of cultural transcendence, then African American theologians hold few prospects for effectively ameliorating the social and existential crises that bind black life. Talk about liberation becomes hard to justify where freedom appears as nothing more than defiant self-assertion of a revolutionary racial consciousness that requires for its legitimacy the opposition of white racism.[91]

These critics claim that Cone's concept of blackness is a blackness produced by whiteness, which actually delimits the range of possibilities for black identity. Cone's blackness is captive to white Euro-American racial reasoning and unable to transcend its dialectical relationship with whiteness, even when it attempts to return to distinctively African American and African sources. In fact, this appears to replicate, or provide a mirror image of, the antagonistic dualism that birthed white supremacist theology—the originating theological factor in the development of white supremacy that I addressed in chapter 2. In this view, Cone is trapped in a binary logic of blackness versus whiteness, and rather than undoing this logic, he simply shifts power from one to the other. J. Kameron Carter suggests that Cone's problem arises because he remains a dialectical thinker (a remnant of his early debt to Barth), wherein the I (that is, whiteness) still maintains its dominant and determining power.[92] Similar to Anderson, Carter sees Cone's concept of blackness as a settlement with "the blackness that whiteness created."[93] By envisaging race in this dialectical and intrinsically competitive manner, Cone trades in "zero-sum terms" that he is incapable of transcending. This account implicates Cone in the same agonistic—even "traditional"—framework in which Hauerwas operates.

An overlapping but perhaps more searing critique emerged within black theology itself when black women theologians reflected on their absence from the discourse. Delores Williams notes that even when Cone realizes and corrects for his use of patriarchal language, he still does not "use the heritage of black female intellection to shape his ideas."[94] This is certainly a failure of Cone, as early womanist theologians including Jacquelyn Grant understood—and a failure of black liberation theology more generally—to address sexism.[95] But the womanist critique goes beyond the fact that "black women have been left out of black liberation theology and its understanding of historical agency." As Delores Williams charges, the neglect of black women voices has led Cone and other black theologians to "masculine models of victimization."[96] Cone's ethic of liberation "by any means necessary" leads to a singular focus that collapses the black experience into one of (masculine) struggle.

While helpfully nuancing white witness theology's agonistic view of story, Cone himself operates with a binary view that neglects the multiple, complex, and intersecting oppressions that black women face. White and black stories may, in fact, be two sides of a shared story, but Cone leaves room for only two sides. While he insists that "blackness" encompasses all forms of oppression and speaks to each community in its own particularity, his account marks communities as either oppressed or oppressor, black or white. Perhaps in the way that Hauerwas's thought produces an unhelpful binary between church and world that aids in his blindness to the church's sin of white supremacy, Cone's parallel binary veiled the way other forms of oppression, including patriarchy and heteronormativity, seep into black theology and Cone's concept of blackness. As Kelly Brown Douglas notes, black theology's emphasis on liberation was inflected by its masculine roots and eclipsed black women's desire for a "politics of wholeness" that confronts racism, sexism, classism, and heterosexism.[97]

Womanist criticisms of Cone open the door for more nuanced expressions of intersectional stories. Womanist theologians illuminate the ways that, in our morally complicated world, some people face multiple forms of oppression and some function as both oppressor and oppressed at different times, in different forms, and to different degrees. I am not talking about white people claiming victimization or disenfranchisement in a way that neglects the empirical benefits of white privilege due to real or perceived loss of hegemonic power. Rather, I mean the complex ways in which most people participate in intricate systems of oppression, often unseen and unexplained, even if they experience oppression themselves. Womanist accounts of this experience break apart binaries like Cone's and suggest that any ethic that is responsible to resisting forces like white supremacy must offer an intersectional narrative of oppressions and liberations.

In fact, womanist theologians' engagement with Cone's work opens a new vista into his concept of blackness that moves it beyond the binary and agonistic logic indicated earlier. While womanist theologian M. Shawn Copeland worries that the concept of race in Cone's project functions too ambiguously, her account of race as a social construct that has very real (life and death) effects—one that aligns with many other womanists' accounts—helps to highlight the fluid, symbolic character of Cone's account of blackness.[98] Blackness is both an objective reality fully encapsulated by the black experience and an ideology in which persons can participate regardless of their skin color.[99]

Rather than serving as a contradiction, I contend that both aspects of Cone's concept of blackness function in equally important and even convergent ways, although his oscillation between the two often leads to confusion over what he means. I agree with Timothy McGee's assessment that, in Cone's work, blackness is neither purely racial essence nor social construction, "yet, it is linked to both, as something that traverses and unsettles the essentialist and anti-essentialist discourses of race."[100] Blackness simultaneously operates on a literal register, identifying black-skinned people or those who have experienced antiblack violence themselves, and a symbolic one, as a category of moral identification and action.

Reading Cone in light of the intersectional focus of womanist theology, the attention to the multiple and intersecting stories that constitute the self and shape communities opens up his concept of blackness in narrative and counternarrative form. In fact, because it is developed in narrative form and expressive of the black community's faith, Cone's concept of blackness is able to contain these ambiguities. Narrative is able to sustain multiple registers at the same time, like the multilayered meanings of "promised land" in slave spirituals or characters in folk tales that Cone identifies as informing his own methodology. His counternarrative absorbs the seeming contradictions in his definitions of blackness and directs them toward opening new horizons of meaning that challenge the conventional story of black and white division.

Becoming Black

My argument is that Cone places greater emphasis on the symbolic level—*blackness* as a synecdoche for anyone who lives under oppression. The term stands in for a larger group while not leaving behind its literal meaning. Rather, the literal referent—blackness—reveals the identifying characteristic of the larger group: anyone struggling for liberation or on behalf of the oppressed.[101] Cone is not always so clear, but he often attempts to explain. "It's not a literal blackness but a symbolic blackness," he claimed late in his career. "God takes on the identity of the oppressed. That's why you can say that God is red, God is brown,

God is yellow, God is gay—anything that symbolizes the victim. I chose 'black' because black identified my experience."[102] Kelly Brown Douglas helps to clarify the symbolic character of Cone's concept of blackness. She identifies the way he drew on Paul Tillich's notion of "ontological symbols" as the only way humans can speak of the divine. In this sense, blackness for Cone represents a way to talk about God's presence, a way to participate in that presence, and a means to open up new ways of comprehending God and human reality.[103]

Cone claims that his concept of blackness is capacious enough not only to include those suffering from oppression but also those who choose to participate in the work of liberation on behalf of others, even if one is not oppressed herself. Cone, from his earliest work in *Black Theology and Black Power* and *A Black Theology of Liberation*, claims that anyone can "become black"—"all those who participate in liberation from oppression"—even white people.[104] He explains that his claims about blackness are not meant to exclude: "whites can become identified with the black Jesus."[105] In fact, he concluded his first published manuscript with this claim:

> Being black in America has very little to do with skin color. To be black means that your heart, your soul, your mind, and your body are where the dispossessed are. We all know that a racist structure will reject and threaten a black man in white skin as quickly as a black man in black skin. It accepts and rewards whites in black skins nearly as well as whites in white skins. Therefore, being reconciled to God does not mean that one's skin is physically black. It essentially depends on the color of your heart, soul, and mind.[106]

In light of this capacious dimension of blackness, Cone extends an invitation to whites to "become black with God!"[107] This means recognizing that God is black—that is, on the side of the oppressed—and therefore whites can only enter in relationship with God "by means of their black brothers."[108] Becoming black means actively working for the destruction of white values, knowing that every element of white supremacy is placed under God's judgment.[109] According to Prevot's analysis, Cone argues for self-emptying and self-giving as active elements of blackness, obligating both whites and blacks in its work: whites must empty themselves in order to receive the gift of blackness, and blacks are called to give themselves as critical witnesses by confronting whites with their racist history and offering the gift of a more faithful account of the gospel. If blackness is the achievement of liberation and ultimate goal of reconciliation—an eschatological reality breaking into world history—this opens the possibility for whites to "share deeply in the passions, sorrows, and resilient hopes of their black brothers and sisters."[110]

When I met with Cone, I spent much of our interview asking about these later claims. When I teach Cone in my undergraduate or seminary classes, his claims that Christ is black and that white people must become black in order to be saved generally draw the most resistance from white students.

I was skeptical for a different reason; I worried that Cone's capacious account of blackness risks whites attempting to put on blackness without enduring the same experience and cultural history of racial oppression—to "[take] on the symbolic register of blackness severed from its particularity."[111] This was an epistemological concern—that whites are incapable of shedding privilege in such a way that assumes the same risks as people of color, and attempting to do so may cause more harm than good. Though I may join in solidarity with the black struggle, my white skin would always allow me to opt out. I may participate in a Black Lives Matter march, but then I could simply drive back to the safety of my home without the same fears of being pulled over by a racist police officer. In fact, in an early dialogue about black theology with a former teacher, Cone himself identified this concern. He claimed, the "difficulty with white students is that they appropriate black symbols without encountering the concrete experiences which gave rise to them."[112] Interestingly, this concern echoes the worries of Hauerwas about instrumentalizing the black story, one of the reasons he does not engage the topic.

When I asked Cone about this concern, however, he explained, "There are [white] people who have become black. Look at John Brown, those students in SNCC [the Student Nonviolent Coordinating Committee] in Mississippi and Alabama with Stokely Carmichael and Robert Moses. They became black." When I asked him what gave him hope that white people would remain in the struggle and not opt out when things became difficult, he replied, "I'm hopeful because I'm a Christian. The gospel won't let you walk away from this." In fact, the gospel gives white Christians the power to break through privilege and actually endure the long and difficult work of liberation. This reveals a deep and transcendent hope in the gospel, the work of God, and the Spirit in the lives of those who attempt to follow this black Christ—a commitment often overlooked in scholarship on Cone.

Narrative Blackness

I believe Cone's concept of blackness needs a better name—one that bears forcefully upon the work white people must do to confront white supremacy. Renee Leslie Hill claims that Cone does not offer an "ontological" blackness but an "ideological" one, by which she means a concept not defined by struggle but designed to cultivate a new consciousness that affirms black humanity in response to the social reality of white supremacy.[113] Similarly, Andrew Prevot argues that Cone's concept is better articulated as a "doxological blackness" that affirms the beauty of blackness and aspects of black culture that affirm its relation to God.[114] These reflections, more accurately than the criticism of scholars like Anderson, describe how the concept of blackness functions in Cone's thought. However, I want to propose another term; I contend that Cone operates with a *narrative blackness*.

I argued above for the narrative foundation of Cone's black liberation theology. It begins in the story of the black experience, rooted in the sources of black culture, and preached from the pulpits of black churches. "The form of black religious thought is expressed in the style of story," he said,[115] and Cone is the storyteller of black faith par excellence. Consequently, it would only make sense for his concept of blackness to also take the form of narrative. Grounded Christologically in the story of the historical Jesus—the black Christ of Palestine who meets the oppressed in their particularity—the story of the gospel enfolds the history of the black experience into its own narrative. At first blush this would seem to align with the focus on narrative proffered by the white witness theology of Hauerwas outlined in the previous chapter. However, this narrative blackness offers for white Christians a more helpful understanding of story than does white witness theology—and also offers crucial points of correction—for three reasons.

First, Cone's narrative theology avoids succumbing to abstraction in the same way we witnessed in Hauerwas's thought. Instead, his theology remains "at the level of concrete history."[116] Blackness must be a tool of liberation, and as he claims, the liberating truth is not easily told in rational discourse; "it must be told in story."[117] Similar to Hauerwas, Cone claims that the truth of the story is dependent on the transformative effect it has on the community that hears the story.[118] If this is true for both authors, then, despite Cone's criticisms of the black church, we can see these effects more clearly in the black church, as both theologians acknowledge.

A narrative concept of blackness holds together both the literal and symbolic dimensions, while preventing it from sliding into abstract theological concerns like God's sovereignty. Narrative avoids essentializing blackness while still attending to its embodied effects. Blackness is a social and cultural construction, but one that marks real effects, written upon the skin.[119] It cannot be severed from the concrete reality of skin color, but "refers to a particular black-skinned people in America."[120] Divisions between the biological and the sociocultural are porous and provisional at best, yet they produce and maintain relations of power and oppression.[121] While blackness is not essential, it is, as Linda Martín Alcoff claims of race, "most definitely physical, marked on and through the body, lived as a material experience, visible as surface phenomena, and determinant of economic and political status."[122] Blackness has real consequences (life and death effects), defining who is loyal and who is a threat, who is fundamentally "American" and who is a suspicious outsider. Though a construct, race still produces material realities that shape bodies through things like public policy, healthcare practices, mechanisms of punishment, and national borders.[123] Cone's concept of blackness, while not trapped in ontology as Anderson charges, shifts the concept back to its concrete reality.

Importantly, this narrative blackness challenges any notions of colorblindness as beneficial to black liberation and provides a direct denunciation of the colorblind pretensions of many white theologians and Christians. In a prescient moment near the end of *Black Theology and Black Power*, written at a time when racism was beginning to shift to its more masked and sinister forms in the wake of the civil rights movement, Cone warns his readers of "whites who insist on making blacks as white as possible by de-emphasizing their blackness and stressing the irrelevance of color while really living as racists."[124] He predicts the coming "racism without racists" and offers a narrative conception of blackness that emphasizes the role of color, tolerating neither essentialism nor blindness. His narrative blackness helps Cone to identify the real, material consequences of racism while also praising the beauty of black culture and offering it as an invitation to more closely witness the gospel by attending to race and its material consequences.

Second, as narrative, blackness serves as an invitation into its story, into a particular community. This invitational narrative distinguishes Cone's concept of blackness from the antagonistic dualisms that generated white supremacy and allows Cone to avoid the deepest criticisms of Anderson and Carter. A story is porous and opens toward others who seek to authentically identify with it. In this way, a story is, in Jacquelyn Grant's phrase, "broad in the concrete."[125] In fact, stories are ways in which people of one culture and history can enter, however provisionally, the story of another people.[126] Cone recognizes that this does not mean that a white person who wants to enter the story of blackness or of the black church will share all of the historical and cultural experiences. Rather, the black religious story provides an opportunity for others to break out of their own constrictive stories and undergo a conversion.[127] "Hearing another story can force us to tell our own story in a different way," argues Robert McAfee Brown, leading to such a transformation "that we can properly call the experience one of conversion."[128] That is, by immersing themselves as best they can; "sharing deeply in the passions, sorrows, and resilient hopes" of the community; taking on the embodied risks of solidarity without pretending that they are the same risks as native storytellers experience; and allowing that story to re-form them, a person can achieve the ability to re-narrate the story themselves—even with a different dialect and from a different perspective.

Third, Cone's narrative theology better recognizes the connection between the "white story" and the "black story." Whereas Hauerwas understands the experiences of the white and black churches as each containing their own internal logic that is incommensurable and untranslatable to those outside the community, Cone's understanding of the history and story of race in the American church does not allow for white people to distance themselves from systemic racism and the material effects it inflicts on the black community. In contrast to the MacIntyrean account of narrative that Hauerwas proffered, they are not two incommensurable traditions, two closed systems, or agonistic communities. In my interview with Cone, he insisted that the black story also "is [the white person's] experience; he can't separate that from himself." Each one impacts and shapes the story of the other. The stories that Reverend Warnock proclaims from the pulpit of Ebenezer Baptist Church are shaped by the stories of Bull Connor and white SNCC members alike. They are forged together out of two experiences of the same history and two reflections on the same gospel.

With this, Cone reflects James Logan's criticism of Hauerwas's theology. Logan argues, "Since Hauerwas appears to understand that the habits of racism and White supremacy have been deeply written into the story of his life, he ought to also know, then, that the story of 'the struggle' is as much his story as it is King's story." It is "one and the same story," he says, "because even Christian disunity is part of a common story."[129] This phenomenon is what Mary McClintock Fulkerson and Marcia Mount Shoop call "dis-membered stories of race." They contend, "Our unique experiences, our shared social contexts, and our bodies' idiosyncrasies create in each of us particular and shared 'tellings' of dis-membered stories of race."[130]

In my interview with him, Cone explained that the supposed "two stories" of blackness and whiteness are inextricably intertwined in ways that other groupings of people are not: "White people have no sense of their own identity without their black brothers." They were formed together, more accurately described as two "tellings" of the same story. "Black people were there when white people achieved their identity," he explains. "We were always there from the beginning, in their fields, in their kitchens. There is not black experience without the white experience right with it."[131] Therefore, it does not make logical sense for whites to say that they cannot engage with the experience of African Americans, because it is the other side of their own story. According to Cone, fear of recognizing and grappling with a part of their own story is what whites want to avoid; in response, they call that part of the story the "black experience" in order to elide it and the guilt that surely accompanies that discovery. Whites' refusal to talk about race is simply a "cheap silence." Then, speaking of Hauerwas, Cone adds, "He has no sense of who he is without me. I'm his bastard brother." Hauerwas's excuse is typical of white theologians, and white Christians in general, Cone claimed. They are afraid to ask what kind of theology comes out of a people that is capable of enslaving others.[132]

Cone's message is not a call to mere integration, assimilation, or eradication of racial difference. It does not collapse the experiences and stories of black and white Christians into one and thus overlook difference. Racial differences remain, written upon our bodies. Yet in Cone's narrative they are potential sites of connection. The stories of blackness and whiteness are inextricable, yet distinct. Cone's message to white Christians is, therefore, a call to conversion—a process of becoming black that I describe as an ethic of responsibility.

5. *Conclusion: Resources for an Ethic of Responsibility*

In this chapter I have offered a reading of James Cone's black liberation theology as a narrative theology that directly challenges white theology's support of white supremacy. Cone's theology does so on the level of story, linking the experiences of blackness and whiteness as processes of racial formation within the same narrative arc, even reconfiguring them within the same salvation history. That is, Cone positions blackness in the role of soteriological ideal. In a move that is unsettling for white people, James Perkinson claims that Cone flips the conventional script: "the greatest uncertainty about salvation must now be predicated not of dark skin, but of light."[133] The burdened question of salvation now becomes, "Can whites be saved by a black Christ?"[134] Cone's answer is, "Yes, by becoming black."

Significantly, Cone is not burdened with providing whites with an account of what it means to become black. He is primarily writing to black people and for their self-determination and liberation. Consequently, he does not offer a process of formation or account of the virtues necessary for discipleship to a black Christ. In other words, "he is not programmatically concerned about white destiny," according to Perkinson. "It is not Cone's purpose to try to work out the soteriological meaning of blackness as a Christological title for white people in their whiteness."[135]

Still, Cone does provide some indication of what it means to shed our whiteness and become black by invoking the process of conversion. At the conclusion to his first book, Cone draws on the three steps Jesus names in Mark 8:34, the three marks of discipleship. There, Cone insists that a process of conversion to blackness "means that white people are prepared to deny themselves (whiteness), take up the cross (blackness), and follow Christ (black ghetto)."[136] In this chapter's conclusion, I outline these three steps of the process, which are fleshed out in Cone's reflections on reconciliation, white conversion, and becoming black. Each of these steps corresponds with one of the three resources I identified in the previous chapter in white witness theology (at its very best): memory, particularity, and concreteness. While we saw the ways in which these concepts were incomplete when expressed through white witness theology, when read through the lens of black theology they take on a refined and powerful character that forms the building blocks of an ethic of responsibility for resisting white supremacy. Though introduced briefly here, together they form the praxis of responsibility laid out in part III of this book.

Memory

Becoming black, like any conversion, begins with a call to remember, to truthfully tell the story of our lives. The New Testament term ἐπιστροφή, typically translated as "conversion," recalls a turning or recollection of something that has been lost or corrupted due to poor formation—that is, sin. Denying whiteness, as Cone urges, begins with remembering our racial malformation and its compelling narrative that convinced us we were superior. Despite our inclinations to forget that past and move quickly forward, as Judith Butler claims, I cannot simply "dispense with the history of my formation." I can only struggle against repeating its effects. "The point is not to eradicate the condition's of one's own production, but only to assume responsibility for living a life that contests the determining power of that production."[137] Just as Christ's resurrected body carried the wounds of his earthly afflictions, our converted "black" selves will always carry the wounds of our whiteness. But this wound always risks growing and requires constant, vigilant resistance.

Resistance begins with remembrance of our collective past. "My hope is that whites will be redeemed from their blindness," Cone says, "and open their eyes to the terror of their deeds so they will know we are all of one blood and what we do to others we do to ourselves."[138] In our interview he told me, "If white people and black people are going to be reconciled, they have to do that looking at the lynched bodies, the enslaved bodies, the Trayvon Martins. You've got to look them in the eye, their mothers, their fathers." Only at that point is conversion possible. This reconciliation does not follow conventional modes, where both parties make strides to come together—often neglecting the deep recesses of pain and violence. No, reconciliation cannot precede liberation. In the case of becoming black, white Christians must first reckon with our history and lay those memories in full humility before the cross and the lynching tree. According to Cone, this means white people must "shut up and listen and get down on your knees and pray that all those people you killed will forgive you without you assuming that is going to happen."[139]

Particularity

Next, conversion to blackness means taking up the cross of blackness—that is, taking on the black story in all of its particularity. Becoming black involves a catechesis in which white allies must submit to the authority of new teachers and exemplars in the struggle for black liberation. As Cone explains, "White converts, if there are any to be found, must be made to realize that they are like babies who have barely learned to walk and talk."[140] White Christians must continually reject their whiteness by submitting in full accountability to black leaders until our "value system is now defined by the oppressed engaged in the liberation struggle."[141] This requires actively destroying whiteness by working alongside the oppressed—taking on their risks as our own—to the degree that a person of privilege is able.

This activity is best described in theological language as *repentance*, which Cone, quoting Alan Richardson, defines as a "reorientation of one's whole life and personality, which includes the adoption of a new ethical line of conduct, a forsaking of sin and a turning to righteousness."[142] Taking up the cross of blackness is the continuous, diligent work of refusing the privileges of whiteness and submitting in accountability to our black sisters and brothers. This is not sympathy, but solidarity and sacrifice—a reorienting of the self and the self's relation to the world around it, giving up power, and placing oneself in a vulnerable position to others.

Concreteness

Finally, becoming black entails a concrete, material change. This is a direct challenge to the abstracting tendencies of whiteness, often predicated on our fear to face the realities we have created, our inability to see beyond the narrowness of our experience. This is why concrete action for Cone must reach beyond the story we tell ourselves as white Christians and move into the black ghetto—to allow ourselves to be confronted and changed by the storytellers of black faith.

Following Christ into the black ghetto is best described by the New Testament word to describe transformation—*metanoia*. Recall Paul urging the Romans to "be transformed [μεταμορφοῦσθε] by the renewing of your minds, so that you may discern what is the will of God—what is good and acceptable and perfect" (Romans 12:2). Metanoia necessarily leads to social, political, and structural change. According to Paul, conversion begins with a conversion of thought—of the mind—but results in a moral transformation, the ability to see that which is good. But transformation's end is not simply an altered worldview. Repentance is completed through acts of reparation. Repentance without material repair is cheap repentance. True solidarity (for Cone, true discipleship) must involve taking on the same risks of those you claim to join. Reparation may take several forms and must be developed in conversation and under the guidance of the oppressed.

The situation of the white church and our theology is dire. Black liberation theology teaches us that we are mired in sin and in need of conversion, and destroying our whiteness is the only way to bring about that transformation. Each of these three steps is difficult, and few white churches and theologians have begun the journey into the "black ghetto." Part III of this book argues that we cannot achieve this transformation through projects of "reconciliation," but following James Cone, we must submit ourselves to an ethic of responsibility.

"Where Do We Go from Here?"

5

An Ethic of Responsibility

The Christian faith begins in stories. White supremacy does too.

THE PREVIOUS FOUR chapters have told a bleak story of white Christianity and its prospects for overcoming racism. The famous words of Frederick Douglass from over 150 years ago are just as poignant today: "Between the Christianity of this land, and the Christianity of Christ, I recognize the widest possible difference."[1] The church's complicity in racial oppression challenges the institution's very legitimacy. But how deep does the brokenness go? Does anything redeemable remain? Perhaps white theology can only be defeated with the emergence of counternarratives of resistance, painful stories of confession, and tales of new creation rising from white-washed tombs and the dry, white bones of a church that has failed.

Jonathan Tran puts the issue pointedly when he writes that white Christians cannot commit all the atrocities they have committed in God's name and "still expect the moral infrastructure in which we committed those atrocities to remain intact. The atrocities demonstrate that either the infrastructure is not to be trusted or we are not to be entrusted with it."[2] Tran argues helpfully that it is within a moral infrastructure—such as the Christian tradition—that we forge a moral standard by which we measure acts and character and deem them racist or not, and then propose less racist alternatives. But, he questions, what if the cause of America's racism is this framework or infrastructure itself? Can we still trust it to guide us? In Kelly Brown Douglas's words, considering the way Christianity has been used for centuries to oppress black people, is "there not something wrong with Christianity itself"?[3] If so, we might come to see morality, or Christianity, "as something about which we can no longer speak with much confidence."[4]

This returns to my point at the end of chapter 1: white supremacy presents a wicked problem—not only a problem without any clean and clear solution, but a problem that indicts the very moral structure we employ to assess it. "Considering such possibilities," Tran suggests, "is what responsibility looks like in the aftermath of the kind of racism we have cultivated in America."[5] The white church has spawned the monster that is white supremacy. After ignoring its devastation for so many years, in the face of growing white nationalism and increasing hate

Witnessing Whiteness. Kristopher Norris, Oxford University Press (2020). © Oxford University Press.
DOI: 10.1093/oso/9780190055813.001.0001

crimes, the hope of the white church lies in awakening to the ways we might destroy the everyday white supremacy that lives within us.

Maybe this all sounds hyperbolic. Perhaps racism shouldn't so deeply indict a tradition, or its doctrines and practices. In fact, I don't suspect that many white Christians are willing to dig that deep, to let go of doctrines and practices they hold dear, despite their distortion. Such letting go requires a suppression of our confidence in those doctrines and practices, an examination of their trustworthiness, and ours with their use. Thus far, white Christians have not proven ourselves in capable of such severe yet necessary measures. While some theologians, Christians, and churches simply ignore the issue of race and racism, many understand the presence of a problem but struggle to address it. In recent years, many white Christians have responded to the moral crisis of whiteness with earnest appeals to and attempts at racial reconciliation.

In this chapter I begin constructing an ethic of responsibility toward white supremacy, first by addressing the inadequacies of projects of racial reconciliation to address the issue's depth and complexity. After outlining the failures of reconciliation, I suggest the concept of original sin as a more comprehensive way to understand white Christians' collective responsibility for white supremacy. At that point I return to this question of how we might respond to a crisis so deeply entangled in Christian thought and practice. While methods like reconciliation fall short, I propose responsibility as a potential method for more sufficiently reckoning with the white church's sin. This ethic of responsibility—entailing practices of remembrance, repentance, and reparation—emerges at the critical convergence of the two streams of theological ethics represented by Hauerwas and Cone—white traditionalist and black liberationist theology, respectively—and suggests that scholars and practitioners within these streams may find resources at their disposal to confront white supremacy. I draw upon Cone, Hauerwas, and Dietrich Bonhoeffer, a figure to whom Cone points as a model for white Christians striving to become black—albeit with certain flaws. Bonhoeffer's account of responsibility, therefore, serves as a guide for my proposal here. As a process of formation, an ethic of responsibility promotes radical, communal action to confront the wicked problem of whiteness through material practices, while also recognizing the lingering challenges of whiteness within a broken and wounded body of Christ. In light of the sins of the white church in America, we can only answer Martin Luther King's question "Where do we go from here?" with an ethic of responsibility.

1. Reconciliation and Its Discontents

Today, white churches and many multiracial congregations remain unreflective about the ways whiteness impacts their theological positions and practices. When they do perceive a problem with race—most often identified as racial division—many well-intentioned congregations propose various models of racial reconciliation, ranging from a simple pulpit exchange or annual fellowship meal to shared mission projects or targeted efforts at creating "diversity." For many sincere Christians, the work of racial reconciliation is integral to their theology and ministry and predicated on a strong biblical imperative. The Apostle Paul writes to the Corinthians that God, who has reconciled the world to God's self, has "given us the ministry of reconciliation; that is, in Christ God was reconciling the world to himself, not counting their trespasses against them, and entrusting the message of reconciliation to us" (2 Corinthians 5:18–19). And as Paul expresses in Ephesians, God's work of reconciling all humanity to God's self opens the path for reconciliation within a humanity divided by ethnic and racial conflict. Paul writes that Christ's work will overcome those divisions and make us "one body through the cross, thus putting to death that hostility through it" (Ephesians 2:16).

In fact, even James Cone employs the term to describe his hopes for racial justice. Reconciliation must be the goal, he insists, because it is a theological necessity: "The Christian faith requires it, and human decency demands it."[6] "I'm for reconciliation," he repeated to me during our interview. "Reconciliation happened on the cross."[7] Yet for him, the problem lies in white theology's distorted views of reconciliation. Cone understands liberation and reconciliation not as two competing interests but as "a single soteriological event." As he puts it, "God's reconciliation is God's liberating work."[8] Liberation is thus a precondition for reconciliation. Most white theologians and white churches permit their desire for reconciliation to overrun the self-interrogative work that liberation requires. In order to better understand the inadequacy of reconciliation, we must first address the twin problems of segregation and integration.

The Problem with Segregation

The ecclesial effects of white supremacy are revealed ostensibly in the segregated character of American congregations. Martin Luther King Jr.'s adage that the most segregated hour in America is eleven o'clock on Sunday morning remains just as true fifty years later. Only 20 percent of U.S. Christian congregations qualify as "multiethnic" by sociological standards (which at anything less than 80 percent of one ethnicity are already quite generous).[9] From the moment

Richard Allen and Absalom Jones left St. George's Methodist Episcopal Church in Philadelphia in 1794 in protest over segregated worship space and founded the African Methodist Episcopal Church—the first independent black denomination in the United States—to the cascade of denominational segregations from Reconstruction through the civil rights struggle, this empirical reality reveals a deeper cultural tendency toward white homogeneity.

The consequences of this segregation are reinforced blindnesses that allow white theologians and white Christians to avoid dealing with race altogether— the privilege of ignorance. The realities of race and racism do not press upon us on a daily basis nor register as a theological concern. In segregated contexts, white people are not confronted with the fact that we also have a racial identity so we have no imperative to reckon with that reality. Alexis de Tocqueville observed nearly two hundred years ago the ways that political and social attitudes were reinforced and spread subtly and indirectly within religious communities. And as these communities remain homogenous cultural-religious enclaves, racial blindness—or even outright racism—is reinforced.[10]

This indictment of racial insulation does not mean that racially specific spaces, churches, or ministries should not exist; often these are vitally important for the health of minority groups that must constantly navigate white-dominated culture. Rather, such an indictment means that white-dominated spaces should also be understood as racialized spaces that are forming—likely, malforming—its congregants in all the ways expressed in chapters 1 and 2.[11] In light of the problems created by homogenous echo chambers of privilege, integration would seem to be the solution.

The Problem with Integration

If the story we tell ourselves about America's racism is primarily one of racial separateness, then togetherness is the logical solution.[12] For many, reconciliation becomes synonymous with and encompassed by integration.[13] Yet the complexity of colorblindness suggests that mere racial integration would prove deeply insufficient as a solution to racism, for three reasons.

First, the act of integration alone masks the deeper issues of racial injustice and constricts our vision of racism to lingering elements of segregation. Most Protestant Christians have been shaped by the prominent legal goals of the civil rights movement to think that division is the true evil and unity is the answer, but this understanding underscores a shallow recollection of history. Early in the movement, grassroots freedom organizers like Ella Baker realized that "even if segregation is gone, we will still need to be free; we will still have to see that everyone has a job." The Student Nonviolent Coordinating Committee (SNCC) founder continued, "Even if we can all vote, but if people are still hungry, we will not be free."[14] Baker's biographer, Barbara Ransby, suggests, "For many people, the movement was about the ballot and defeating Jim Crow," but Baker and eventually King himself began pushing "against those cramped ambitions to draw people toward a more comprehensive vision."[15] Asserting integration as the goal ignores the deeper resources of history.

Second, integration leaves problematic theological convictions of whiteness unchallenged. Michael Emerson and Christian Smith, in their extensive study of religious attitudes toward racism, discovered that views on the country's "race relations problem" came down—unsurprisingly—to competing narratives: black Christians identified social and structural forms of oppression, and whites circumscribed the problem to prejudiced individuals. Emerson and Smith suggest three theological convictions that continue to shape white Christians' perception of race relations: "accountable freewill individualism, relationalism, and antistructuralism."[16] White Christians, and white evangelicals especially, operate with a view that "individuals exist independent of structures and institutions, have free will, and are individually accountable for their own actions."[17] This is why their explanations for racial disparity, even in reconciliation efforts, are often lost in translation. The pietistic language they often employ locates salvation within a singular relationship between God and the individual, robbing salvation of any socially transformative possibilities. Individualized notions of salvation and sin contribute to an emphasis on personal responsibility and obscure any collective perspective. If sin is limited to individuals, then racial problems are simply individually caused and individually resolved through personal relationships or personal responsibility.

Third, a focus on integration as the solution leads to an emphasis on sameness across racial differences. At first blush, this may not present as a problem, yet this push for unity as the totality of reconciliation risks the loss of identity for minority selves or communities as they integrate with majority communities.[18] Often, the traffic pattern of integration flows one way; what white Christians mean by "integration" is for black Christians to join white churches. This only reinforces the white tendency to maintain power even within multiracial churches. Multiracial congregations elevate the common spiritual identity of the individual congregants and subordinate their various racial identities; the result is often to reproduce racist structures within the power dynamics, organization, and leadership of the church.[19] Because these congregations too often leave dominant white frames and assumptions unchallenged, everything from the worship style to leadership positions remains unchanged.[20] Thus, even within integrated churches, the minority race disproportionately bears the costs of integration. I remember as a seminarian being troubled by fellow students of color who cited "worship style" as a reason they did not actively pursue multiracial churches (as if this was their responsibility in the first place). Yet what appeared to me at the time as a trivial matter reflected my ignorance of the particular history of the black church. The lack of institutions open to African Americans during slavery and Jim Crow meant that the black church became "the most logical institution for the pursuit of racial self-help," according to Evelyn Brooks Higgenbotham. It was "an agency of social control, forum of discussion and debate, promoter of education and economic cooperation, and an arena for the development of leadership."[21] Black Christianity thus developed its own highly distinctive culture and liturgy, and most integrated churches struggle to incorporate these distinctive elements into a common congregational life.

Put simply, though, togetherness is not enough. An integrated church that fails to meet deeper cultural and liturgical needs, as well as include the more expansive social roles that the historical black church has filled, will continue to replicate racial inequality. Typical approaches to reconciliation that identify separateness as the problem fail to see it, instead, as a symptom of a deeper problem of unjust social, political, and economic structures.[22] The call for racial diversity as the true and sufficient sign of reconciliation neglects these structural injustices, risks placing minorities in positions in which they lose their power and identity, and emphasizes sameness to the expense of particularity in a way that encourages colorblindness.

The Problem with Reconciliation

All of this points to the difficulty, even impossibility, of racial reconciliation in our time. African Americans have long had good reasons to be suspicious of white desires for reconciliation. Ta-Nehisi Coates captures this suspicion well in his memoir, *Between the World and Me*. He begins by recalling the moment he and his son heard the news that Michael Brown's shooter would go unpunished. He writes to his son, "Here is what I would like you to know: In America it is traditional to destroy the black body—it is heritage."[23] Though Coates is not religious, his despair is revealing and representative. Proposals for reconciliation, primarily originating from white America, "ring hollow in a country whose existence was predicated on the torture of black fathers, on the rape of black mothers, on the sale of black children."[24] At best, they are colorblind attempts to make us "all beige and thus the same 'race.'"[25] He ends the book with this somber warning to his son: "I do not believe we can stop them . . . and still I urge you to struggle. But do not pin your struggle on their conversion."[26]

White theologian Jennifer Harvey takes up this issue in her book *Dear White Christians*, arguing that the "reconciliation paradigm" has failed. The eagerness of most advocates of reconciliation pushes them to reach for shallow solutions and premature solidarity. For Harvey, the problem with reconciliation is that it rests on the universalist ethic that buttresses whiteness. Whites are trained to see our perspectives as objective and universal, and thus normative.[27] Our colorblindness projects our own particular experiences universally onto all others; it presumes that "all differences are different in the same way."[28] And thus, it imposes one uniform standard to which we can hold one another accountable across racial difference. This universalism also functions to block self-awareness: whites are obstructed from seeing how our own identity contributes to our privileged social condition as well as the oppression of others. The consequence of this universalist preoccupation with sameness is the belief that everyone equally bears the burden of reconciliation. Such universalism promotes the same duty owed to one another and entails the same urgency for unity on all parties, despite one's location of privilege or oppression. As Harvey argues, an awareness of cultural particularity and the fact that whites bear more responsibility is "flattened" into a universal and equal call to action.[29] Reconciliation thus becomes a more costly endeavor for black Christians than for whites, while failing to address the deeper collective problem of white supremacy.

Since the white Christian tradition invented white supremacy, it is easy to see how its resources may prove inadequate to overcoming it. The fact that white people want to move so quickly to "reconciliation," James Cone contends, is a symptom of white people's short memories.[30] But white people cannot be trusted to define the terms of reconciliation because we have been "enslaved by [our] own racism."[31] Oppressors cannot define what reconciliation looks like. Because our theological tradition was so distorted in the birth of white supremacy, contemporary manifestations of racism appear to outstrip its capacity to address it. Likewise, whatever models of reconciliation we come up with are themselves shaped by our inevitable white supremacy and thus insufficient. Reconciliation will never be possible (at least!) until the white church and white theology first confront the white supremacy that has deformed our churches and theologies and then release our own expectations of what reconciliation looks like in exchange for those of the oppressed.[32] Reconciliation can still be an eschatological reality that ought to guide our ethics, but in our present condition any attempts to actualize it will likely replicate harm. The result is that, in the interim, white Christians should stop promoting the task of racial reconciliation.

If the story we tell ourselves about racism is that it is a phenomenon birthed outside of Christianity that has infected our churches, it is easy to see how reconciliation becomes the solution. But this story shields us from rightly seeing—and telling—our history and reality. We need a better story to account for the ways white supremacy begins and manifests itself in and through our white

Christianity. The age-old concept of original sin offers a better, more truthful story about our church.

2. The Church's Original Sin

It has become popular today to talk about the racism that generated slavery as America's original sin.[33] James Cone forcefully did so for fifty years.[34] As stories in the book of Acts and Paul's epistles reveal, ethnic divisions were the early church's original sin as well, as it struggled to include ethnic others as members of the body of Christ (see Acts 15; Galatians 2:1–10). The concept of original sin illuminates a more comprehensive narrative, one that promises to better express the reasons white American Christians living today are implicated in white supremacy even if we were not alive during colonialism, slavery, or Jim Crow, and even if we do not view ourselves as racist. If my argument is that racism is something for which white Christians must take responsibility and for which we must repent and repair, it is important to offer an account of why we are responsible for the sins of Christians past—as well as for the ways we benefit from and behave within the systems constructed by that history. Framing white supremacy in terms of original sin does this. As Ryan Newson argues, "Even though sin is not 'genetically' passed on or the same thing as creatureliness, it quite literally becomes body—is written onto creatures—thus creating systems of injustice that are transmitted to and transmuted into all."[35] The sins of our forebears can cause our own sin, which still does not let us off the hook: "Sin becomes at once each of our inheritance, as well as a reality of our own making."[36]

While Augustine popularized the belief that sin is passed on "biologically" through procreation, several twentieth-century theologians provided updated versions of original sin for a post-Enlightenment age. Reinhold Niebuhr identified anxiety as the underlying cause of sin, fundamentally presenting as pride, a sin that inflicts every human person capable of rationally or emotionally reckoning with human finitude. He claimed that humans seek to overcome their insecurity by a will-to-power that attempts to overreach the limits of their creatureliness.[37] Within this insecurity, "sin posits itself."[38] Marjorie Suchocki, a relational theologian, alternatively suggests that theologians should look to a "violence-engendered anxiety" rather than a "finitude-engendered anxiety" as the presenting cause of sin.[39] I do not see the need to choose between these two accounts; in many ways I think anxiety and violence are mutually enforcing: violence triggering anxiety that inflicts more violence, or vice versa. Both accounts converge and when taken together provide a compelling case for defining white supremacy as original sin.[40] But how is sin "original"—in both senses of originating and of ubiquity?

First, scientific evidence of the earliest human groups suggests that human development (physically, socially) depended upon violence over territory and resources, and this inheritance continues to mark and shape human consciousness. While humans have gradually evolved to reduce the scope of this violence, a tendency toward aggression was built into the human species through its instinct to survive.[41] Violence is an innate, even natural part of human instinct that is transmuted psychically to subsequent generations.

Second, this sin is passed on. As Walter Rauschenbusch noted, "The evils of one generation are caused by the wrongs of generations that preceded, and will in turn condition the sufferings and temptations of those who come after."[42] For him, sin is incomprehensible alone; it must be accounted for collectively. It becomes a society's collective memory embodied within its institutions designed to protect the privileges of the dominant group. These institutions, in turn, shape the institutions, structures, and consciences of each new generation.[43] Recall from chapter 1 that cognitive scientists argue that environmental cues literally shape the brain development of future generations by offloading cognition into the world—cues like gated communities of white people or "dangerous" urban schools of people of color. The environment, then, shapes the brain development of future generations to interpret the world through these cues. Human cognition is therefore extended across time; the accumulated knowledge (and sins) of previous generations is passed on to new ones.[44] Sin becomes lodged in the social customs, environment, and institutions of society, and each overlapping generation then absorbs the norms of the social environments it inherits from the past, which are mediated by social institutions; "each generation corrupts the next."[45] According to Suchocki, institutions and social systems serve as the "bearers of sin to which the children will adhere before they even have the means of assent."[46] Original sin simply creates sinners, because we each are caught in the clutches of sin without ever giving it consent. The theological concept of original sin provides a habituating model by which Christians can make sense of our culpability and responsibility not only for the sins we commit each day but for those committed by our ancestors that still haunt our culture and institutions.

This original sin is then made ubiquitous by the interrelatedness of all humans. The sin that is transfused through institutions and imaginations impacts and implicates all humans. Racism, economic deprivation, crimes, wars, political oppression, and psychic oppression are "relationally internalized" and dispersed throughout the human race.[47] Even if we deny our participation in them and therefore leave unexamined the systemic forms of our complicity, we cannot extract ourselves from their deployment or harm. As James Cone perceptively notes, none of us is free of committing acts of violence—even when we are blinded from recognizing the structural violence we inflict on others by our privilege (through the products we buy, the policies we endorse, the injustices we ignore): "No one can be nonviolent in an unjust society."[48] To claim to be nonviolent is simply to accept the oppressors' values and participate in their violence. The fall dictates that all of humanity is bound in sinful solidarity—and responsibility.[49]

This account of original, ubiquitous sin means that, in Suchocki's words, "responsibility is diffuse"; it is masked but pervasive.[50] Since we participate in institutions that transmit corrupted ideals, norms, and worldviews—as well as maintain privilege or profit for some at the expense of others—we each bear some degree of responsibility for the structure of society. In this way, racism—preserved, mediated, and transmuted through the institutions, norms, and values of each generation—is the church's original sin. As theologian Erin Kidd summarizes, "The doctrine of original sin can appear paradoxical—as if human beings are in some way responsible for sins they did not commit, or cannot help but commit."[51] Yet, supported with this theological and scientific data, it gives us a theory with which to understand how I may be responsible for something I have never intended or performed.

This narration of white supremacy as original sin reflects Copeland's observation: "Racism is no mere problem to be solved; it is a way in which we define our reality, live the most intimate moments of our lives. Racism is not something out-there for us to solve or fix; racism is in us, sedimented in our consciousness."[52] This account therefore expands the scope of moral responsibility, extending it across time and into the present. White Christians today may not be to blame for the origins of white supremacy and more than five hundred years of oppression performed in its name, but the theological concept of original sin, supported by historical and scientific data, demonstrates that we are indeed responsible for it.

3. The Meaning of Responsibility

In this book so far I have been building a case for the responsibility of white Christians for the sins of white supremacy. At this point I finally turn to this ethic of responsibility and explain what I mean (and don't mean) by the term. What does responsibility involve? What is its substance and its praxis? In light of the failure of other approaches, such as reconciliation, why advocate for this one? In the remainder of this chapter I flesh out the contours of this ethic of responsibility. I believe that in light of the devastation of white supremacy, both to the bodies of nonwhite people and to the theological doctrines and practices of the white Christian church, accepting responsibility for this devastation is the only choice white Christians have.

Hauerwas, Cone, and Responsibility

Responsibility may appear to be an odd constructive concept for a project predicated upon the work of Cone and Hauerwas. Neither theologian employs the term often; in fact, Hauerwas outright rejects a form of its use. In terms of constructive vocabulary, he prefers the language of *witness*, and Cone, *liberation*. Neither of these terms achieves exactly what I'm aiming for here: *witness* neglects the malformation practiced in and proclaimed by the church to the world, and *liberation* assumes a struggle against an outside force. (One could presumably speak of white people liberating ourselves from white supremacy, but that kind of language obfuscates our role in its persistence and risks recentering us as its victims.) Yet both terms point at the type of responsibility I'm advocating in this book. An ethic of responsibility encompasses the fundamental concerns of witness and of liberation.

The common threads that I identified in white witness theology and black liberation theology make up the substance of this ethic, even if their proponents do not use the term *responsibility* to describe them. These common threads, even if misdirected in Hauerwas's thought, are grounded in a fundamental epistemological assumption: there is no Archimedean point from which one can objectively observe and adjudicate between differing truth claims and moral perspectives. The very idea that one could occupy a neutral view from nowhere (or an objective view from above) already emerges from a particular location, or tradition of inquiry, and has been shaped by a particular social context. Therefore, no system of thought possesses an objective and universal claim to truth, despite white people's best efforts to believe this. As finite creatures and moral agents, we are unable to see the world clearly or in whole; we see partly, through a glass dimly, restricted by the contingencies of our subjective experience and the provisionality of our communal commitments. We are never able to escape our own parochial particularity, because we are always and everywhere embedded concretely in formative narratives and communities that shape our perceptions, limit our knowledge, and direct our attention.[53]

In light of this claim, theologian Sean Larsen sees a continuity between Hauerwas's project and black, feminist, womanist, queer, or postcolonial ethics: they all reject the modern project of granting deference to the dominant subject of universal rationality (white, heterosexual, male). Larsen argues, "Though Hauerwas and subversive ethicists may differ in degrees about whether a form of traditional Christian orthodoxy can avoid reintroducing the same hegemonic subject, both similarly deconstruct progressive Protestantism"[54] and important characteristics of whiteness, to some degree.

Yet, as philosopher Walter Mignolo suggests, simply affirming that knowledge is situated or that reality is constructed doesn't take us far enough in overcoming the abstraction and universalisms found in whiteness (or, using his term, "coloniality"). That is just one step. The second step, "and most important one is to ask how is it constructed, by whom, why, what for, and whose interest does it serve if we construct reality in A or B manner? And what are these constructions saying to those who are affected by the construction of reality without having the opportunity to participate in such construction?"[55] Both theologians take the first step, but Hauerwas stops there, restricting his capacity for ecclesial self-reflection. Cone ventures the second step, interrogating the interests behind the situations and constructions: Whom do they help? Who is left out? For Cone, the matter is not limited to identifying the subjective contextuality of all theology, but also identifying the interestedness of theology as a justice issue.

While the commitment to deconstruction falls short in Hauerwas's thought, when amended and corrected by Cone's account of story, it serves as the foundation for an ethic of responsibility. The contours of responsibility reside in the shared commitments to the formative concepts of narrative, memory, concreteness, and the moral particularity of communities. While narrative shapes the methodological approach to an ethic of responsibility, mutual attention to the roles of memory, particularity, and concreteness provides the substance and practice. The thought of these two figures converge at these three points to suggest that any potential path forward for white Christians to take responsibility for white supremacy, and to have any hope of beginning a process of conversion to blackness, begins here. Within an ethic of responsibility for white supremacy, the concepts of memory, particularity, and concreteness issue in practices of remembrance, repentance, and reparation. Memory calls white Christians to remembrance of our collective history and the original sin that continues to pollute our theology and practice. Particularity suggests that any attempt to universalize the roles of black and white Christians in reconciliation or to abstract race into colorblindness are doomed to fail. Rather, "becoming black" necessitates repentance, or true submission to and solidarity with the black community. Finally, concreteness demands material conversion. Recognition and apology are not enough; moral transformation is contingent upon structural change. I examine the practice of responsibility in this book's final chapter, but it is important first to analyze the structure of this ethic.

Bonhoeffer and Responsibility

The language of responsibility and commitment to particularity also invoke the ethics of the only theological figure to whom both Cone and Hauerwas consistently appeal: Dietrich Bonhoeffer. Due to his shared influence on Hauerwas and Cone, Bonhoeffer's thought serves as an important guide for this ethic, and I especially attend to the way Cone draws on his work in this account of responsibility. Hauerwas often appeals to Bonhoeffer's work and even devotes a book to his theology.[56] Likewise, Cone references Bonhoeffer consistently, from his first book (nine times) to his posthumous memoir published fifty years later. Bonhoeffer remains the only white theologian he appeals to constructively after other white sources fall out.[57] Perhaps his most revealing reference to Bonhoeffer comes from *A Black Theology of Liberation*, in which he explicitly removes Bonhoeffer from his criticism of the heresy of "white theology" because Bonhoeffer attended to the suffering of the oppressed as a central element of his theology.[58]

I have another reason for my turn to Bonhoeffer. As I previously observed, Cone insisted that white people must "become black" if we are to be of any help in the struggle against racism. Cone describes this as a process, employing the language of conversion, yet he does not provide white Christians with an account of formation into "blackness" or examples of practices that lead to solidarity—nor does he need to. This is not the task of black theology. Rather Cone leaves this work up to white people to determine what such a process entails and to find our own models of conversion by listening to people like Cone and other black and womanist theologians. I believe Bonhoeffer provides such a model because Cone points to Bonhoeffer as a model of a white Christian attempting to follow the "black Christ." In his interview with me, Cone pointed to John Brown and white members of the SNCC as white people who became black. In his theological writings, Cone points to Bonhoeffer.

I recognize the limitations of turning to a European as a model for white Christians in confronting white supremacy, as well as the risk of re-centering European figures to address distinctively American issues.[59] Bonhoeffer was embedded within an ideology of whiteness and remained so throughout his life, even as he tried to contest it—much like all of us who attempt such work. But since this book is by a white theologian primarily addressing other white theologians and Christians about our role as oppressors, I think turning to a white person as a model for other white people—especially one highlighted by the father of black theology and one who experienced a theological transformation after immersing himself in the black church—is an important part of white Christians doing our own work without further burdening theologians of color to address our sins.

Importantly, Bonhoeffer's account of responsibility, as well as the model of conversion he provides white Christians in America, is not one that points to himself or his own thought. His life demonstrates how his own work was influenced by attention to the reality of the marginalized. Bonhoeffer exemplifies what it is like to have our stories interrupted by the counternarratives of those we once neglected or disparaged. Bonhoeffer's model directs us back to the stories of the subjugated and calls us to look to the voices in our own time and place that challenge us and disrupt our own stories of colorblindness, white fragility, and evasion.

That is, Bonhoeffer's particular concept of responsibility anticipates both the turn toward formation we find in Hauerwas and other postliberals, as well as the attention to concrete reality in liberation theologies. This concept also anticipates the focus on particularity and contextuality that I have identified in Cone. Bonhoeffer's account of responsibility avoids abstraction and subsists in the concrete and bodily behavior of human beings, and therefore offers an important link between the thought of these two figures. But it does so because it is a product of his own submission to and learning from black Christians about how to think about responsibility for others.

In *The Cross and the Lynching Tree*, Cone affirms the impact of Bonhoeffer's immersion in the black church during his year in Harlem while attending Union Seminary—befriending black students, attending Abyssinian Baptist Church, and reading and writing on African American literature. He contrasts that with other American theologians like Reinhold Niebuhr who always maintained a distance from the black community.[60] In our conversations Cone also acknowledged his reliance on Bonhoeffer because of his participation in the black church during his time in New York, and suggested that because of that immersion, Bonhoeffer is able to provide a vision of the cross that allows us to see God's suffering in the oppressed and to hear a call to radical conversion.

As a young theologian and pastor, Bonhoeffer's preaching presaged the racist nationalism that would overtake Germany in a few years. In a 1928 lecture Bonhoeffer spoke of ethics as a "matter of blood and . . . of the soil." He claimed that the German race possessed a God-given freedom to subdue other nations, "even if it disregards the lives of other peoples."[61] Yet just over a year later he would engage and embrace these "other peoples" and witness the struggle and spirit of the black church in Harlem. Reggie Williams lays out the argument that Bonhoeffer's experience at Abyssinian, which he attended in 1930–1931, triggered a conversion from white theology to the "black Jesus."[62] There Bonhoeffer "met a counter-narrative to the white racist fiction of black subhumanity"[63] that clearly impacted him: he would write in defense of the nine Scottsboro Boys falsely accused of rape, collect gramophone records of spirituals to later play for his Finkenwalde students, and claim in letters home that in the United States he "only heard a genuine proclamation of the gospel from a Negro."[64] One of

his seminary friends recalled his time in Harlem as "the beginning of his identification with the oppressed which played a role in the decision that led to his
death."[65]

Bonhoeffer credits his "impressions abroad" for his "turning from the phra-
seological to the real."[66] That is, his immersion in the lived experience of the
gospel at Abyssinian and observation of real suffering—and the black resistance
to that suffering—caused him to leave behind the abstract theology of his previous education. He now began to understand the Christian faith and task of
theology as emerging from the reality of the oppressed. In fact, Williams suggests that Bonhoeffer's particular notion of responsibility may have been influenced by a consistent homiletic theme of Abyssinian's legendary pastor Adam
Clayton Powell Sr.: the church's "responsibility to act in accordance with the love
of God for creation and to meet the needs of the community." Williams claims
that Powell's emphasis on "Christian responsibility" portrayed a "Christ-centered
interpretation of community among the socially marginalized that helped to
develop Bonhoeffer's sense of the Christian community and impacted the way he
understood what the church should be doing when the [German] church struggle began."[67] Upon returning to Germany and witnessing Hitler's rise, Bonhoeffer
would immediately oppose the Nazi racial laws targeting Jewish people. The
counternarrative of resistance to racism that he encountered in Harlem would
lead to his conversion from proclaiming a theology of "blood and soil" to one
that began to see "history from below, from the perspective of the outcasts . . . the
oppressed and reviled, in short from the perspective of the suffering."[68] These sentiments resonate with James Cone's claim to do theology "from the bottom and
not the top, from the experience of the powerless black oppressed."[69]

In light of these experiences I believe that Bonhoeffer provides white
American Christians, churches, and theologians with a model of conversion to
blackness, one by which to repent for the collective sins we have inflicted on the
world through our whiteness. This is not to say Bonhoeffer is a perfect model. He
began his ministry by preaching the same ethnonationalist theology that would
later support the Third Reich, and for most of his life he remained more concerned about the future of the church in Germany than about liberating those
decimated by the genocidal Nazi machine. His conversion to solidarity with
the oppressed was slow and stumbling. Yet, as a white, privileged Christian in
a nation and church that were exacting racial terror, as the United States and its
predecessor colonies have for over four hundred years, Bonhoeffer recognized
the urgency of the problem and forfeiture of easy solutions. Through his theology
and sacrifice on behalf of the oppressed, he offers an ethic of responsibility to help
other white, privileged Christians to confront our own.

Clarifying Responsibility

Bonhoeffer claims, "Each individual is Adam; everyone is entirely responsible."[70] With this, Bonhoeffer points us to the difficult starting point of responsibility, the product of his listening to and learning from black Christians and marginalized voices in a process of conversion. This casts his version of responsibility in quite a different form from other versions of the concept. Responsibility became one of the most prevalent and debated ethical concepts during the twentieth century. Before fleshing out the contours of this ethic of responsibility, therefore, I should first provide a few clarifying comments about what responsibility does *not* mean in light of popular versions of the concept.

First, *responsibility* is not the same as *guilt*. Though no white person can claim innocence, I do not think the term *guilty* is theologically or practically helpful in identifying the precise relationship of white Christians in the present to the church's legacy of racial oppression. Language of innocence and guilt further obscures the moral complexity of our current reality. Instead, responsibility identifies a deeper collective sense of claiming this heritage as one's own without the forensic baggage of a term like guilt. (Guilt requires freedom to do otherwise, to opt out of a system, but one can participate in a sinful and oppressive system without consenting to it, or even having knowledge of it.) To be transparent, this is also a rhetorical choice; as Elizabeth Vasko notes, "Guilt is not a particularly effective tool for engendering social responsibility."[71] Out of her work as a trainer on issues of racial justice, Robin DiAngelo observes that white guilt too often paralyzes action.[72] This concern is not to preserve white people's feelings, and certainly not to claim that people of color should do so. Emotions like shame and guilt are shaped politically and can be politically powerful tools (for good or bad). I simply believe that *responsibility* more fully captures this reality in all of its complexity and call to action.

As a member of a body (the church as body of Christ) that persists through time, I inevitably possess a collective sense of responsibility. My membership in a body larger than myself burdens me with responsibility for what my collective body has done to others. Bonhoeffer's articulation of responsibility, as *verantwortung übernehmen*, often translated as to "take on responsibility," means, more precisely, to accept or to bear the responsibility that has already been placed upon us. Responsibility is simply a necessary response to the encounter of the other (be it God's direct command or God speaking through the demand of a neighbor) in light of the responsibility that we already bear.

Thus responsibility more properly entails a claim of identity—it is we who are encountered with this reality. It means taking hold of—accepting, assuming, bearing—the heritage of racism that already permeates our church, which means we have a responsibility to act. While Bonhoeffer uses the peculiar idiom "taking on guilt" in his discussions of responsibility, Jennifer McBride interprets his phrase as "the active determination to take responsibility for sin."[73] Guilt means choosing to respond to our sinful reality without seeking or calculating our own self-justification. In fact, Bonhoeffer models the acceptance of collective responsibility when he claims that all Germans—even those active in the resistance movement—were responsible for the crimes of their country prior to and during the war.[74]

To put this in our context, I may not be responsible for the system of white supremacy, but because I necessarily participate in it (even if I don't consent to it or even understand it), I am therefore response-able to it. *Responsibility*, etymologically, is rooted in the juridical system and means "giving an account of oneself," a testimony before a court or witness.[75] Responsibility most directly demands a response; it calls us as a witness to the evil deeds of our faith, church, and theology, and demands we give account and tell its story—our story.

Second, despite popular theological uses of the term in the last century, *responsibility* does not mean *reasonable*. This was the way the Niebuhr brothers, especially, employed the concept.[76] H. Richard, in defining "the responsible self," focused on the concept of the "fitting" action. For an action to be fitting, it must involve layers of interpretation and moral calculation. For him, the responsible self is a self that does not directly respond to the needs or claims of the other but "to interpreted action upon us . . . insofar as they are made in anticipation of answers to our action."[77] While this account of responsibility recognizes the power of sin and the way it entangles all of our moral choices, the problem with it as fitting or reasonable action is twofold. First, Niebuhr's account of reasonableness includes filters of anticipation and interpretation which abstract responsibility in layers of moral calculus and distance the responsible one from the particularities of those suffering in ways that often preserve the status quo. Second, the moral calculus to discern the reasonable action easily shifts self-justification, which undercuts the genuine posture of repentance necessary to take responsibility for white supremacy and neglects Cone's challenge to white people to ask for forgiveness without "assuming that is going to happen."[78]

In contrast, Bonhoeffer insisted that Christians have "overestimated, time and again, the importance of reasonableness."[79] His notion of responsible action does not place judgment within one's own moral calculation, but lays it bare before God and the concrete other. Judgment and moral determination lie in the direct encounter with the other, without domesticating the other person or sliding into self-justification. For Bonhoeffer, "genuine responsible action is characterized by a deliberate turning of one's back on the responsible self."[80] Responsible action disavows reasonableness and perceives responsibility as a direct response to the particular situation of the neighbor.

This commitment links the three theologians, Bonhoeffer, Cone, and Hauerwas, in their rejection of ethics as problem-solving in favor of ethics as responding to Christ in the neighbor or community—"Who is Christ actually for us today?"[81] (Hauerwasians, and Hauerwas himself, may find this connection over responsibility surprising, yet I contend there is an important affinity.[82]) As Bonhoeffer writes, "We can and should speak not about what the good is, can be, or should be, for each and every time, but about how Christ may take form among us today and here."[83] All three theologians are united in resistance to ethical certainty determined by abstract principles and isolated from the living community and reality of Christ.

The Structure of Responsibility

I can now turn to the structure of this ethic of responsibility. Here again, Cone highlights the particular ways Bonhoeffer's version of responsibility offers a model for white Christians in response to white supremacy. Cone identifies several elements in Bonhoeffer's thought that give form to this ethic. First is Bonhoeffer's conception of the connection between relationship and freedom, the foundation of his vision of the "responsible life." In *A Black Theology of Liberation*, Cone argues that white theology's promotion of rationality and the goodness of humankind—liberal Protestantism's view of human progress—seemed to forget about black enslavement and colonialism. In contrast to "liberalism's confidence in man," Cone turns to Bonhoeffer's concept of the *analogia relationis*: humans are not defined by rationality but relationship, which also underscores a commitment to human freedom—a freedom to be for others.[84] For Bonhoeffer, the term *responsibility* describes a response, given at the risk of one's life and not for one's self but "for Jesus Christ" and "for human beings before Christ."[85] And as Cone highlights, this response is constituted by two commitments: (1) a bond in relationship to Christ and to others, and (2) the freedom of one's life. I address both commitments in turn.

The bond to Christ and others is further divided into two forms: what Bonhoeffer calls *vicarious representative action* and *living in accordance with reality*.[86] First, if responsibility is fundamentally Christological, then it is discipleship to the one who lived and died on behalf of others. Taking responsibility as a representative of Christ, then, must be a response to and on behalf of others. Second, if at the base of Bonhoeffer's account of responsibility is the belief that all action is responsive—it gives an account, a witness, or answer before Christ and Christ-in-the-other—then all actions occur within a particular context. All responsible action, therefore, must take place "in accordance" with that person's or group's reality,[87] which means responding to the "concrete neighbor in their concrete reality," not in a way that is filtered through ethical systems or principles or determined in advance.[88] Rather, the response "develops together with the given situation"; the context is not "the raw material on which they want to impose or imprint their idea or program, but instead it is included in their action as the formation of the act itself."[89] Bonhoeffer emphasizes that responding in accordance with reality does not serve the status quo (unlike Niebuhr's realist account of responsibility we recall from chapter 2) nor stage a "principled" rebellion against it; rather, it means responding as Christ does—in love, judgment, and reconciliation—to a world that seeks to remain world but is already reconciled to Christ.[90]

The second commitment, to freedom, also contains two forms: the responsible life is lived in *accountability* for one's actions and in *the venture of the concrete decision*.[91] First, the accountability of freedom means that "to accept responsibility for others also involves willingness, in following Christ's example, to bear the guilt of others."[92] While, again, I worry about the usefulness of the term *guilt*, Jennifer McBride helpfully interprets Bonhoeffer's language of "acceptance of guilt" as "the church's acknowledgment of its complicity in social sin."[93] It simply means taking the risk of faith to act without recourse to self-justification or moral calculation. Second, the venture of the concrete decision implies the acknowledgment of a responsibility that dislodges us from concerns over our own self-justification. "The fact that the world has been reconciled sets the agent free to act in response to reality without scruples about his moral purity," Guido de Graaff explains.[94] The responsible action of vicariously representing others means accepting their free judgment as well as accepting the collective sinfulness of our own position without promise of forgiveness. It is, in Cone's words written thirty years later, a "situation of freedom in which the burden is on us to make the decision without a guaranteed ethical guide. This is the risk of faith."[95]

Cone's appeals to Bonhoeffer help to frame the way his vision of responsibility reveals four implications about responsibility for white supremacy. Cone generally frames these insights in reference to Bonhoeffer's emphasis on "costly grace" over the "cheap grace" of much of white theology.[96] Cheap grace fails to see the cross as a symbol of liberation and political resistance, Cone writes.[97] In contrast, costly grace commits one to action, in response to God's calling, on behalf of the suffering and oppressed as the "concreteness of Christ's continued presence today."[98] In the costly work of responsibility we begin to understand how to confront the disease of white supremacy.

First, in the context of white Christianity's sin of white supremacy, responsibility demands responding in solidarity with African Americans by "taking on the guilt" of the entire white church while not excluding our own contribution to that sin. Responding without "any knowledge about its ultimate justification" resonates with Cone's emphasis on "the risk of faith."[99] White Christians must take a similar risk, witnessing to our own sin and prostrating ourselves before the judgment of God and the world. It is responsibility without justification, consistent with Cone's claim that white people must beg forgiveness from black people without assurance that we will be forgiven.

Second, responsibility entails a concrete response within the situation in which one finds oneself. Because an individual only exists in relationship to an other, Bonhoeffer writes, a "person exists always and only in ethical responsibility."[100] He insists, in contrast to the popular idealism of his day, that humans do not exist "unmediated," but "in responsibility vis-à-vis an 'other.'" In fact, a "person" is created in the first moment of encounter with the other.[101] The ethical person does not exist by universal principle or in a state of moral obscurity, but "grows out of the concrete situation" and recognizes the ethical demands and boundaries presented by the concrete other.[102]

Bonhoeffer believed that ethical principles reduce the complexity of the world and its multiple claims upon us to one singular imperative.[103] Thus, they place God and God's commands at human disposal and easily become instruments of self-justification, thereby keeping us from acting responsibly toward our neighbor.[104] Bonhoeffer writes that those who act based upon an ideology or set of principles consider themselves "justified by their idea." In contrast, those who act responsibly "place their action into the hands of God and live by God's grace and judgment."[105] The Niebuhrian account of responsibility as reasonableness, that seeks self-justification, trades in the universalizing elements of whiteness that we witnessed in previous chapters, because they claim to know what is righteous in all contexts and situations.

Bonhoeffer's disavowal of universalized and principled ethics reflects womanist ethical accounts of virtue. Stacey Floyd-Thomas argues that the "universalizing" idea of virtue proffered by most white, male theologians only brings about "desired ends for members of the privileged class," but not the dispossessed.[106] Instead, as Katie Cannon demonstrates from the wisdom of enslaved black women, virtue should not "appeal to the fixed rules or absolute principles of what is right or wrong or good or bad," that is, of "the white-male-capitalist value system." Rather communities must "embrace values related to the causal conditions of their cultural circumstances."[107] Virtue is contextual; it is identified and discerned within the particular story of the community. For example, she recalls the ways enslaved women refused the docile moral precepts exhorted by slave preachers but "learned to consider their vices as virtues in their dealing with whites."[108] Affirming their God-granted dignity denied them in their moral situation under slavery, they developed an ethics focused on survival as their central virtue. Virtue involved deceiving the master in order to avoid punishment or looking for means of escape whenever possible.[109] Actions deemed deviant by white society were virtuous in the ethical code developed within the concrete situation of the black community, suggesting the particular and communal shape of ethics. This is important for our context because responsibility is the direct antithesis of a universal ethic awash in whiteness. It entails discerning who Christ is in the here and now, in direct connection (and response) to a particular situation.

Third, if responsibility is Christological and the church is "Christ existing as community," as Bonhoeffer claims, the church takes on this responsibility as its very structure—it exists for the sake of others.[110] Yet, like Cone, Bonhoeffer envisions those outside of the institutional church as also capable of participating in Christ (Christ has taken on all of humanity) and, thus, responsible agents who also take action on behalf of others: "All human responsibility is rooted in the real vicarious representative action of Jesus Christ on behalf of all human beings."[111] Bonhoeffer recognizes the agency of those the responsible one joins in solidarity. This is not a paternalistic ethic but respects boundaries and alterity: "Other people who are encountered must be regarded as responsible as well."[112] This sense of responsibility honors others as responsible agents themselves to whom the church should listen and from whom the church should learn.

Simply, white Christians must respect the limits of empathy and solidarity. Many black and womanist theologians identify the limits of any attempt to enter another's subjectivity—in this case, to "become black." Emilie Townes notes how "categories of otherness and difference can swerve toward abstractions at best and become tools for hegemony at worst."[113] Empathy is not the same thing as experience, and the hubris to think that we can fully empathize with those who have radically different experiences is damaging; it does not recognize the messiness of life and often results in either romanticization or trivialization.[114] In many ways, these expressions parallel Hauerwas's concern about colonizing the story of African Americans. He rightly perceives the white tendency to possess that which we desire, though it paralyzes his account of story.

Postcolonial pastoral theology echoes these concerns but suggests the generative possibilities of "misunderstanding stories" across cultural and racial contexts. Melinda McGarrah Sharp redirects empathy and solidarity as primarily dealing with the subject rather than the object. Empathy is often expressed by the colloquialism "walking in another's shoes," although McGarrah Sharp identifies how such expressions fail to grasp the boundedness of our experience and understanding. Instead, these actions should be provisional endeavors: I respect that your shoes are yours and that I could be wrong in trying to understand how it feels to wear them. Empathy imagines in dialogue with you what the contours of your shoes might feel like on my feet.[115] This means, for white people, solidarity is not primarily about better understanding another's blackness, but about comprehending our own whiteness first. It is allowing our whiteness to become visible to us. Then we may begin to understand how that whiteness affects the world and affects the other's story.

Finally, responsibility is a process of formation. Understood as conversion—attending to others in accordance with their reality until one is able to take action on their behalf—responsibility is the formation of character. As all three theologians remind us, the key questions of formation, who am I and how I should live, cannot be addressed without reference to others, suggesting that formation necessarily entails responsibility. Bonhoeffer, Hauerwas, and Cone view the world as deeply contingent, so no moral category can be perceived independently from historical reality. All three theologians reject the abstractions of foundationalism: Bonhoeffer by emphasizing the concrete, Cone by focusing on the particular history and context of the community making decisions, and Hauerwas by championing a narrative description of the world. There can be, therefore, no abstraction into ethical principles or criteria that float above the concrete phenomena of this world. The concrete Christian ethic of responsibility, on the other hand, means that "we can and should speak not about what the good is, can be, or should be for each and every time, but about how Christ may take form among us today and here."[116] This question is impossible to determine for all times and places. We must, as Bonhoeffer later says, attend to the "particular context of experience, responsibility, and decision, from which we cannot withdraw without ending up in abstraction."[117] Christ forms us in a concrete manner to act in accordance with the reality in which we find ourselves. Since the world and God have been unified through Christ, and the renewal of the world has begun, it is only in this way that we can perceive reality. For all three theologians, this means that we must be conformed to the authoritative form of reality, that is, Christ. "Formation occurs only by being drawn into the form of Jesus Christ," Bonhoeffer says, "by being conformed to the unique form of the one who became human, was crucified, and is risen."[118] In sum, Christ forms us, in our particular and contingent contexts, times, and locations into the body of Christ.

We cannot afford to understand challenging white supremacy in terms of solving problems. This is the flaw in models of racial reconciliation—they perceive racism as a "problem" that we can handle with preconceived and manufactured solutions. Recall Copeland's observation: "Racism is not something out-there for us to solve or fix; racism is in us, sedimented in our consciousness."[119] It is a question of what type of community we will be. As a process of formation, an ethic of responsibility promotes incremental, communal action to confront the wicked problem of whiteness through material practices, while also recognizing the lingering challenges of whiteness within a broken and wounded body of Christ.

4. The Cost of Responsibility

My turn to Bonhoeffer as a model for white Christians is not a hero story of a white theologian easily converting to "blackness." Such conversion can never be heroic work, only a stumbling journey of missteps and mistakes, ventured penitently with no assurance of success or acceptance. Bonhoeffer's theology, even after his "Harlem sojourn into black church life," as J. Kameron Carter puts it, was still bound to the constraints and distortions of whiteness.[120] This part of the story is just as instructive as the positive moments for those of us seeking to confront our whiteness.

The foibles and failures of Bonhoeffer are helpful because they express the same patterns of colorblindness evident in our contemporary context, and demonstrate the ways all white people are shaped by a system of white supremacy— and the costs required to challenge it. Even as I point to Bonhoeffer as a model, and follow Cone in doing so, Bonhoeffer also demonstrates the complicated ways that white Christians and theologians remain tethered to whiteness even as we try to resist white supremacy. Resistance is sure to be costly.

Bonhoeffer's Colorblindness

We can see Bonhoeffer's colorblindness emerge, following Carter and Michael DeJonge, almost immediately after his return from Harlem to the chaos of the church struggle in Germany when the "German Christian" movement began supporting the Nazi government. In response to this theological upheaval, he maintained that race was not a proper theological concern. The church struggle was troubling for Bonhoeffer not directly because of the mistreatment of Jewish people but because it jeopardized the free preaching of the gospel (an issue of religious liberty). DeJonge claims, "Bonhoeffer, in [his] 1933 writings, frames the treatment of Jews as an ethical and political issue with theological and confessional implications, but it is not in itself a theological and confessional issue."[121] To make it so, in Bonhoeffer's thought, "would be to confuse theology, proclamation, and confession with humanitarian and political activity."[122] That is, part of Bonhoeffer's response to the German Christians' embrace of Nazism—specifically their adoption of the Aryan Paragraph that excluded from church leadership and eventually membership anyone of Jewish descent—was to contend that, in normal circumstances, race is not a "gospel matter," but an "indifferent" one.[123] For this reason, the German Christians were wrong: they elevated an "indifferent" issue like race to a criterion of church membership.[124]

Only in emergency circumstances in which the state of the Gospel is jeopardized, what Bonhoeffer called *borderline cases*, or *grenzfall*, could "indifferent" matters like race be treated as theological issues. Thus, in 1933 in its adoption of the Aryan laws, German Christians were making race a gospel issue when it shouldn't be. In his response to this emergency, Bonhoeffer also invokes race as a gospel issue, because now, for him, the gospel was at stake.[125] That is, according to DeJonge, "When others make the heretical error of turning race into a central theological category, then (i.e., *in casu confessionis*) race becomes a theological concern."[126] Race had become an issue of proper theological concern in this emergency case only because the German Christians had made it one that threatened the very "substance of the church."[127]

In some ways, his colorblind theology allowed Bonhoeffer to quickly perceive the German Christians' heresy. Yet, in ways similar to many white theologians and Christians today who think of race as peripheral to the church's mission or proclamation, Bonhoeffer bracketed race as possessing no theological significance.[128] Like the white theologians I addressed in chapter 3, Bonhoeffer said that racism was the world's problem to solve, not the church's. This is the type of theological abstraction that upholds the dualistic thread of the Christian tradition, subjugates bodies to spiritual matters, and fails to perceive racial oppression "in normal circumstances." Bonhoeffer, thus, serves also as an example of the way white supremacy remains a part of us against which we must continually struggle.

In an essay written seven years after his contentions that race is not a gospel issue Bonhoeffer does finally recognize race as a theological, even Christological, matter. Briefly anticipating Cone's claim years afterward, Bonhoeffer insists that we must understand Christ in his particular, historical form as "the promised Messiah of the Israelite-Jewish people." The National Socialist and German Christian efforts in "driving out the Jews from the West must result in driving out Christ with them, for Jesus was a Jew."[129] This emphasis on Jesus's racial identity falls off quickly, and this is the only instance in which Bonhoeffer includes race within his account of the gospel, but it does signal a change in conformity with his radical political actions.

Costly Responsibility

In this cautionary tale—relieving "well-meaning" white Christians of our self-justification and thoughts of cheap reconciliation—we also find an element useful for narrating our own context of responsibility. Bonhoeffer's response to the racism of the German Christians was to identify a *grenzfall*, or emergency case.

While Cone, in his favorable reflections on Bonhoeffer, does not attend to his colorblindness, Cone would likely agree with Bonhoeffer that this was an emergency, requiring a response. And it still is.

Just as in Bonhoeffer's time, the white church in America has been "silent witnesses of evil deeds . . . learned in the arts of obfuscation and equivocal speech."[130] It has witnessed racial oppression and failed to act. It has "looked on while injustice and violence have been done under the cover of the name of Christ," and inflicted that injustice and violence itself.[131] In both contexts, the role of the church in oppression has rendered everything questionable and jeopardized the state of the gospel. Since the advent of white supremacy within the Christian church, the white church has always existed in an emergency situation.[132] There are no "normal circumstances" in which the faithfulness of the church in an age of white supremacy is not suspect. And in such cases, racism is a gospel issue: the proclamation of the gospel is proclamation of a black Christ; the church's service is resistance to white supremacy; the church's community is one of formation into blackness. White supremacy means that our everyday, ordinary time is an emergency situation. In emergencies like ours, nothing is of greater importance, and responsibility will be costly.

In the wake of a church-sanctioned genocidal regime, as he witnessed the literal and figurative ashes of the church around him, Bonhoeffer speculated to his friend Eberhard Bethge that perhaps all that will and should remain of the church after this moment was prayer and righteous action.[133] "It has become incapable of bringing the word of reconciliation and redemption to humankind and to the world," he lamented. "All Christian thinking, talking, and organizing must be born anew, out of that prayer and action."[134]

And here is the payoff, a central claim of this book: a faith, theology, and church capable of inventing white supremacy, justifying racial slavery, or supporting National Socialism must be stripped to its studs—everything called into question and most of it dismantled. We have witnessed the temptation to rush too quickly to models of racial reconciliation without doing the difficult work of self-examination. But as Bonhoeffer warned during his moment, every attempt the white church makes to develop a solution too prematurely "will only delay its conversion and purification." [135] For us, this process must begin with living responsibly in the face of what we have done. In Bonhoeffer's words this will certainly require the white church to

> give up our privileges without a struggle, recognizing the justice of history. Events and circumstances may arise that take precedence over our wishes and rights. Then, not in embitterment and pride, but consciously yielding to divine judgment, we shall prove ourselves worthy to survive by

identifying ourselves generously and selflessly with the whole community and the suffering of our fellow human beings.[136]

This purging will mean letting go of our control over doctrines that have been tainted by white supremacy, or doctrines that birthed it. We saw in chapter 2 the way soteriological exclusivism and Christian attitudes toward religious difference paved the way for racial hierarchy. If this history and these doctrines have aided and abetted Christianity's participation in gruesome levels of racial oppression, we must clear the threshing floor and burn the chaff with fire.

In the next chapter I turn more directly to the work the white church must do, but perhaps this is the task for white theologians: white theology must tear itself down and start anew with the bare essentials of liberative praxis and a "worldly nonreligious interpretation of Christian concepts."[137] That is, Bonhoeffer directs us to listen to the stories of those outside the church and white academy—the worldly, the activist, the marginalized, and oppressed—and allow that perspective from outside, "from below," to reinterpret our faith. We must venture the risky work of uncovering and breaking our own white supremacy and submit our efforts to the judgment of black and womanist scholars and ministers, and to the grace of God (a vulnerability I feel even writing these words). The white church has avoided this difficult work for too long, it seems, out of concern for its own self-preservation. (It cannot risk its own legitimation descending into crisis.) If white theologians dig too deeply into its sordid past and discover the distortion of white supremacy permeating our own thought and practice, that jeopardizes its existence—and our own. Yet, it is not clear whether its existence has been a help or hindrance to the movement of God in the world.

For Bonhoeffer, responsibility meant the difficult choice of wishing and working for the collapse of his nation. "I must say that I pray for the defeat of my country," he once told a friend, "for I believe that is the only possibility for paying for all the suffering that my country has caused in the world."[138] Perhaps soberly facing the severity of suffering and evil we have unleashed on the world and reflecting on the wicked ways white supremacy has become entangled in our theology and practice, our only option is to pray—and actively work for—the death of the white church in America. Perhaps the only way to cleanse our toxic baptismal waters is to drain them and start anew. Only in its utter defeat and destruction can a new creation be resurrected.

5. Responsibility as the Wounded Body of Christ

White theologians like Hauerwas blame the world outside the church for the white supremacy that has infected the church. As he claims repeatedly in his sparse treatments of racism, it is the result of the atomizing effects of liberalism that create division and hierarchy among and within a people called to be one in Christ. This is the effect of the nation-state supplanting Christian identity and colonizing the soul. Because the church is to be nothing less than "a community capable of forming people with virtues sufficient to witness to God's truth in the world," the moral crisis of whiteness that has infected the church is simply a failure of the church to be the church.[139] Like most white theologians, however, he misidentifies the source of the sin of white supremacy. While Hauerwas rightly discerns the role of the nation-state in solidifying racist power, this account neglects the role of the church and its theology of generating racial hierarchy in the first place. This is not most accurately an issue of the church accommodating the liberal, sinful world, or even failing to "be the church." Such diagnoses only further evade the question of the church's role in inventing white supremacy.

However, this book is arguing that the problem is not one of shielding the church from the racist world outside its doors but coming to terms with the white supremacy we have given to the world. Its doctrines and practices—from its soteriology and theological superiority, body-soul dualisms, and sacraments like baptism that bound black enslaved people to their masters rather than setting them free—all contributed to developing and proliferating white supremacy. The issue is not one of allowing liberalism to loosen the ties that bind us in ecclesial unity, but of "being bound improperly." As Katie Grimes helpfully identifies, "White supremacy operates not just by rending human beings apart from each other but also by binding them together perversely and for the sake of white power."[140] The solution to racism cannot be simply "more church," but deconstructing the church and its malforming doctrines and practices in light of its moral failing.

Cone's concept of narrative helpfully corrects the closed, antagonistic account of narrative found in Hauerwas's thought. The church's formative narrative does not need to be insulated from the world. It is already broken. For Cone, the story-formed character of the black church is one that accommodates multiple formative narratives and allows for critical introspection. Because of the multisite nature of the black church—as a political, social, and spiritual institution from its very origin—it understands the ways that these multiple identities converge to shape the worldly story of the church. Not only are the black story and white story not two separate narratives, but the stories that make up the white and black churches contain many interacting and overlapping sources—gospel, history, social context. Just as all theology is contingent upon the location of the person doing the theologizing, so too is each ecclesial community shaped by the context and history in which it finds itself.

Another way to put this is that the body of Christ is not sealed. Rather, like actual human bodies, it is porous and open to the world. It shares sin and sacrament. While this porosity frightens many white theologians who worry about the capacity of the church to resist a sinful, racist world at its door, it is good news for others who recognize that the white church has proven itself incapable of reforming itself from within.[141] The white church cannot save itself. Rather it must take a cue from the model of Bonhoeffer, who points us to marginalized voices and stories from which to learn. It must listen to black theologians like James Cone, Kelly Brown Douglas, and Bryan Massengale and engage with black churches and (even non-Christian) prophets like James Baldwin and Malcolm X.[142] If we are to take responsibility for the white supremacy we have inflicted upon the world and be responsible to the victims of that oppression—and rightly remember, repent, and repair—we must listen to the voices and stories that call us to this work. And we must look for models like Bonhoeffer, who—albeit imperfectly—show us what these practices might look like in the face of the moral collapse of the white church, and even press us to work toward its death.

The Pauline image of the church as the body of Christ has perhaps been the most significant ecclesial concept through Christian history.[143] The image shapes much of Bonhoeffer's ecclesiology as well. His is a rather literal understanding that the church "*is* the body of Christ."[144] The church is of course provisional, and morphs into different visible forms, yet, "there is no relation to Christ in which relation to the church is not established as well."[145]

In agreement with Bonhoeffer, Shawn Copeland asserts, "The flesh of the church is the flesh of Christ in every age." But she further pushes churches to remember that this flesh is marked just as Christ's was by race, sex, gender, sexuality, and culture. "These marks differentiate and transgress, they unify and bond."[146] Therefore, the body of Christ takes in all, as they are in their own bodies. This is an "incorporation" of difference, not its "erasure, not uniformity."[147] As Christians, we are indeed reoriented, remade, and remarked beneath the foot of the cross of Jesus, but being incorporated into his body "preserves the integrity and significance of our body marks" and does not overwhelm them.[148]

Yet recognizing the church as the body of Christ that bears the marks of Jesus's flesh forces Christians to reckon with what was done to Jesus's flesh. Bonhoeffer's assertion that the church literally is the body of Christ is not a triumphal claim, as some have taken it, positing a pure and sinless church in contrast to a tainted and sinful world. Rather, it is a claim that like the physical human body of Jesus of Nazareth, with flesh prodded, pierced, and beaten, the church bears those same marks—some given to it by the world, but many perpetrated on itself; a long history of oppression against persons of color reveals these self-inflicted wounds, which scar church members of all races. The church is not the body triumphant, but the body of the suffering servant who was "wounded for our transgressions" and, certainly, by our transgressions. As we recall the beautiful, grotesque, wounded, and porous body of Jesus, we recall the bare lives that the church has so often refused to see—bodies hanging from a tree, bleeding in the street, walking to the death chamber. The cross demonstrates the power of redemptive love, Copeland comments, but we must be careful to never reduce it to a cheap solution to evils like racism. Instead, placing the cross next to the lynching tree—the maimed, lynched bodies next to the wounded body of Christ—"reinforces the sacramentality of the body, contests objectification of the body, and honors the body as the self-manifestation and self-expression of the free human subject." The image of the wounded body of Christ can shape us and remind us that we are people in need of grace, a people in need of healing, and a people who need to do the hard work of repairing these breaches. Therefore, when we begin to understand ourselves, the church, as the wounded body of Christ—that carried a cross to his own death—and not just the transfigured body triumphant, we can, "as his body," according to Copeland, "embrace with love and hope those who, in their bodies, are despised and marginalized."[149]

6. Conclusion: The Church in the World and the World in the Church

As a theologian influenced by Hauerwas and bound by practices of whiteness, for years my theological focus was on maintaining the distinctive witness of the church—a triumphal body of Christ. Facing issues of injustice like racism, I contended that it was not the church's responsibility to be effective in confronting these evils, but simply to witness to an alternative way. I concluded that the church should be wary of social and political partnerships with any groups that do not share our same spiritual and moral convictions. I believed Christians and their partners not only ought to share goals but also the reasons for those goals and the same means for achieving them. Bracketing the deeper forces that generate these shared ends—the fundamental and comprehensive beliefs, stories, and moral truths that constitute these communities—only results in shallow networks destined to break down as soon as motivations conflict. Or worse, it might result in the church sacrificing its own identity and moral purity for a so-called greater good.

Yet August 12, 2017, in Charlottesville, Virginia, cemented a growing concern that these self-protective efforts limit the church's ability to be faithful to its mission. I was, and am still, haunted by Dietrich Bonhoeffer's question written to his fellow conspirators ten years after Hitler assumed power: "Are we still of any use?" In light of the moral crisis of whiteness and the white church's utter failure to confront it, much less to confess its own role in its devastation, there are many days I believe our "usefulness" to a world in need has run its course—if we were ever useful in the first place. Charlottesville is a pivotal moment in the life of the church in America because, like Bonhoeffer's melancholy question from a prison cell, it revealed the limits of the church. In moments like this, the beloved community that Martin Luther King Jr. hoped for appears to be a far-off dream.

Whatever usefulness the church possesses in this time is likely to be revealed only in unlikely actions and allies. This will also compel us to discover "church" in unlikely places and allies in unlikely people. The struggle against white supremacy means forming coalitions across religious and political communities. Alliances with Muslims and Jews, atheists and anarchists may be difficult and complex. But Christians will need partnerships, not only to protest and plan marches but also for the grueling daily work of racial justice: criminal justice and immigration reform, police accountability, education equality. Sometimes church comes upon us unexpectedly, in the midst of the world, and we must be open to receiving it.

On August 12 a line of clergy formed the first wave of nonviolent resistance to the armed and approaching white nationalists. But when police stood idle during the moments of confrontation, clergy lives were threatened by a white nationalist horde amped up on a cocktail of fear, rage, and hate. Members of Antifa and Christian clergy, Jewish and Muslim protesters, were all intermingled in a broad coalition of resistance. We shared not only a common goal but also communication devices and protest space. And when violence broke out and law enforcement failed, clergy and antiracist protesters found a common safe haven in a nearby bar. The rainbow flags hanging in the windows signaled this safe space as a potential target for the armed right-wing gangs now roaming the streets after the rally was dispersed. A siegelike afternoon ensued with bomb threats forcing us to shelter in place, a militia member with an assault rifle posted across the street forcing us to retreat from the windows, and a murderous vehicular rampage on the street outside sending clergy into pastoral action. Through it all, for the owner and his same-sex partner, this was their act of defiance, and a welcome offering for those needing safety. He opened his doors as sanctuary for Christian clergy, a category of people he would have every reason to suspect. Instead, as we sheltered in place for hours, he brought us a buffet of food and poured pints of beer as neo-Nazis and rifle-toting militias marched outside. A coalition of people of faith and no faith, black, white, and brown, gay and straight, we broke bread and shared a cup, bonded liturgically by our common cause—a motley, beloved community of love and hope.

6

Remembrance, Repentance, Reparation

Reconciliation to God means that white people are prepared to
deny themselves (whiteness),
take up the cross (blackness), and follow Christ (black ghetto).

—JAMES CONE[1]

1. The Promise and Problem of Practices

Stories do not remain mere stories. They do not linger on the level of cognition or emotion, content to simply shape our beliefs or affections toward a topic, event, or person. They are material.

As I contended in chapter 1, stories "lie in the realm of the given"[2] by structuring reality through the practices they inculcate within a society. That is, they frame our social imaginations by cultivating social and cultural practices, and in turn are refashioned and retold by those very practices. They construct a shared understanding and ethic of a community in a way that makes that ethic seem natural by shaping (and sometimes controlling) bodies through practices. Mary McClintock Fulkerson and Marcia Mount Shoop begin their account of race in white churches as follows: "Our stories tell us who we are, at least that is what Christianity tells us. Our salvation story, the stories of scripture, and testimonies of faith define us and inform our religious identities." Yet the authors wonder, "What about when our stories are incomplete? Or worse yet, what about when our stories about ourselves are lies? What about when stories dis-member or contort part of the body of Christ by denying truth, silencing dissonance, or ignoring wounds?"[3] Though Scripture and liturgy continually remind us that we embody a shared story as followers of Christ, "instead of seeing all nations and tongues represented at the table, often we look around and see people just like us."[4]

We witnessed the mutually enforcing power of story and practice in the interlocking relationship between stories of Jewish host desecration or usury and practices of marking and segregating Jewish populations from Christians in European history. Stories and practice mutually enforced supersessionist logic and action. We see this today at the convergence of the American stories of autonomous

Witnessing Whiteness. Kristopher Norris, Oxford University Press (2020). © Oxford University Press.
DOI: 10.1093/oso/9780190055813.001.0001

individualism and black welfare recipients with political practices that neglect historical systemic racism.[5]

Sociologist George Yancey defines *whiteness* as a historical process of hegemony and privilege that "forces bodies of color to the margins"—a process expressed through "cultural, political, interpersonal, and institutional *practices*."[6] White supremacy, as the form of the church's original sin, is passed on to each new generation by infestation of its institutions, but—importantly—it does so through the repetition of social and cultural practices. Therefore, if Yancey is correct, any attempt to resist or subvert whiteness must also do so through practices. These practices must acknowledge our racial history, grant all a voice and power to influence communal decisions, and generate the refusal of privilege and power by placing the burden on the shoulders of whites and requiring us to submit to minority authority.

For many white theologians like Hauerwas who deem white supremacy a problem external to the church, or one with which the church has simply become complicit, the solution to racism may be more church. It is through church practices, liturgy, and formation that one can excise this racist intruder. Postliberal theologians, especially, focus on the formative potential of Christian practices—how practices like baptism, prayer, or the Eucharist conform Christian practitioners into the likeness of Christ. They insist that people must learn the language and practices of the Christian tradition before knowing what they means when proclaiming, "Christ is Lord," or "God will make all things new." Hauerwas contends that practices make the church "a community capable of forming people with virtues sufficient to witness to God's truth in the world."[7] But these theologians often project abstract or ideal descriptions of the practices and their effects. In these accounts, misperformance of Christian practice, or damage that ensues from practice, is left out of the picture. And when it is taken into account, blame is directed at forces external to the church and its practice of these idealized rituals.

Even most white theologians who identify the ways church practices have failed to produce more virtuous or moral Christians, such as the ones I identified in chapter 3, suggest that the reason these practices still produce malformed people is due to something exterior to the practices themselves. For example, for James K. A. Smith, white supremacy is the result of a rival tradition, of worldly liturgies, forming us; it is not inherent to the church's tradition itself. The church and its practices embody a tradition that is in competition with these sinful worldly liturgies. His solution to the problem of "deformation" is for church leaders to be better ethnographers capable of diagnosing the way "churchgoers are shaped by 'the world.'"[8] A more realistic sense of the dangers of worldly liturgies can help the church identify these alien influences and allow its liturgical practices to more purely "[form] a people who are sent out for the sake of the common good."[9] Yet, if the problem is actually within the church—one the church itself invented—then simply more church is likely to exacerbate the problem.

In light of these realities, Lauren Winner argues that "many current discussions of Christian practice are too rosy—are pristinated—and fail to acknowledge, let alone account for or respond to, the sin entailed by those practices."[10] Of course, some things go wrong in uncharacteristic ways. That is, they are damaged or deformed externally, from the outside. But some go wrong in characteristic ways, deformations intimate with the form and goods of the practice.[11] Winner takes concrete cases, and displays, for example, the ways the internal logic of the Eucharist—consuming the Jewish flesh of Christ—generated the deformed "host desecration narratives" that falsely accused Jews of inflicting harm upon the communion host, and often led to their execution. Practices like the Eucharist, baptism, or prayer carry within themselves the possibilities of their own deformation. Katie Grimes similarly recognizes that ecclesial practices like baptism and the Eucharist have historically lacked the power to disrupt the church's white supremacy; in fact, in many ways they were used to support it. Slavers forcibly baptized newly captured Africans as a way of symbolically severing them from their familial and ancestral identity and binding them to their new white masters.[12] The historic complicity of these practices suggests that the church cannot reform itself from within, relying on the morally formative powers of its practices.[13] This claim aligns with one of the arguments of this book, that Christianity itself in its theology and practice possessed the resources to concoct and disseminate white supremacy. This malformation was internal to Christianity itself.

It might seem surprising, then, that in conclusion I turn to "practices" as a way to address this deformation. In spite of the many ways practices can go wrong, Winner and others—mostly feminist, queer, and womanist theologians—still contend that some counter-practices (though perhaps ones found external to what are deemed conventional Christian practices) may be tools for rehabilitating the deformations of Christianity and Christian practice. For example, feminist theologian Mary McClintock Fulkerson and womanist theologian M. Shawn Copeland both turn to church practices—in ways consistent with and moving beyond postliberals—as means of contesting white supremacy, despite recognition of the ways practices have often been used as tools of harm.

Copeland recognizes that racism advances as a set of practices that "infiltrates, permeates, and deforms the institutions of politics, economy, culture, even religion."[14] Yet, because racism exists as a practice, she understands that cognitive and affective modes of resistance will remain inadequate; it must be challenged by embodied practices of solidarity.[15] She identifies the Eucharist and table fellowship as practices that challenge racist ideologies and practices in the church. Though the Eucharist has been a trigger of supersessionist and racist violence, according to Copeland the radical bodily inclusion that is also inherent to the practice makes it a possible means of liberation and solidarity. This is due to the ways it appreciates bodily differences, while still bonding bodies together in the consuming of "one body."[16] The Eucharist can also function as a "countersign" to the devaluing of black bodies by serving as a memorial for all of those who, like Jesus, are victims of oppression. Copeland claims, in the "humble embrace of different bodies, Eucharistic celebration forms our social imagination, transvalues our values, and transforms the meaning of our being human, of embodying Christ."[17] The concreteness of the symbol in actual bread and wine generates a communal commitment to resistance when practiced in full view of the violence of the cross and the lynching tree.

Fulkerson, a white feminist theologian seeking to uncover means of antiracism within white-majority communities, recognizes that practices are inevitable as a part of communal experience.[18] In her ethnographic study of a multiracial church in the South, Good Samaritan Church, Fulkerson argues that incorporative practices, as embodied ways of communicating meaning—from liturgical practices to communal meals—generated the conditions for cross-racial solidarity and hospitality to the stranger.[19] This does not mean that some of the church's practices were not damaged. She notes how some of its inscriptive practices—methods of Scripture interpretation—or practices of welcome still invoke colorblindness. Good Samaritan was both conformist and resistant; in some ways its commitment to "not see race" contributed to complicity and projection of premature reconciliation. But through self-criticism and improvisatory openness to challenge, other practices of Good Samaritan refused that script: "Creative thinking originates at the scene of a wound," she argues.[20] This could only occur as the church appropriated categories foreign to traditional theological reflection and reevaluated what counted as orthodox.[21] It needed a "worldly theology" that granted fuller attention to the complexity of the world, a theology that thematizes the complex and dense subject matter of the contemporary situation.

These theologians demonstrate that we must deal in practices; we cannot get rid of them. Despite his faults, Hauerwas resonates with these theologians in his insistence on the formative potential of practices. He claims that the problem with conventional models of ethics, which often abide in a problem-solving mode, is that they are "trying to make a better world without us needing to become better people."[22] If my account of responsibility understood as formation and conversion is correct, we need practices in order to become better. (In fact, if we consider that one of the earliest Christian documents, the *Didache*, was a set of liturgical and moral practices long before the creeds codified orthodoxy, we must conclude that the root of Christianity exists in praxis.)

In the aftermath of the Holocaust, Dietrich Bonhoeffer stripped the institution that participated in national genocide of all its formality, religiosity, and piety and claimed that it could proceed only in two practices: prayer and righteous action. For the white church in America, in the afterlife of the Middle Passage, plantation, and lynching tree—of mass incarceration, colorblindness, and cheap reconciliation—we find ourselves in a similar moment. In light of our distorted theology and malformative practices, we cannot rid ourselves of practices, but we must strip the church and its practice down to the studs. Even more, we must look beyond our conventional modes and sources of practice, and expand what counts as theology and what marks a community as church. Our old models have not served us well, and other, often silenced voices and counternarratives may be directing us to other practices. These may be theologians neglected by white theologians and the white church—liberation, black, womanist, queer, and *mujerista* theologians. They may be stories from outside of what we typically call the church, but parts of broad coalitions and beloved communities. Most likely the church will be constituted by practices of interruption—difficult and painful practices that challenge the status quo. They are risks of faith because they may seek sources outside of orthodoxy, or they may force us to tell a new and truer story of ourselves.

In what follows I take my cue from James Cone, who argues that for white people and the white church to ever "become black"—that is, to be reconciled to God and live in full solidarity with people of color—we must deny our whiteness, take up blackness, and follow the black Christ into the black ghetto.[23] Cone draws from Jesus's words to his disciples in Mark 8:34 to identify three steps in his call to conversion. I have argued that this is what it means to take responsibility for white supremacy. These three steps correspond to the three resources for an ethic of responsibility I identified in part II of this book—memory, particularity, and concreteness—and issue in the three practices of remembrance (recognizing the power of our whiteness and denying it), repentance (confessing and turning away from white supremacy), and reparation (joining the movement for black liberation in submission and solidarity). In the remainder of this chapter I flesh out these three practices, drawing on Scripture and providing examples of congregations that attempt these steps. These examples are not meant to be glorifying or even sufficient, but to provide practical and concrete (and, like the model of Bonhoeffer, imperfect and instructive) models for other white churches seeking to take responsibility for white supremacy.

2. Remembrance

The Gospels record two interactions between Jesus and Canaanite women. In the more troubling story, as Jesus has ventured far into Gentile territory, a Canaanite or Syrophoenician woman approaches him, shouting for him to heal her daughter.[24] Jesus at first ignores her and then responds, "I was sent only to the lost sheep of the house of Israel." Gaining her composure she kneels next to Jesus and again begs for his help. This time he offers one of the most perplexing lines in the Gospels: "It is not fair to take the children's food and throw it to the dogs."[25] Undeterred by his insult, the woman replies, "Yes, Lord, yet even the dogs eat the crumbs that fall from their masters' table." At this, Jesus praises her faith and heals her daughter.

Many exegetes and preachers attempt to sanitize this story with some account that saves Jesus from his own words. Despite his apparent cruelty, the irresistible smile of Jesus and a twinkle of his eye would have connoted the truth—or perhaps his statement was some sort of ancient inside joke.[26] Unfortunately, there is not good evidence to suggest either. Other modern interpreters refuse attempts to soften the scandal and suggest that we must read Jesus's remarks as a "rejection of the Syrophoenician woman based on her race and ethnicity."[27] On this reading, we are left with an image of Jesus rejecting this woman's request simply because she was not a member of the proper ethnic group. He was sent to the Jews, not to her people. On the one hand, this is a good reminder to those of us prone to supersessionism: white supremacy has no legitimacy in our salvation history because we are all outsiders to God's election, begging like this woman to be grafted into the salvation promised to Israel. But on the other hand, this raises the fearful question: Was Jesus racist?

Postcolonial, feminist, and womanist theologians have consistently read this episode as an overcoming of Jesus's ethnocentric outlook through the clever subversion of this anguished woman.[28] Kelly Brown Douglas notes that the story moves from a presentation of Jesus as "controlled by the biases of his society" to one in which "Jesus realizes how he had succumbed to the privileges of being Jewish and male in that particular society."[29] Marilyn McCord Adams suggests that Jesus learned to outgrow his racism "under the tutelage" of this woman.[30] Facing a verbal wall of ethnic division, she persisted and won the argument. Jesus learns from her and changes his mind.[31] The Gospel lesson is one of openness to hearing the stories of others, willingness to learn from those stories, and recognition of the difficulty and risk of entering those stories.

And though it does not say it explicitly, the story is also a lesson of remembering. With his education from the Canaanite woman, perhaps Jesus "remembers" the universality of his mission—breaking through the cultural and religious stories of his context. Perhaps he remembers that Israel was once an alien and stranger and was now called to remember that history and care for the stranger in its midst. Perhaps he remembers his own parable about the Samaritan helping the wounded Jewish man alongside the road. Perhaps he remembers his namesake, Joshua, who is said to have slaughtered countless Canaanites several hundred years earlier and laments. Perhaps he doesn't remember—the inner life of the mind of Jesus remains a mystery. But this story surely calls us to remember the triumphs and tragedies of our own faith journey and then listen, learn, and change.

The Work of Remembrance

In her recounting of lynching narratives from eyewitnesses, now catalogued and analyzed in her book *Lynched*, womanist theologian Angela Sims gives voice to the story of Reverend Clarence Walker Kidd from Louisiana. During their interview, Kidd took Sims to a spot near his church, now in the center of an upper-income, mostly white neighborhood, where still stands a lynching tree. Kidd's childhood memories of the horrors that took place, the bodies hanging from that tree, are seared into his mind. "Walking past that hangman's tree," he told her, gives him a feeling of "excruciating fear" that goes "as deep as I can imagine." He says, "The innermost part of myself was frightened beyond the ability to move." His sister adds that every time she passed that tree, "you just had to look up because you had a feeling what went on there."[32] Sims ponders how one's personhood, or sense of self, is shaped by daily life in the shadow of a lynching tree.

These memories do not just affect African Americans, however, but the children who gathered with families at these public spectacles—memorialized in postcards and photographs—and the white people whose characters are formed and deformed by the decisions to hide the tree within an upper-class white neighborhood, rendering the memories of their atrocities invisible. Black residents of this town cannot help but recall the stories and the horror "etched forever in the recesses of the mind" when they pass this tree;[33] white people's memories are stunted and fragmented by the ways these symbols and the stories they tell are hidden from our view and conscience.

When whiteness takes form, in Peter McLaren's words, as "a form of social amnesia" or even willful ignorance, memory takes work.[34] To remember is to fight through the veils we use to shield our conscience or the stories we tell ourselves to refract reality. Remembrance gives voice to those who were silenced by fear, oppression, and death, and provides a glimpse into their realities and strategies of resistance. Recall Saidiya Hartman's claim that the stories we tell about the past "redound" in the "ethical and political stakes of the present."[35] According to Sims, the narratives of lynchings compel us to discern the camouflaged forms in which lynching persists in "economic policies and sentencing guidelines that seek to disrupt our mental-emotional-cultural constructions that shape our notions of that which is ultimately just."[36] She says, "to name multiple shared narratives" is an invitation to a process of truth telling and self-examination.[37] That is, without remembering all of the stories, our current perceptions are distorted. Truth telling requires giving voice to the people and events that have been silenced, "to the ways in which justice has been misconstrued and misrepresented by architects of domestic terror whose sole purpose is to benefit from artificially constructed fragmentations."[38] The "racial perception gap," whereby whites and blacks interpret current events in drastically different ways, is a symptom of this fragmented memory—an intentional effort to silence stories that reveal the full history of white supremacy, because of what they might reveal about who we really are. Yet, as Alice Walker says, "We are who we are largely because of who we have been."[39]

Remembrance sheds light on our present reality and illuminates injustices for what they are. In fact, Hauerwas resonates with these claims and even anticipates the turn toward repentance when he writes that genuine peace never emerges from simply forgetting past wrongs, but "must come from encompassing those wrongs in a history of forgiveness."[40] As Kelly Brown Douglas notes, remembrance is "the beginning of 'white' America taking responsibility for the past that it carries within it."[41] White Christians cannot begin to reject the privileges of our whiteness—to deny ourselves, as Cone admonishes—without remembering our whiteness and its effects on the world, past and present.

Yet "remembering is terrifying," Copeland writes, "especially when the perpetrators of wrong are no longer available, when death and decades disrupt the possibility of apology or direct reparations of survivors."[42] She contends that remembrance is an imperative for the church and its theology because of their wicked entanglement in white supremacy. Theology is not meant to aid our evasion of reality, as white theology does, but to take on things as they really are and with what they really demand. The terrorism of lynching is one acute historical moment for which the church must reckon. But this "ethical responsibility of memory," as Copeland puts it,[43] extends to the Middle Passage, plantation, and prison-industrial system that still attempts to control black bodies. It extends to the theological construction of white supremacist colonialism, supersessionism, and Christian superiority that produced slavery in the first place.

White theologians and churches must begin to cultivate practices of remembrance—retelling the collective history of the church's endorsement of racism. This could mean more self-conscience writing from white theologians, naming our position and privilege and then attending to the gaps, hidden assumptions, and silenced voices in our work. Within congregations it could mean efforts to address the history of the church or denomination, to seek out the ways the congregation still participates in and benefits from a system of racism, and to retell their story in a more truthful key.

Practicing Remembrance: Calvary Baptist Church

Calvary Baptist Church was founded in the midst of the Civil War in the heart of the Union's capital, Washington, DC. Splitting from another congregation that wanted to remain silent on issues of secession and slavery, Calvary was planted in 1862 and later became the inaugural congregation of the Northern Baptist (now American Baptist) Convention. Though consistently a white-dominated congregation, it has long prided itself on its abolitionist history. The story it has told about itself—during anniversary celebrations, on its website, in newspaper articles—is that it was founded by abolitionists, and this heritage precipitated its progressive activism to this day, especially its concern for racial justice. One *Washington Post* article reads, "According to church historians, Amos Kendall, a prominent District businessman, led a break from the E Street Baptist Church after that congregation opposed praying for the Union forces during the Civil War. *Founded by abolitionists*, the then-white Sixth Street Baptist Church was later renamed Calvary Baptist Church." The article continues, "From *opposing slavery* in the 1860s to supporting the civil rights struggles in the 1960s, Calvary has always been more progressive than traditional Baptist churches." [44] Now a truly multiethnic congregation, the church has been forced to reexamine and now re-remember that history.

Research that began in the congregational archives recently unearthed the truth that the church did not have abolitionist origins or even abolitionist values during its founding in the middle of a war fought over slavery. At a worship service earlier this year, the church leadership revealed this new narrative to the congregation, led by pastors Sally Sarratt, Maria Swearingen, and Elijah Zehyoue, and member John Appiah-Duffell. [45] In the historical records, they explained, there is "nothing to suggest that any founder or early member was abolitionist." [46] The dissenters who left E Street Baptist to found their own congregation were simply pro-Union activists: Baptists and citizens against secession, patriots who simply wanted to preserve the unity of the nation. "They were open to compromising," the pastors said, "even on the issue of slavery, if it meant keeping the country together." [47] The founders recorded nothing in their formative documents or foundational meeting minutes opposing the institution of slavery, but pledged loyalty to national authority. In fact, the congregation's primary benefactor, Amos Kendall—a man whose name the sanctuary building still bears—intervened to prevent abolitionist mailings while serving as President Andrew Jackson's postmaster general and was himself a slave owner. He worried that abolitionism was a danger to the unity of the nation. [48]

In light of these facts, the church must set the record straight, the church leaders said, and no longer claim that it has an abolitionist history.[49] They paused for a moment to remember "Daniel," the only known name of one of Kendall's enslaved people, and then called on the congregation to remember this history rightly.[50] Daniel was never given voice to "tell his truth," but Calvary Baptist now can tell its truth, and in doing so, hopefully model a process of right remembering and truth telling for other churches, communities, and people. In much the same way that colorblind white Christians content themselves with a rosy, sanitized history, or shield themselves from guilt with stories that they are not racist (or their ancestors didn't own enslaved people), or prioritize civility and unity over justice, this church had told itself a formative story that embellished the virtues and embargoed the vices. But this story was not true. They had to, in the words of James Baldwin, "go back to where you started, as far back as you can, examine all of it, travel your road again and tell the truth about it."[51] They had to remember rightly and retell their own story, now in a penitential key.

3. *Repentance*

Christians often take the story of Saul on the road to Damascus in Acts 9 as the paradigmatic conversion narrative. It is understood, like Augustine's conversion tale in his *Confessions*, to be a momentary spiritual event that leads to confession and then repentance, signaling a sudden change in one's soul due to a newfound awareness of one's utter sinfulness. Yet this spiritualized account of repentance neglects the broader social and political dimensions of repentance, as well as the ongoing difficult work of conversion as a process.

Biblical scholar Brittany Wilson offers an account of Saul's conversion that highlights these important elements of repentance. As Saul was riding along the road, on his way to find and imprison followers of Jesus in the town of Damascus, a light from heaven blinded him, and the voice of Jesus ordered him to proceed into the city and there he "will be told what you are to do."[52] Wilson explains that Saul's conversion immediately rendered him dependent upon others due to his newfound blindness. This opened him to vulnerability and compelled this leader—who commanded garrisons and possessed the power to bind and execute—to give up self-control over his own life.[53] Yet also, significantly, after the visit from the disciple Ananias three days later, Saul's vision was restored; "something like scales fell from his eyes," and he was immediately baptized.

Saul's blindness displaced him and set him on a new way after his first moment of conversion, a way of submission, dependence, and vulnerability. His restoration came from the hands of a man he was persecuting. But this recovery of sight, a kind of seeing that compelled him to immediately go and be baptized, signaled a new way of seeing the world. Instead of persecuting the Damascus disciples, he stayed and learned from them, despite threats on his life now. His conversion entails a new solidarity—accepting the risks, joys, tragedies, hopes, injustices, and redemption of the least of these in the world until he becomes embedded within their story. His repentance would lead him to take on the same responsibilities and same sufferings as those he once oppressed.

The Work of Repentance

In 1942, under the cover of conducting intelligence work for the German Abwehr, Dietrich Bonhoeffer met with British bishop and Member of Parliament George Bell in Sigtuna, Sweden. He was hoping to relay a message to the British government of the assassination plot against Hitler and seek assurances of an Allied peace settlement after the Fuhrer's deposal.[54] During this clandestine conversation, Bonhoeffer confided to his friend that no German was immune from responsibility for Germany's crimes. All owed repentance for what was happening, and this applied especially to the church in Germany because it was tasked with calling the people to confession.[55] He added that even the resistance movement, of which he was part, must be engaged as an act of collective repentance and offered without the guarantee of forgiveness. Rather than simply repenting on behalf of others, however, Bonhoeffer vicariously took their responsibility onto himself, along with his own. He stood in the solidarity of sin, his own mixing with the collective, calling "everyone into a community of confession."[56]

This story underscores the importance of linking repentance—the act of turning away, taking up one's own cross—with confession. Lauren Winner suggests during her account of damaged Christian practices that the best way to address, and perhaps correct for, malformed Christian practices is to perform them in a confessional key. Confession is diagnostic and as a frame for practice may help us to see the ways we are likely wrong in our performance. But she reminds us that confession itself is "hardly immune from deformation."[57] Confession can be done halfheartedly, competitively, and self-righteously like the religious leaders who stand on the street corner and make long prayers only to appear pious (Matthew 23:14). It can be done in an attempt to justify our actions or to relieve ourselves of the responsibility to do more in response to injustice. In such cases, confession is a form of cheap grace when it does not proceed in repentance—*metanoia* or turning away from that sin and back toward God. Confession only works as a diagnosis and corrective to malformation if it is done without prior knowledge of good and evil, without the assurance of forgiveness—from God and those we oppress. It only works if it is done in the spirit of Christ's prayer: "Thy will, not mine, be done" (Luke 22:42).

Jennifer McBride draws on Bonhoeffer when offering an account of what it means for the white church to repent for its racism. Her use of the phrase "confession unto repentance" captures Bonhoeffer's meaning by framing repentance as "taking on responsibility for sin."[58] In this way, repentance links original sin and responsibility. Repentance requires us to accept responsibility for our actions and our collective history, and often this requires us to listen to the voices of others who can renarrate our story in ways to which we are blind.[59] This is a key lesson for white theologians and churches. We must take the risk of listening to the stories of others explain the ways we have harmed them. In this way, repentance decenters us, offering our story and "laying it at another's feet, for another's adjudication," as Charles Mathewes observes. This is an ultimate act of "turning toward the other"—both God and fellow—and requires an openness to "transforming, and being transformed by, the other."[60] The work of repentance, then, necessarily begins with acts of public confession—exposing and acknowledging one's sin—but proceeds in the church's conformation to the crucified Christ.

Bonhoeffer's Christology claims that, on the cross, Christ literally took on the guilt of the sinful world and became guilty himself. He declared himself responsible for the sins of the world.[61] As McBride comments, this account "stretches Christological language beyond the church's familiar and potentially domesticated understanding of the righteous and sinless Christ."[62] It pushes the church—"Christ existing as community"—to take a deep and painful look at its own sin. The church offers its most important witness by witnessing to its own sin, just as Christ witnessed to the sin he took upon himself, on the cross.[63] Therefore, if the church witnesses to its own whiteness in conformation to the witness of Christ, it takes responsibility for the sin of the world—and especially its own—and repents by forsaking its own pretensions to innocence and its own (misused) power.

Repentance thus cannot be a private, pious act, but a public witness. This is a challenge to a white church that often expresses itself through individual, private, or spiritual practices. Applying Bonhoeffer's criticism to our own context, in our "sanctuar[ies] of private virtuousness," white churches "close their eyes and ears to the injustice around them" and place personal innocence above responsibility for others.[64] Public repentance is the true risk of faith that Bonhoeffer and Cone (and in some ways Hauerwas) call the church to undertake because it automatically sullies the hands of the church and displays those dirty hands to the world; it forsakes the sanctuary of virtuousness and reveals this image as a lie. It is renouncing faith in the stories that give white people their meaning while recognizing that no response is going to be pure and perfect. The white church's witness in a time of white supremacy is not in "showing the world how it turns to God in pious devotion," McBride charges, but in its penitence.[65]

White churches and theologians, especially during a time of declining membership and resources, often fear radical steps, especially those that may make the church look bad. The church can only represent the world, Bonhoeffer says, "by following Christ under the cross"[66]—and, we add, the lynching tree. And this can only happen in vulnerable and public displays of the church's own sinfulness—regular public reminders offered directly to African Americans for our crimes against them. Here Bonhoeffer resonates with Cone—in its confession before God and others, the possibility of forgiveness is opened, but not guaranteed. Repentance is a risky business because confession before others does not always result in the offer of forgiveness. The risk of true repentance can only take place without self-justification.

Practicing Repentance: Mount Vernon Place United Methodist Church

On October 8, 2017, on the one-hundred-year anniversary of the laying of its sanctuary cornerstone, Mount Vernon Place United Methodist Church offered a Service of Remembrance and Repentance for its role in slavery. In her sermon that day, pastor Donna Claycomb Sokol explained how conversations during a church book series on racial justice sparked a desire to learn more about the history of the congregation and what the words "Methodist Episcopal Church, South," engraved into the white marble façade of the sanctuary, actually mean. The church had to face the question: "How does a church tell its unvarnished truth, particularly a congregation that gathers in a glorious space built as a monument to the Methodist Episcopal Church, South—the church that splintered off in 1844 so its members could uphold slavery?"[67]

Reverend Sokol recalled the history of the church's Methodist denomination and its own founding. "Methodists gathered in Baltimore in 1780 and condemned slavery as 'contrary to the laws of God, man, and nature, and hurtful to society,'" she said, even passing legislation to expel any member of the church who held a slave.[68] However, by 1808, the Methodist Church published one thousand special copies of the *Book of Discipline* to be sent to its southern conference that didn't include the statement and rules on slavery. H. Shelton Smith reported, "Everywhere except in New England the conferences were dominated by preachers who tried to check antislavery militancy within Methodism."[69] When debate over whether a bishop could possess enslaved people ensued in the 1840s, the "Methodist Episcopal Church, South" was formed with five hundred thousand members in response to the irreconcilable differences on slavery. Southern Methodists "contended that slavery was a strictly civil institution exclusively in the custody of the civil power, and that the church should leave that institution strictly alone."[70] Reverend Sokol writes, "The church was so entangled in the sin of human bondage that every person elected to be a bishop in the Methodist Episcopal Church, South between 1846 and the start of the Civil War was a slave-holder."[71] Mount Vernon Place was soon founded in 1850 to be the "representative" church of the Methodist Episcopal Church, South, and its slaveholding values, in the heart of the nation's capital.[72] The website explains, "A church was formed over bondage, and sinful statements of white supremacy were sounded from pulpits, in newsletters and small group meetings." As she ended the sermon, she explained, "We cannot change what people most treasured in the past. But we can repent. . . . We can turn away from whatever has a grip on us, and reorient our lives to a vision of God's best ways for the world."[73]

To conclude the service, the church engaged in a "Litany of Remembrance and Repentance," to "name the sin of racism and repent for our roots in white supremacy." The litany began by invoking Jesus's words: "The truth will make you free,"[74] while confessing that even with painful truths, "the only way to be free is to tell the truth—the unvarnished truth." The congregation confessed, "Our church was founded as the 'representative church' for the Methodist Episcopal Church, South, the denomination formed in 1844 to support its members who wanted to hold slaves. . . . Our church was part of a denomination in which every bishop was a slaveholder. . . . We gather in a building constructed as a monument to America's original sin." The congregation continued, "We lament a history in which people valued property over people. We lament the ways in which this church contributed to the wounds of an entire nation. We lament the proclamation of white supremacy and the belief that such a proclamation is consistent with the gospel of Jesus Christ." They concluded by asking for forgiveness, not just for themselves, but importantly for "those who came before us." After this service, the words "We repent for our roots in white supremacy" were printed on a large banner that the congregation signed and hung from the columns of the church building. This act of public confession unto repentance represents one way in which congregations can begin the work of disrupting their own whiteness, a pivotal public step toward conversion.

4. *Reparation*

One day, as he was passing through the city and became swarmed by the crowds, Jesus spotted a man "short in stature" sitting in a tree. This begins the brief but powerful conversion story of the chief tax collector of Jericho, Zacchaeus, in the Gospel of Luke. Another paradigmatic conversion narrative, Zacchaeus's conversion, like Saul's, is punctuated by a profound social and political transformation. But in Zacchaeus's case, this takes form specifically in financial reparation. After a life of stealing money from the poor, enabled by the power of empire, he commits to giving half of his possessions to the poor, and "if I have defrauded anyone of anything, I will pay back four times as much."[75] The story of Zacchaeus builds on the conversion of Saul, modeling the role of reparation in the narrative of conversion; the Gospel itself sanctions reparations. Repentance is not complete, or should we say true, until it is made concrete by material acts of atonement for one's sins.

The Work of Reparation

On the eve of a 2019 House of Representatives committee hearing on H.R. 40, the bill proposed by John Conyers that would launch a commission to study reparations, Republican Senate Majority Leader Mitch McConnell told reporters, "I don't think reparations for something that happened 150 years ago, for whom none of us currently living are responsible, is a good idea."[76] The next day, during testimony before the House committee, writer Ta-Nehisi Coates concluded his opening statement with, "The thing about Senator McConnell's 'something': It was 150 years ago. And it was right now." Coates continued, "The question really is not whether we'll be tied to the somethings of our past, but whether we are courageous enough to be tied to the whole of them."[77] He stressed that the dream of America is one that extends beyond personal reach—it is a collective vision of future and inheritance. And the "dilemma posed by reparations is just that: a dilemma of inheritance."

During the period in which I've been writing this book, reparations for African Americans has become a hotly contested topic, even among the public debates of presidential candidates. *Reparations* generally refer to programs designed to account for and redress historic, group-based harms. The term often connotes financial compensation but may also take the form of rehabilitation or other forms of satisfaction.[78] Regarding the issue of reparations for African Americans, this is not a (relatively) simple calculation of payments due to ancestors for the exact costs of slave labor. In his testimony Coates noted that it is tempting to divorce from contemporary forms of racism the institution of slavery and its immediate after-effects as a tragic period that ended 150 years ago. Yet "the logic of enslavement, of white supremacy, respects no such borders and the guard of bondage was lustful and begat many heirs."[79] In his article "The Case for Reparations," published three years before his testimony, Coates outlines an intricate story of the federally sanctioned practice of redlining, the racial prejudice intrinsic to the housing market, an impotent G.I. Bill that excluded black veterans, and the crafting of Social Security and unemployment insurance in a manner that excluded African Americans, all resulting in a "concentration of disadvantage . . . paired with a concentration of melanin."[80] For example, President

Franklin Roosevelt's New Deal barred sharecroppers and domestic workers from its benefits, which disproportionately affected black workers.[81] Or, with its practice of redlining, the Federal Housing Administration marked out black neighborhoods as areas ineligible for home mortgages, which "locked blacks out of the greatest mass-based opportunity for home ownership and wealth accumulation in American history."[82] These were deliberate and active attempts to keep black people at a financial and political disadvantage, and maintain the social and political power of whites.

This legacy of elusive equality is what Saidiya Hartman termed "the afterlife of slavery." White supremacy developed well before American slavery, and its impact dwells on long afterward. The list of restrictive policies, individual and collective prejudices, and compounding gaps in education, opportunity, and wealth result in "skewed life chances, limited access to health and education, premature death, incarceration, and impoverishment," Hartman explains. "Black lives are still imperiled and devalued by a racial calculus and a political arithmetic that were entrenched centuries ago."[83] This means we must think beyond reparations for slave labor alone and seek repair for the many variegated ways that white supremacy has cost people of color their freedom, labor, and lives.

Coates turns to Germany as an example, with its reparations to Israel for the Holocaust. Even though 29 percent of the West German population opposed reparations to Jews, the country finally agreed to pay Israel the contemporary equivalent of $7 billion, as well as individual payments to some survivors and families. However modest this amount may seem, it resulted in significant infrastructure improvement in Israel and GNP growth.[84] There are also a few national precedents for reparations. In 1994 Florida paid $2.1 million to descendants of the black victims of the 1923 Rosewood massacre, and the 1988 Civil Liberties Act established a Civil Liberties Public Education Fund and paid twenty thousand dollars to each Japanese American who was incarcerated in internment camps during World War II. Early in American history, Quakers in New England, New York, and Baltimore made church membership contingent upon compensating one's former slaves.[85]

Reparation is the concrete third step of taking responsibility for white supremacy. It requires the diligent and painful work of remembrance of past wrongs and the ways they may continue into the present. And it is the practical, ethical outgrowth of true repentance. As Cone puts it, this represents white Christians committing to follow the black Christ into the black ghetto. Becoming black entails a lifetime of struggling to materially shed privilege while contributing to the political, economic, and social liberation of people of color. It is primarily listening to black and womanist theologians and church leaders, holding oneself accountable to black authority, and placing one's body in the risk of solidarity with those who are oppressed. It may take many forms, but I am convinced that one of those forms must be financial repair. Still, the final answer has to come from the oppressed communities themselves. Reparations must be contextual and must respond concretely to the wishes of the aggrieved. The form of repair may look different for every white congregation or denomination, but responsibility remains incomplete without it.

Still, we must remember that reparations will always be limited, always insufficient to repair the damage that has accumulated and compounded over time. Harvard Law professor Martha Minow writes, in *Between Vengeance and Forgiveness*, that reparations do not offer "tidy endings."[86] They are not a final resolution or a means of squaring accounts. They are necessary but ultimately insufficient means of enacting the justice that is called for. Yet, at a time when even progressive Christians prefer to focus on "class struggle" as a colorblind means of coalition building and others wring their hands over the practical details of reparations, we see how these continued maneuvers of evasion and obfuscation fail to produce policies—and theologies—poised to address this history that is not past.

Reparations are the best practical step to allow for healing and restitution to African Americans and the black church that has been hard pressed on every side.[87] However inadequate reparations may be, they are what is required for the nation, and the white church, to at least see ourselves rightly and to tell the story truthfully about our past and present. They force us to recognize ourselves as the villains in the story—Cain murdering his brother in cold blood or Pharaoh enslaving God's people. We are Zacchaeus, who spent a lifetime robbing the poor; Saul, who spent years oppressing religious minorities; or Jesus, who neglects the Canaanite woman pleading for help. We are those responsible to try and repair the damage we have done by learning from those we injured and joining in their struggle for liberation.

Practicing Reparation

I do not conclude this section with an example. A few Christian institutions are initiating processes of reparation, specifically offering forms of financial redress to descendants of enslaved people on whose labor the institution was built.[88] When it comes to ecclesial models of reparations, the examples are few. Both Calvary and Mount Vernon Place, while doing the good work of remembering and repenting for their racist origins and their failures to address that history, have yet to move to the point of reparations. Conversion is a process, and both congregations are processing next steps. Congregations and denominations struggle, if not with resisting the very idea of paying reparations, then with discerning what this would mean in their context. Like many churches who lament their past and recognize their captivity to white supremacy, they struggle to discern what the work of repair entails, and what their responsibility looks like.

A few denominations have made attempts.[89] In 2016 the Episcopal Diocese of Maryland accepted a resolution to begin reviewing the details of financial reparations in its context. The "Reparations Investment" proposal would give the diocese a chance "to set an example for the church at large and other congregations whose endowed wealth is tied to the institution of slavery," according to a statement from the eight white clergy who sponsored it. Specifically, the clergy asked the diocese to provide "at least 10% of the assets of its unrestricted investment funds to the diocesan chapter of the Union of Black Episcopalians."[90] After three years of review, at its 2019 Convention, the diocese unanimously passed a "Resolution on Racial Reconciliation." In this resolution, the direct focus on reparations had been replaced with the paradigm of reconciliation, though the agreement still urged each congregation within the diocese "to examine how their endowed wealth is tied to the institution of slavery."[91] The focus on reparations was ultimately replaced by language of reconciliation (presumably so that the resolution would pass diocesan vote). This is still an important step, but represents the distance of most churches from this third step of responsibility.

The lack of examples, and the tendency to shift back to a reconciliation paradigm, should signal not only the difficulty of reparations but also the power of white supremacy to convince us that they are not necessary. Resisting white supremacy is a costly endeavor, and so far, not many churches have been willing to bear those costs. Following Christ into the black ghetto is not easy. But until white churches take that risk of faith and begin the work of reparation we will only continue our work of oppression. In other words, disavowing white supremacy is not sufficient; it must be followed by dwelling with the marginalized, or in Cone's words, following Christ into the black ghetto. It may mean, practically, living in a different neighborhood (with no gentrifying expectations to conform that neighborhood to your own way of life), shopping at different stores, writing on different topics, choosing a different career, or joining a different church. It is having our stories shaped by those with whom God dwells, the outcast and oppressed whom God ordains to be our teachers. It is participating in God by being where God is, among the marginalized, among the poor, among those seeking liberation. It is seeing the church as, and working to transform the church into, a community that seeks after God by joining the work of God, in prayer and just action, in remembrance, repentance, and repair.

Conclusion

THE LAST PUBLISHED words of James Cone still haunt me. In the conclusion to his posthumously published book, he invokes the story of Cain and Abel (Genesis 4:1–12):

> Cain can be viewed as a metaphor for white people and Abel for black people. God is asking white Americans, especially Christians, "Where are your black brothers and sisters?" And whites respond, "We don't know. Are we their keepers?" And the Lord says, "What have you done to them for four centuries?"
>
> *The blood of black people is crying out to God and to white people from the ground in the United States of America.* The blood of Sandra Bland in Texas and Tamir Rice in Ohio; the blood of the Emanuel Nine in Charleston, South Carolina, and Eric Garner in Staten Island, New York; the blood of nearly five thousand lynched blacks; the blood of Nat Turner, Denmark Vesey, and Gabriel Prosser, and the "many thousands gone," millions gone on the auction block, under the lash, and during the Middle Passage. Black blood is crying out to God all over this land. Is anybody listening to the cries of black blood, that "strange fruit" that Billie Holiday sang about, "blood on the tress and blood at the root"? The cry of black blood that I heard in Detroit (1967) nearly fifty years ago is still crying out all over American today. White people didn't hear it then, and they still don't hear it now.[1]

In his final address to the Southern Christian Leadership Conference on the tenth anniversary of the Montgomery bus boycott, Martin Luther King Jr. cautioned, "In order to answer the question, 'Where do we go from here?' which is our theme, we must first honestly recognize where we are now."[2] In this book

Witnessing Whiteness. Kristopher Norris, Oxford University Press (2020). © Oxford University Press.
DOI: 10.1093/oso/9780190055813.001.0001

I have attempted to do that in the context of white theology and white churches in America—to assess "where we are now." King's favorite description of the kingdom of God, that eschatological reality in which all of humanity is reconciled to God and to one another, was the *beloved community*. And in assessing where we are now we realize that the beloved community remains a faint dream: the Pentecostal vision of "every tribe and tongue" worshiping in harmony, a distant prayer. As Cone lamented, white Christians failed to hear the cry of black blood crying out from the ground fifty years ago, and we fail to hear it today. We fail, even, to witness our own whiteness.

Can our whiteness be redeemed? Is there any hope in whiteness? The answer must be *no*. I'm sure the reader has noticed that I have used the terms *whiteness* and *white supremacy* interchangeably in this book. It is characteristic of whiteness to seek and presume supremacy at all costs. (I have noticed a recent troubling cultural trend to identify white supremacy with individual actors—Dylann Roof, perpetrators of hate crimes, neo-Nazi marchers in Charlottesville—in a way that distances supposedly "good" and "nonracist" white people from white supremacy. But this fails to articulate white supremacy as a system that inescapably implicates and indicts all white people. Whiteness touches us all.) I'm not interested in saving whiteness; it must be destroyed. And the white church must go down with it, and with God's grace be born again into something completely new.

The *no* that we are forced to utter to our whiteness is the only sign of hope to which we can cling. It is a hope that emerges from the painful practices of remembrance, repentance, and reparation, but it is the only hope capable of challenging our bondage to white supremacy. But even then, we must ask if hope is enough. In his book *Embracing Hopeless*, theologian Miguel de la Torre argues that hope is a privilege that soothes the consciences of those complicit in oppressive systems. It "leads to complacency with the oppressive status quo and breeds apathy" because it convinces us that there is always more to lose in attempts to change social structures.[3] The cost is too high. Instead, he wants a theology of "desperation that leads to hopelessness," because in desperation and hopelessness, one has nothing left to lose and no choice but to act. Hopelessness is to embrace a faith without certitude—action with no assurance of success or of self-justification. Hopelessness, de la Torre says, provides "an impetus to our praxis, for hopelessness is the precursor to resistance and revolution."[4] But until the white church recognizes that there is more to lose by remaining bound to whiteness than in actively working to defeat it, there is no hope.

More specifically focusing on whiteness in an article titled "For What Are Whites to Hope," Vincent Lloyd argues that when it is employed by those in positions of privilege, hope is always distorted by white supremacy, "affirming the status quo even as they promise transformation."[5] That is, the material conditions of our lives as white people—shaped by white privilege—can only distort our perspective and limit the options visible to us to ones that "preserve privilege, and systematic racial injustice."[6] Even if hope signals a refusal to be limited to the possibilities of the present, or the present ordering of the world, this longing for the new possibilities of the beloved community often promotes a colorblindness that disregards whiteness, and thus still supports the status quo.[7] Even Hauerwas in the waning years of his career has reckoned with a more chastened view of the church's potential. White churches are "inheritors of histories that involve cruelties so horrible there can be no way to make what was done undone," he writes. And despite his frequent slips into ecclesial triumphalism, he admits, "There is indeed something the church cannot do. The church cannot make the difficulty of reality less difficult. What I hope the church can do . . . is help us bear the difficulty without engaging in false hopes."[8]

In light of these realities, Lloyd proposes that for the white church, despair must precede hope. Despair is a training in true hope because it wipes away false hopes, those dictated by white supremacy, and forces us to come naked and humbly before God. Only then can hope become a virtue, a characteristic and disposition oriented by God.[9] Becoming black requires whites to despair, Lloyd argues, because it is nearly impossible work. Hope, for whites, is a "hope for hopelessness" by renouncing privilege and whiteness and joining the struggle of black liberation with black people, as Cone says, without the assurance that our sins against them will be forgiven.

On this side of the eschaton, the ways our lives are formed by whiteness will never fully disappear, never stop shaping our desires, perspective, and actions. We must be ever diligent. Our hope and our work will always be a different work from those who have had their lives shaped by being on the underside of whiteness. We will enter into the work of black liberation through taking responsibility, step by step—through the painful and difficult work of remembering, repenting for, and repairing what we have done. King's answer to his own question—where do we go from here?—was a call for America to "be born again," which, he said, meant a complete restructuring of American society.[10] That same answer can be directed at the white church fifty years later—we must be born again through a complete restructuring of everything that has made us oppressors.

A white church hoping for hopelessness and trained by despair—seeking its own destruction and rebirth into something that can no longer be called "the white church"—may seem like a far cry from the ways we are typically trained to think of the church's mission, a shadow of the conventional ecclesiologies that have captivated postliberals and many white theologians and pastors. Yet it is not a far cry from the biblical imagery of the church, which speaks of the church primarily with two metaphors that convey a community bound to contingency yet moving toward another story.

The church is the *body* of Christ, a body wounded by the lash of empire and divided by the sins of white supremacy.[11] While in Christ there is no white or black, the body of Christ bears the marks of our black and white flesh, and bears the wounds inflicted on those bodies—both in its resurrected form awaiting the redemption of all things, and in the church, the earthly form of the body of Christ awaiting the same.

The church is also the *Way*, not a claim of soteriological or epistemological exclusiveness, but a recognition that redemption is a process. This metaphor identifies the church as a body moving toward reconciliation, yet always revising, always adjusting, and always self-correcting through the voices of God's prophets. This means we must understand the church not as a fixed institution, but as a body "on the Way."[12] It is a community of formation, of people bound in relationship and free for responsibility, and this means it is a community contingent, provisional, aspiring, failing, and confessing—a church on "the Way" to glory and virtue while currently bound by the limits of our creaturely finitude.

In the context of our responsibility for white supremacy, I have argued, the practice of conversion proceeds in remembrance, repentance, and reparation; it also proceeds in mistakes and missteps. As Gillian Rose observes, any true process of learning, and we might say, of conversion, "works precisely by making mistakes, by taking the risk of action, and then by reflecting on its unintended consequences, and then taking the risk, yet again, of further action, and so on."[13] Bonhoeffer reminds us that "no one has the responsibility of turning the word into the kingdom of God, but only of taking the next necessary step."[14] Consequently, the story of the church on this side of the eschaton may be one not "of rejoicing but of groaning, not yet a place for exultation but still a place of lamentation."[15] The white church is a place, a body that may only experience its rebirth through its death, by the grace of God.

I hope by now it is clear that this book is not a retrieval project. I am not attempting to retrieve any neglected, pure, or unproblematic elements of the Christian tradition "before" things went wrong. I'm not sure any exist. If my account of original sin is correct, there are no uncorrupted elements of the tradition. Rather, this is a project of self-reflection and self-interrogation, turning our gaze and analysis inward to the ways whiteness shapes Christian theology and practice. The three practices that I proposed are not uncontaminated practices—but after the difficult work of stripping white Christianity to the studs and observing what, if anything, is left, they are potential ways of navigating the ruins.

Instead, this book is a call to conversion. Put more specifically, it is an invitation to white theologians and Christian leaders to interrogate our own work and uncover the ways our thought and practice are inflected by its formation in whiteness, and then to confess those ways to the world. In what ways do we participate in universal abstractions, in projections, in evasion? What has our color-blindness blinded us from seeing? What do we need to remember? Of what do we need to repent? How do we begin the work of repair? I submit these three practices, and practical examples of their successes and failures, as the "prayer and righteous action" for our context. After the painful work of peeling away all the layers of our faith tainted by white supremacy, all that is likely to remain is the Gospel call to conversion, Jesus's invitation to deny ourselves, take up our cross, and follow him.

The white church must take the risk of surrendering what we hold dear to the movement of God—liberating the oppressed from our oppression and calling us in the midst of our ruins to be made anew. In the end, we may not be capable of creating the beloved community during this world—only a community capable of walking together on the Way to its Beloved, who welcomes all and out of death promises to make all things new.

Notes

1. Frederick Douglass, "Slaveholding Religion," in *African American Religious History*, ed. Milton Sernett (Durham, NC: Duke University Press, 1985), 104.

2. Jeffrey Stout, *Democracy and Tradition* (Princeton, NJ: Princeton University Press, 2004).

3. James D. Hunter, *To Change the World: The Irony, Tragedy, and Possibility of Christianity in the Late Modern World* (New York: Oxford University Press, 2010).

4. A note on categorizing these threads. First for Hauerwas: The label *New Traditionalist* connotes both an inheritance of Roman Catholicism and a debt to the work of Alasdair MacIntyre on the concept of *tradition*. Jeffrey Stout includes scholars like MacIntyre, John Milbank, and Hauerwas in this group. *Neo-Anabaptist* signals less the emphasis on "tradition" and more a focus on the distinctive "witness" of the church and an understanding of the church's radical separation from the world. James Hunter focuses most specifically on John Howard Yoder and Hauerwas when he employs the term. *Postliberal* best signals the genealogy of this mode of theological thought, invoking the Yale School of Hans Frei and George Lindbeck, and focuses more exclusively on Hauerwas as their most influential inheritor. For Cone: *liberation theology* signals the broad scholarly grouping that coupled itself to actual movements of resistance and opposition to empire and oppression. According to Dwight Hopkins, Cone's 1969 *Black Theology and Black Power* was the very first book written on liberation theology (Hopkins, ed., *Black Faith and Public Talk: Critical Essays on James Cone's Black Theology and Black Power* (Maryknoll, NY: Orbis Books, 1999), 4). Though it was intentionally contextual and particularly focused on the situation of African Americans in the United States, Cone's book birthed the larger movement. Cone began exclusively with a focus on the liberation of African Americans. Liberation theologies in Latin America, feminism, and queer theologies began simultaneously, though in many ways independently. While they maintained similar structures, themes, and methodologies, they did not interact or integrate initially. However, in his later works, Cone has extended his vision to include other liberation theologies, especially at the prodding of black womanist theologians.

5. Walter Rauschenbusch, *A Theology for the Social Gospel* (New York: Abingdon, 1917), 5. See Walter Rauschenbusch's *Christianity and the Social Crisis* (New York: Macmillan, 1907) and *Christianizing the Social Order* (New York: Macmillan, 1912).

6. See especially, Reinhold Niebuhr, *Moral Man and Immoral Society: A Study of Ethics and Politics* (1932; Louisville, KY: Westminster John Knox Press, 2002); *The Nature and Destiny of Man: A Christian Interpretation* (New York: Charles Scribner's Sons, 1943); *The Children of Light and the Children of Darkness* (New York: Charles Scribner's Sons, 1944); and *The Irony of American History* (New York: Charles Scribner's Sons, 1952).

7. Luke Bretherton, "Exorcising Democracy: The Theo-Political Challenge of Black Power," *Journal of the Society of Christian Ethics* 38, no. 1 (2018): 5. He writes, "Black Liberation Theology heralded a seismic shift in Protestant social ethics and the use of Christian Realism as a dominant framework for thinking about political and social questions. From Cone's work onwards, liberationist paradigms, of one sort or another, became increasingly normative in North American liberal Protestant circles and determinative points of reference and critique in others."

8. Though originating with black liberation theology, liberation theologies and ethics expanded quickly in diversity and global reach. This included Latin American liberation theologies of the poor. The most prominent of these is Gustavo Gutiérrez. See especially his groundbreaking *A Theology of Liberation: History, Politics, and Salvation* (1973; Maryknoll, NY: Orbis Books, 1988). For a more comprehensive historical picture, see Leonardo Boff and Clodovis Boff, *Introducing Liberation Theology* (Maryknoll, NY: Orbis Books, 1987), and Miguel A. De La Torre, *Handbook on U.S. Theologies of Liberation* (St. Louis: Chalice Press, 2004). It also included feminist theologies, beginning with the work of Mary Daly, especially *The Church and the Second Sex* (Boston: Beacon Press, 1968); *Beyond God the Father: Toward a Philosophy of Women's Liberation* (Boston: Beacon Press, 1973); *Gyn/ecology: The Metaethics of Radical Feminism* (Boston: Beacon Press, 1978); and Rosemary Radford Ruether, *Sexism and God-Talk: Toward a Feminist Theology* (Boston: Beacon Press, 1983). More recently is the emergence of queer theologies; see especially the early works of John Michael Clark and Marcella Althaus-Reid, and womanist theology, pioneered by Dolores Williams, Alice Walker, Katie Cannon, and Jacquelyn Grant. I turn to specific sources and contributions of womanist theology in later chapters.

9. Brian Bantum, *Redeeming Mulatto: A Theology of Race and Christian Hybridity* (Waco, TX: Baylor University Press, 2010), 2–3.

10. Bantum, *Redeeming Mulatto*, 3.

11. Kelly Brown Douglas, *What's Faith Got to Do with It? Black Bodies / Christian Souls* (Maryknoll, NY: Orbis Books, 2005), xiii.

12. Douglas, *What's Faith*, 9; Willie Jennings, *The Christian Imagination* (New Haven, CT: Yale University Press, 2011), 6.

13. Shelly Rambo, *Resurrecting Wounds: Living in the Afterlife of Trauma* (Waco, TX: Baylor University Press, 2017), 93.

14. Ta-Nehisi Coates, *Between the World and Me* (New York: Spiegel & Grau, 2015), 7.

15. For the concept of "wicked problem" see H. W. J. Rittel and M. M. Webber, "Dilemmas in a General Theory of Planning," *Policy Sciences* 4, no. 2 (1973): 155–169.

16. Reinhold Niebuhr, "Christian Faith and the Race Problem," in *Love and Justice: Selections from the Shorter Writings of Reinhold Niebuhr*, ed. D. B. Robertson (1957; Louisville, KY: Westminster/John Knox Press, 1992), 128–129.

17. Reinhold Niebuhr, "The Confession of a Tired Radical," in Robertson, *Love and Justice*, 120.

CHAPTER 1

1. James Baldwin, *No Name in the Street* (New York: Vintage Books, 1972), 46.

2. Ta-Nehisi Coates, "The First White President," *The Atlantic*, October 2017, http://www.theatlantic.com/magazine/archive/2017/10/the-first-white-president-ta-nehisi-coates.

3. Michelle Alexander has famously labeled the U.S. mass incarceration system "The New Jim Crow," citing the fact that in the nation with the highest incarceration in the world, in which people of all colors have been shown to use and sell drugs at similar rates, black men are admitted to prison on drug charges at rates twenty to fifty times higher than white men (*The New Jim Crow: Mass Incarceration in the Age of Colorblindness* (New York: New Press, 2010), 6–7).

4. James Baldwin, *Notes of a Native Son* (Boston: Beacon Press, 1955), 8.

5. The long history of racism in the United States is well documented. I focus here on recent trends as they bear considerably on the particular forms of white supremacy we now experience and attend to the longer history of white supremacy in chapter 2.

6. James Cone, "Theology's Great Sin: Silence in the Face of White Supremacy," *Black Theology* 2, no. 2 (2004): 139–152.

7. Toni Morrison, "Unspeakable Things Unspoken: The Afro-American Presence in American Literature," in *The Black Feminist Reader*, ed. Joy James and T. Denean Sharpley-Whiting (Malden, MA: Blackwell, 2000), 34.

8. James Cone, "Christian Faith and Political Praxis," *Encounter* 43, no. 2 (Spring 1982): 136.

9. James Cone, *For My People* (Maryknoll, NY: Orbis Books, 1984), 116.

10. Jeff Tiberii, "North Carolina Gerrymandering Trial Could Serve as Blueprint for Other States," National Public Radio, July 15, 2019, https://www.npr.org/2019/07/15/740842847/north-carolina-gerrymandering-trial-could-serve-as-blueprint-for-other-states.

11. While some initial reports from white pundits attributed Trump's success to economic factors, more thorough studies have debunked that myth and attributed

his election to the factors of religious (i.e., evangelical) defense or outright racism. One interesting study combines these factors into a nuanced treatment of "Christian nationalist ideology" as the most significant predictor of voting for Trump, suggesting that racism and religion combine to form an influential political ideology. This ideology operates in ways similar to colorblindness—as I show later—by influencing political action through mythical narratives about America's heritage (Andrew L. Whitehead, Samuel L. Perry, and Joseph O. Baker, "Make American Christian Again: Voting for Donald Trump in the 2016 National Election," *Sociology of Religion: A Quarterly Review* 79, no. 2 (Summer 2018): 147–171). For the now outdated arguments for economics, see Nate Cohn, "Why Trump Won: Working Class Whites," *New York Times*, November 9, 2016, http://www.nytimes.com/2016/11/10/upshot/why-trump-won-working-class-whites, and Alec MacGillis, "The Original Underclass: The Despair of Poor White Americans," *The Atlantic*, September 2016, http://www.theatlantic.com/magazine/archive/2016/09/the-original-underclass. A couple monographs that these articles appeal to are J. D. Vance, *Hillbilly Elegy: A Memoir of a Family and Culture in Crisis* (New York: Harper, 2016), and Nancy Isenberg, *White Trash: The 400-Year Untold History of Class in America* (New York: Viking, 2016). For the role of racism, see Sean McElwee and Jason McDaniel, "Economic Anxiety Didn't Make People Vote Trump, Racism Did: New Data Provide a Compelling Answer to This Vexing Question," *The Nation*, May 8, 2017, http://www.thenation.com/article/economic-anxiety-didnt-make-people-vote-trump-racism-did. For religion and how Trump was perceived to protect evangelical interests (rather than express their beliefs), see Gerardo Martí, "The Unexpected Orthodoxy of Donald J. Trump: White Evangelical Support for the 45th President of the United States," *Sociology of Religion: A Quarterly Review* 80, no. 1 (Spring 2019): 1–8.

12. Melani McAlister, "A Kind of Homelessness: Evangelicals of Color in the Trump Era," *Religion and Politics*, August 7, 2018, religionandpolitics.org/2018/08/07/a-kind-of-homelessness-evangelicals-of-color-in-the-trump-era.

13. Robert P. Jones, "The Rage of White Christian America," *New York Times*, November 10, 2016.

14. Robert P. Jones, *The End of White Christian America* (New York: Simon & Schuster, 2016). The percentage of U.S. citizens who identify as white and Christian has now dropped below 50 percent (Jones, "Rage of White Christian America").

15. Jones, *End of White Christian America*, 38–39.

16. See Amos 6.

17. Randall Balmer, "The Real Origins of the Religious Right," *Politico*, May 27, 2014, http://www.politico.com/magazine/story/2014/05/religious-right-real-origins. Balmer writes, "It wasn't until 1979—a full six years after *Roe*—that Evangelical leaders, at the behest of conservative activist Paul Weyrich, seized on abortion not

for moral reasons, but as a rallying cry to deny President Jimmy Carter a second term. Why? Because the anti-abortion crusade was more palatable than the religious right's real motive: protecting segregated schools."

18. In 2012 a Public Religion Research Institute (PRRI) survey revealed that one in four Americans believed that the president, who had been in office already for four years, was a Muslim, and a 2010 CNN poll found that the same number doubted his U.S. citizenship (the "birther" controversy initiated and promulgated by Trump) (Jones, *End of White Christian America*, 81). Jones notes how the *New York Times* concluded that "it is inconceivable that this campaign to portray Mr. Obama as the insidious 'other' would have been conducted against a white president" (Jones, *End of White Christian America*, 82, citing "A Certificate of Embarrassment," *New York Times*, April 28, 2011).

19. See Carol Anderson, *White Rage: The Unspoken Truth of Our Racial Divide* (New York: Bloomsbury, 2017), and Kelly Brown Douglas, *Stand Your Ground* (New York: Orbis Books, 2017), 116–131. Anderson writes, "The trigger for white rage, inevitably, is black advancement. . . . It is blackness that refuses to accept subjugation, to give up. A formidable array of policy assaults and legal contortions has consistently punished black resilience, black resolve."

20. Michelle Alexander also offers an important account of the lingering effects of the Southern Strategy in *New Jim Crow* (40–96).

21. William J. Barber II and Jonathan Wilson-Hartgrove, *The Third Reconstruction: Moral Mondays, Fusion Politics, and the Rise of a New Justice Movement* (Boston: Beacon Press, 2016); these items come from pp. 54, 63, 68, and 120. Barber cites Republican strategist Lee Atwater: "You start out in 1954 by saying 'Nigger, nigger, nigger.' By 1968, you can't say 'nigger'—that hurts you. Backfires. So you say stuff like forced busing. States' rights and all that stuff. You're getting so abstract now [that] you're talking about cutting taxes, and all these things you're talking about are totally economic things and a byproduct of them is [that] blacks get hurt worse than whites" (quoted in Alexander P. Lamis, ed., *Southern Politics in the 1990s* (Baton Rouge: Louisiana State University Press, 1999), 8).

22. Barber and Wilson-Hartgrove, *Third Reconstruction*, 54.

23. Barber and Wilson-Hartgrove, *Third Reconstruction*, 63.

24. Barber and Wilson-Hartgrove, *Third Reconstruction*, 120.

25. Jones, *End of White Christian America*, 153–154.

26. "Portraits of American Life Survey," Association of Religion Data Archives, 2012, http://www.thearda.com/Archive/Files/Analysis/PALS_2/PALS_2_Var708_1.

27. A PRRI survey from 2012 found that whites are 20 percent less likely to report experiencing a range of challenges in their neighborhoods (Jones, *End of White Christian America*, 157).

28. On the sources of the racial perception gap, see Jones, *End of White Christian America*, 155–166.

29. Sociologists identify a single-race church as one with over 80 percent of its membership consisting of a single race. A 2015 study found that only 20 percent of U.S. congregations are racially "mixed," meaning they have at least a 20 percent minority demographic in its membership (Michael Lipka, "Many U.S. Congregations Are Still Racially Segregated, but Things Are Changing," Pew Research Center, http://www.pewresearch.org/fact-tank/2014/12/08/many-u-s-congregations-are-still-racially-segregated-but-things-are-changing). Using the same measure, a 2010 Faith Communities Survey discovered less than 14 percent of congregations are racially mixed, signaling an uptick during the 2010s (cited in Josh Chen, "Minority-Dominant Spaces, Reflexive Vulnerability, and Blended Integration," unpublished essay draft. I thank Josh for permission to use).

30. H. Richard Niebuhr, *The Social Sources of Denominationalism* (Gloucester, MA: Peter Smith, 1987), 6, quoted in Jones, *End of White Christian America*, 164.

31. Korie L. Edwards, Brad Christerson, and Michael O. Emerson, "Race, Religious Organizations, and Integration," *Annual Review of Sociology* 39 (July 2013): 211–228.

32. Jason E. Shelton and Michael O. Emerson, *Black and Whites in Christian America: How Racial Discrimination Shapes Religious Convictions* (New York: New York University Press, 2012), 172–175. For more on the impact of the Protestant work ethic on racial and racist attitudes see Emilie Townes, *Womanist Ethics and the Cultural Production of Evil* (New York: Palgrave Macmillan, 2006), 120–124.

33. Charles W. Mills, *Black Rights / White Wrongs: The Critique of Racial Liberalism* (Oxford: Oxford University Press, 2017), xvii.

34. Jennifer M. McBride, *Radical Discipleship: A Liturgical Politics of the Gospel* (Minneapolis: Fortress Press, 2017), 46.

35. Jones, *End of White Christian America*, 51.

36. Jones, *End of White Christian America*, 41, citing Sam Roberts, "Minorities in U.S. Set to Be Majority by 2042," *New York Times*, August 14, 2008, https://www.nytimes.com/2008/08/14/world/americas/14iht-census.1.15284537.html.

37. Jones, *End of White Christian America*, 87.

38. The phenomenon of ressentiment derives from the work of philosopher Max Scheler, who developed the concept introduced by Friedrich Nietzsche (see Max Scheler, *Ressentiment*, trans. William Holdheim, ed. Lewis A. Coser (1912; New York: Schocken Books, 1972)). Referencing current trends in Christian political engagement, James Davison Hunter describes this as a form of political psychology based upon a "narrative of injury, or at least perceived injury; a strong belief that one has been or is being wronged" and rooted in a sense of entitlement (James Hunter, *To Change the World: The Irony, Tragedy, and Possibility of Christianity in the Late Modern World* (New York: Oxford University Press, 2010), 107). American studies scholar Melanie McAlister further describes the sentiment of victimization and persecution in contemporary American evangelicalism in *The Kingdom of God Has No Borders: A Global History of American Evangelicals* (New York: Oxford University Press, 2018).

39. Jones, "Rage of White Christian America"; Jones, *End of White Christian America*, 43.

40. Jones, *End of White Christian America*, 44. A survey from Jones's PRRI organization discovered that white evangelicals are the only religious group in America who believe that Christians face more discrimination in America than Muslims (Emma Green, "White Evangelicals Believe They Face More Discrimination Than Muslims," *The Atlantic*, March 10, 2017, http://www.theatlantic.com/politics/archive/2017/03/perceptions-discrimination-muslims-christians.

41. Jones, "Rage of White Christian America."

42. Melvin Rogers, "White Supremacy, Fear, and the Crisis of Legitimation," *Public Seminar*, January 1, 2017, http://www.publicseminar.org/2017/01/white-supremacy-fear-and-the-crises-of-legitimation.

43. Max Weber, *Economy and Society: An Outline of Interpretive Sociology* (Oakland: University of California Press, 1978), see esp. chapter 3, "The Types of Legitimate Domination"; Weber, *Basic Concepts in Sociology* (New York: Citadel Press, 1993); or Weber, *The Theory of Social and Economic Organization* (New York: Free Press, 1964), for treatments of this topic.

44. Jürgen Habermas, *Legitimation Crisis*, trans. Thomas McCarthy (Boston: Beacon Press, 1975), 10, 93.

45. Habermas, *Legitimation Crisis*, 46.

46. Habermas, *Legitimation Crisis*, 2.

47. Habermas, *Legitimation Crisis*, 121.

48. Peter Berger and Thomas Luckman define *symbolic universes* as "bodies of theoretical tradition that integrate different provinces of meaning [detached realms of reality] and encompass the institutional order in a symbolic totality" (Berger and Luckman, *The Social Construction of Reality: A Treatise in the Sociology of Knowledge* (Garden City, NY: Anchor Books), 94–95). Such "universes" explain and justify institutional orders, creating a world of meaning in which a person, group, or nation finds itself (96). In other words, "It puts everything in its right place" until "the entire society now makes sense" (98, 103) by offering authoritative or traditional texts, explanatory cosmological narratives, compelling rules or structures of existence, or charismatic leaders. The symbolic universe provides the ultimate legitimation of the institutional order and roles within a system of order by locating them within a comprehensively meaningful and normative "world."

49. Berger and Luckman, *Social Construction of Reality*, 107.

50. Berger and Luckman, *Social Construction of Reality*, 113. System leaders typically apply conceptual machinery in two manners: therapeutically, ensuring that any deviant persons of ideals stay within institutional definitions of reality, or nihilistically, conceptually liquidating everything outside the universe and denying the reality of phenomena or interpretations that do not fit that universe (113–114).

51. Barber and Wilson-Hartgrove, in *The Third Reconstruction*, notes that this crisis has occurred before with devastating consequences. When those in power feel threatened, they tend to lash out in direct and nuanced ways that inflict harm on

those most vulnerable. Barber cites, as a historical example, the threat to southern white power during the years of Reconstruction. After nearly thirty years of Reconstruction, a period in which sixteen African Americans were elected to the U.S. Congress and more than six hundred African Americans held offices in southern state legislatures (56), the 1890s brought this crisis to a climax and resulted in the overthrow of black politicians, codified segregation in the 1896 *Plessy v. Ferguson* case, as well as the prominence of the Klan's terrorism and rise in the number of lynchings (62).

52. Baldwin, *No Name in the Street*, 46.

53. Melvin Rogers cites an example of one of these subtle narratives. He writes, "White supremacy creates a condition wherein the 'natural' or 'normal' status of black people easily mingles with traits of criminality in the minds of observing citizens and conditions their behavior toward black people, regardless of any observable nonthreatening conduct on display." This renders black bodies subject to arbitrary domination (Rogers, "White Supremacy, Fear, and the Crisis of Legitimation," *Public Seminar*, January 1, 2017, http://www.publicseminar.org/2017/01/white-supremacy-fear-and-the-crises-of-legitimation).

54. Rogers, "White Supremacy."

55. The essay was titled "The White Man's Guilt." For a contemporary commentary on this idea, see Eddie Glaude's *TIME* magazine essay, "James Baldwin and the Trap of Our History," August 18, 2016, http://www.time.com/4457112/james-baldwin-eddie-glaude.

56. Baldwin, *Notes of a Native Son*, 45.

57. Eduardo Bonilla-Silva, *Racism without Racists: Color-Blind Racism and the Persistence of Racial Inequality in America* (Lanham, MD: Rowman and Littlefield, 2006), 2.

58. Douglas, *Stand Your Ground*, 227.

59. Bonilla-Silva, *Racism without Racists*, 27–34. For a study of the ways the criminal justice system creates tropes of black criminality that further justify prejudiced policies and treatment, see Muhammad Khalil Gibran, *Condemnation of Blackness: Race, Crime, and the Making of Modern Urban America* (Cambridge, MA: Harvard University Press, 2017).

60. Robin DiAngelo, "White Fragility," *International Journal of Critical Pedagogy* 3, no. 3 (2011): 61.

61. Thor Berger presents substantial evidence that areas with more prevalent slavery at the outbreak of the Civil War exhibit substantially less upward mobility today (Berger, "Places of Persistence: Slavery and the Geography of Intergenerational Mobility in the United States," *Demography* 55, no. 4 (2018): 1547–1565).

62. James W. Perkinson, *White Theology: Outing Supremacy in Modernity* (New York: Palgrave Macmillan, 2004), 1.

63. H. Richard Niebuhr, *The Responsible Self: An Essay in Christian Moral Philosophy* (New York: Harper and Row, 1963), 96. Niebuhr goes on to say that this epistemological

handicap often results in the Self responding to the other in a mode of defense. The inability to accurately interpret the other's experiences and intentions results in the Self operating out of fear and anxiety with an "ethic of defense" or "ethic of survival" (99).

64. Bonilla-Silva, *Racism without Racists*, 64–74.

65. Bonilla-Silva, *Racism without Racists*, 60.

66. Bonilla-Silva, *Racism without Racists*, 63.

67. DiAngelo, "White Fragility," 63; drawing on data from Louise Derman-Sparks, Patricia Ramsey, and Julie Olsen Edwards, *What If All the Kids Are White?: Anti-Bias Multicultural Education with Young Children and Families* (New York: Teachers College Press, 2006).

68. George Yancy, *Black Bodies, White Gazes: The Continuing Significance of Race* (Lanham, MD: Rowman and Littlefield, 2008), 72.

69. Erin Kidd, "The Subject of Conceptual Mapping: Theological Anthropology across Brain, Body, and World," *Open Theology* 4, no. 1 (2018): 117–135, at 133. Kidd draws on the idea of the "extended mind," developed by philosophers and cognitive scientists Andy Clark and David Chalmers. Cf. Clark and Chalmers, "The Extended Mind," *Analysis* 58, no. 1 (January 1998): 7–19; Clark, *Being There: Putting Brain, Body, and World Together Again* (Cambridge: Cambridge University Press, 1997); Clark, *Supersizing the Mind: Embodiment, Action, and Cognitive Extension* (Oxford: Oxford University Press, 2008); and the idea of the "embodied mind" in George Lakoff, "The Embodied Mind, and How to Live with One," in *The Nature and Limits of Human Understanding: The 2001 Gifford Lectures at the University of Glasgow*, ed. Anthony J. Sanford (New York: T&T Clark, 2003), 47–108.

70. Richard Delgado, "Storytelling for Oppositionists and Others: A Plea for Narrative," *Michigan Law Review* 87, no. 8 (1989): 2411–2441, at 2438. Delgado was an early contributor to what became known as Critical Race Theory, emerging out of legal scholarship, by focusing attention on the power of narrative.

71. Bonilla-Silva, *Racism without Racists*, 96.

72. Bonilla-Silva, *Racism without Racists*, 96.

73. Delgado, "Storytelling for Oppositionists and Others," 2412.

74. Bonilla-Silva, *Racism without Racists*, 118. Bonilla-Silva identifies two forms of story. Storylines are "socially shared tales that are fable-like." These stories take place in situations where the storyteller and audience share a representational world—a common perspective—and they function to strengthen this collective worldview (97). In terms of racial ideology, common storylines of whiteness are that "the past is the past," which denies the effects of historic discrimination as well as the ways it persists into the present. Testimonies include the storyteller as a character and are useful in persuasion. Though more personal, they tend to share a similar structure among themselves suggesting they still represent and create a racial habitus (107).

75. Delgado, "Storytelling," 2414. This is what Bonilla-Silva calls a *racial habitus*— or in the case of white people, a "white habitus." This is a racialized socialization

process that conditions and creates our views, perceptions, and attitudes on racial matters (Bonilla-Silva, *Racism without Racists*, 121).

76. Delgado, "Storytelling," 2413. See also Adalberto Aquirre, "Academic Storytelling: A Critical Race Theory Story of Affirmative Action," *Sociological Perspectives* 43, no. 2 (2000): 320.

77. Charles Mills, *The Racial Contract* (Ithaca, NY: Cornell University Press, 1997), 59.

78. Baldwin, *Notes of a Native Son*, 16.

79. DiAngelo, "White Fragility," 56. White theologian James W. Perkinson offers another good definition of *whiteness* as "perceived difference from, economic exploitation of, political dominance over, and presumed social superiority to, peoples 'of color'" (Perkinson, *White Theology: Outing Supremacy in Modernity* (New York: Palgrave Macmillan, 2004), 153). Whiteness presumes to operate not as equal and inverse of blackness, but its judge. The concept of being "white" came into existence, Jennifer Harvey argues, around 1680 as a term of self-identification, emerging out of the logical, social, and economic systems developed to exploit those with darker skin (Jennifer Harvey, *Dear White Christians: For Those Still Longing for Racial Reconciliation* (Grand Rapids: Eerdmans, 2014), 51). In this sense, whiteness was birthed through violence, was constituted by systems of violence (like slavery), and continues to imply complicity with systems of violence. Therefore, whiteness is not something that can ever be celebrated (52).

80. Ruth Frankenburg, *The Social Construction of Whiteness: White Women, Race Matters* (Minneapolis: University of Minnesota Press, 1993), 1.

81. Townes, *Womanist Ethics*, 73.

82. Bonilla-Silva, *Racism without Racists*, 129.

83. James Cone, *The Cross and the Lynching Tree* (Maryknoll, NY: Orbis Books, 2011), 159.

84. Joe R. Feagin and Eileen O'Brien, *White Men on Race: Power, Privilege, and the Shaping of Cultural Consciousness* (Boston: Beacon Press, 2004), 5.

85. Richard Dyer, *White: Essays on Race and Culture* (New York: Routledge, 1997).

86. James Cone, *God of the Oppressed* (Maryknoll, NY: Orbis Books, 1973), 126.

87. Perkinson, *White Theology*, 153.

88. Townes, *Womanist Ethics*, 72.

89. Townes, *Womanist Ethics*, 70.

90. James Baldwin, *The Fire Next Time* (New York: Vintage Books, 1962), 165.

91. Townes, *Womanist Ethics*, 113.

92. Angelina E. Castagno, "Multicultural Education and the Protection of Whiteness," *American Journal of Education* 120, no. 1 (2013): 101–128, at 108.

93. "We are often trapped in our unexamined particularities," Townes says. "My point is that this makes us dangerous when from this stance we then try to shape public policies that affect the nation and the world" (*Womanist Ethics*, 113).

94. John Danforth, *The Relevance of Religion: How Faithful People Can Change Politics* (New York: Random House, 2015), 165.

95. Townes, *Womanist Ethics*, 120–124.

96. Itagaki shows that many calls for civility (i.e. politeness and respect for authority) only strengthen the racially unjust power relations of American society since they reinforce a sense of meritocracy that suggests that those who are civil deserve societal and material advantages. Lynn Mie Itagaki, *Civil Racism: The 1992 Los Angeles Rebellion and the Crisis of Racial Burnout.* (Minneapolis: University of Minnesota Press, 2016), 67–68.

97. DiAngelo, "White Fragility," 54–70. See also Robin DiAngelo, *White Fragility: Why It's So Hard for White People to Talk about Racism* (Boston: Beacon Press, 2018); all references to DiAngelo in this chapter are to the article of the same name.

98. James Cone, "Martin, Malcolm, and Black Theology," in *How Long This Road: Race, Religion, and the Legacy of C. Eric Lincoln*, ed. Alton B. Pollard and Love Henry Whelchel Jr. (New York: Palgrave Macmillan, 2003), 61.

99. DiAngelo, "White Fragility," 58.

100. DiAngelo, "White Fragility," 57.

101. DiAngelo, "White Fragility," 64.

102. DiAngelo, "White Fragility," 63.

103. See Bonilla-Silva, *Racism without Racists*.

104. Barber and Wilson-Hartgrove, *Third Reconstruction*, 120.

105. David Gilborn, "Educational Policy as an Act of White Supremacy: Whiteness, Critical Race Theory and Education Reform," *Journal of Education Policy* 20, no. 4 (July 2005): 488.

106. M. Shawn Copeland, "Overcoming Christianity's Lingering Complicity: In the Shadow of Charleston," Syndicate Theology, 2015, http://www.syndicate.network/symposia/theology/in-the-shadow-of-charleston.

107. Rogers, "White Supremacy."

108. While Willis Jenkins invokes the term when discussing climate change in *The Future of Ethics: Sustainability, Social Justice, and Religious Creativity* (Washington, DC: Georgetown University Press, 2013), 21, the term originated with H. W. J. Rittel and M. M. Webber, "Dilemmas in a General Theory of Planning," *Policy Sciences* 4, no. 2 (1973): 155–169.

109. Jenkins, *Future of Ethics*, 20–21. I more closely examine in chapter 3 the ways in which the idea of "tradition" itself has caused racial harm.

CHAPTER 2

1. Michelle Alexander, *The New Jim Crow* (New York: New Press, 2012), 26.

2. Orlando Patterson, *Slavery and Social Death: A Comparative Study* (Cambridge, MA: Harvard University Press, 1985), 8–9; Katie M. Grimes, "Breaking the Body of Christ: The Sacraments of Initiation in a Habitat of White Supremacy," *Political*

Theology 18, no. 1 (2017): 22–43, 26. For an extensive and personal account of the Atlantic slave route from slave dungeon to plantation, see Saidiya Hartman, *Lose Your Mother: A Journey along the Atlantic Slave Route* (New York: Farrar, Straus and Giroux, 2008).

3. Brad R. Braxton, "Lifting the Veil: The *Shoah* and the *Maafa* in Conversation," *Perspectives in Religious Studies* 38, no. 2 (2011): 188. Information on Elmina from Hartman, *Lose Your Mother*, 58. Hartman notes that by 1540, between ten thousand and twenty thousand slaves had been confined within the walls of the fort (62).

4. Frederick P. Bowser, "Africans in Spanish American Colonial Society," in *The Cambridge History of Latin America*, vol. 11, ed. Leslie Bethell (Cambridge: Cambridge University Press, 1986), 371.

5. Brad Braxton, guest lecture in "Faith, Politics, and Public Square" course, Wesley Theological Seminary held at the Smithsonian Museum of African American History and Culture, Washington, DC, April 23, 2018.

6. Quotes from Ryan Andrew Newson, *Inhabiting the World: Identity, Politics, and Theology in Radical Baptist Perspective* (Macon, GA: Mercer University Press, 2018), 135, and James K. A. Smith, *Awaiting the King: Reforming Public Theology* (Grand Rapids: Baker, 2017), 208. I examine these texts more in the next chapter.

7. Willie Jennings, *The Christian Imagination* (New Haven, CT: Yale University Press, 2011), 6, 9.

8. Joe R. Feagin, *The White Racial Frame: Centuries of Racial Framing and Counter-Framing*, 2nd ed. (New York: Routledge, 2013), 39, 26.

9. As noted in the title of an essay by another sociologist, Santiago Slabodsky, "It's the Theology, Stupid!" in *Anti-Blackness and Christian Ethics*, ed. Vincent Lloyd and Andrew Prevot (Maryknoll, NY: Orbis Books, 2017), 19–40.

10. Kelly Brown Douglas, *What's Faith Got to Do with It?* (Maryknoll, NY: Orbis Books), xiii.

11. Joseph R. Washington, *Anti-Blackness in English Religion, 1500–1800* (Lewiston, NY: Edwin Mellen Press, 1984), 107.

12. Rolando Mellafe, *La esclavitud en Hispanoamerica* (Buenos Aires: EUDEBA, 1964), 59–60; cited in Rivera, *A Violent Evangelism*, 182; Adam Hochschild, *Bury the Chains: Prophets and Rebels in the Fight to Free an Empire's Slaves* (Boston: Mariner Books, 2006), 3.

13. Hochschild, *Bury the Chains*, 3.

14. Jamelle Bouie, "The Enlightenment's Dark Side," *Slate*, June 5, 2018, http://www.slate.com/news-and-politics/2018/06/taking-the-enlightenment-seriously-requires-talking-about-race. See also Robert Bernasconi, "Who Invented the Concept of Race?" in *Race*, ed. Robert Bernasconi (Malden, MA: Blackwell, 2001), 11–36.

15. Emmanuel Chuckwudi Eze, ed., "Introduction," in *Race and the Enlightenment: A Reader* (Oxford: Blackwell, 1997), 5.

16. Cornel West, *Prophesy Deliverance!: An Afro-American Revolutionary Christianity* (1982; Louisville, KY: Westminster John Knox Press, 2002), 53. For example, while

West acknowledges that "biblically based accounts of racial inferiority flourished" prior to the Enlightenment and cites racist folktales, mythologies, and stories that predate the seventeenth and eighteenth centuries, he contends that the authority of the church prohibited nonreligious, pre-Enlightenment accounts of racism (Cornel West, *Prophetic Fragments: Illuminations of the Crisis in American Religion and Culture* (Grand Rapids: Eerdmans, 1988), 100; and West, *Prophesy Deliverance*, 54).

17. Ivan Hannaford, *Race: The History of an Idea in the West* (Baltimore: Johns Hopkins University Press, 1996), 187.

18. Terrence Keel, *Divine Variations: How Christian Thought Became Racial Science* (Stanford, CA: Stanford University Press, 2018), 5.

19. For an example of the way scientific accounts of race were predicated on theology consider German anatomist Johann Blumenbach's 1785 *Outline of the History of Humanity*. It was touted as one of the first scientific accounts of racial development. Keel traces Blumenbach's claim that the white Caucasian was the progenitor of humanity, the "autochthones of mankind," to earlier parallels in the theological anthropology of Martin Luther, who also allegorically positioned European Christians as Adam and Eve—the original humans (Keel, *Divine Variations*, 41, citing Blumenbach, *The Anthropological Treatises of Johann Freidrich Blumenbach*, trans. Thomas Bendyche (London: Longman, Green, Longman, Roberts, and Green, 1865), 269). Keel appeals to the marginal notes in one of Luther's Bibles for direct evidence, which strikes me as a rather weak argument. But he goes on to show compelling resonances between Luther's and Blumenbach's notions of creation, the fall, beauty, and the image of God (Keel, *Divine Variations*, 40–42).

20. One can see a convergence of liberalism and theology in the thought of Immanuel Kant or a quintessential modern theologian like Adolf von Harnack. J. Kameron Carter recognizes this convergence of Christian theology and Enlightenment rationality in the thought of Kant, who gave the world "rigorously scientific and philosophically sophisticated, and hence, its first fully developed theory of race," but did so in concert with a Christian worldview (Carter, *Race: A Theological Account* (New York: Oxford University Press, 2008), 42). "Christianity as a rational religion and Christ as the 'personified idea of the good principle,'" Carter writes, guarantee that whiteness serves as the continuation of Christ's work—the development of Western civilization (89). Likewise, the early-twentieth-century German Protestant Adolf von Harnack, in magisterial works like *What Is Christianity?* and *The History of Dogma*, writes in a way that presumes objective observation of the entire landscape of Christianity and an ability to speak universally to it and about it. For him, Christianity was a "universal religion" that was able to absorb all cultural differences into itself and, therefore, "sums up everything." In doing so, Christianity "conquered . . . and "subdued all the world to come" (Harnack, *The Mission and Expansion of Christianity* vol. 2, trans. James Moffatt (New York: G. P. Putnam's Sons, 1908), 313, 337).

21. Feagin, *The White Racial Frame*, 156.

22. For example, see legislation passed by the Virginia legislature in 1667 cited in T. W. Allen, *The Invention of the White Race,* vol. 2: *The Origin of Racial Oppression in Anglo-America* (Brooklyn: Verso Books, 2012), 197; and the Maryland legislature in 1664 and others in Albert Raboteau, *Slave Religion: The "Invisible" Institution in the Antebellum South* (Oxford: Oxford University Press, 1978), 99.

23. Historians, philosophers, and anthropologists have spilled a great deal of ink in an attempt to determine race and racism's historical origin. For example, "Many scholars see in the later Middle Ages a tendency for racial discrimination to become sharper and racial boundaries to be more shrilly asserted," beginning with "the hardening of anti-Jewish feeling between the eleventh and the fifteenth centuries" (Robert Bartlett, *The Making of Europe* (Princeton, NJ: Princeton University Press, 1994), 236). Geraldine Heng argues that while many factors lead to this phenomenon of religious difference bleeding into racial difference, in the Middle Ages there certainly existed a "hierarchical politics of color" (Heng, *The Invention of Race in the European Middle Ages* (New York: Cambridge University Press, 2018, 42). See also Heng's discussion at 24–26 in that volume).

24. This is not an original claim, just one that white Christian theologians and ethicists have not adequately addressed. In addition to the sources cited and analyzed here, for a later historical account, see Rebecca Anne Goetz, *The Baptism of Early Virginia: How Christianity Created Race* (Baltimore: Johns Hopkins University Press, 2012).

25. Heng, *The Invention of Race*, 78.

26. Robert C. Stacey, "The Conversion of Jews to Christianity in Thirteenth-Century England," *Speculum* 67, no. 2 (April 1992), 263–283, 278.

27. Heng, *The Invention of Race*, 80. For a more detailed account of this history see 55–109 in that volume.

28. Heng, *The Invention of Race*, 61.

29. Heng, *The Invention of Race*, 67.

30. Lauren F. Winner, *The Dangers of Christian Practice: On Wayward Gifts, Characteristic Damage, and Sin* (New Haven, CT: Yale University Press, 2018), 20ff.

31. Between 1208 and 1290, John Edwards notes, almost a third of the canons enacted by councils of the English church "touched on Jewish matters" (Edwards, "The Church and the Jews in Medieval England," in *Jews in Medieval Britain: Historical, Literary, and Archaeological Perspectives*, ed. Patricia Skinner (Rochester, NY: Boydell Press, 2003), 85–96: 91).

32. Heng, *The Invention of Race*, 15; Hannaford, *Race*, 114. "The badge that distinguished people who could not be set apart by their physical appearance in later times," Hannaford argues, "became the mark of Cain and then absorbed by logic and association of ideas into the mark of race" (126). Interestingly, Hannaford, who insists that racism didn't begin until the late seventeenth century, identifies these historical (and certainly, theological) precursors to the scientific developments that

he contends generated white supremacy—though he fails to understand them as theological.

33. Fourth Lateran Council, Canon 68; cited in Winner, *The Dangers of Christian Practice*, 26.

34. Heng, *The Invention of Race*, 70.

35. Heng, *The Invention of Race*, 32.

36. Hannaford, *Race*, 121.

37. Hannaford, *Race*, 122.

38. Luis N. Rivera argues that it is anachronistic to speak of fifteenth- or sixteenth-century Spanish discussions of blood purity as "merely" racial or racist (Rivera, *A Violent Evangelism: The Political and Religious Conquest of the Americas* (Louisville, KY: Westminster/John Knox Press, 1992), 50). Rivera observes that in the context of the Inquisition *blood purity* refers primarily to demarcating religious identities and unifying Spanish national and Christian identity. This may be true, noting Rivera's qualification that the term did indeed possess some racial significance—"merely." But this does not mitigate my larger point that even if such terminology, concepts, and categories did not refer explicitly or in total to racial classification, they began to obscure or conflate religious and racial identities and, further, invented theological concepts and categories that were easily applied to racialized bodies.

39. Enrique Dussel, *The Invention of the Americas: Eclipse of "the Other" and the Myth of Modernity* (New York: Continuum, 1995), 13.

40. Rivera, *A Violent Evangelism*, 12. Though Alexander VI was chronicled by Machiavelli in *The Prince* (trans. George Bull (Baltimore: Penguin Books, 1961), 100), as possessing a loose relationship with the truth and frequently ruling through deception, this should not cause us to attribute the origin of these pronouncements to one morally compromised or unusually cruel pontiff or obscure the fact that the Roman Catholic Church invoked these documents for centuries to justify their conquest and brutality. These doctrines effectively express the consent and will of the full array of ecclesial leaders of the time.

41. "Bull Romanus Pontifex, January 8, 1455," in *European Treaties Bearing on the History of the United States and Its Dependencies to 1648*, vol. 1, ed. Frances Gardiner Davenport (Washington, DC: Carnegie Institution of Washington, 1917), 23; cited in Jennings, *The Christian Imagination*, 29.

42. Dussel, *The Invention of the Americas*, 54–55. See also James W. Perkinson, *White Theology: Outing Supremacy in Modernity* (New York: Palgrave Macmillan, 2004), 155, and Michael Omi and Howard Winant, *Racial Formation in the United States, from the 1960s to the 1990s*, 2nd ed. (New York: Routledge Publishing, 1994), 61–64.

43. According to Pagden, on August 8, 1444, a shipment of 235 Africans from Senegal arrived at the Portuguese port of Lagos for inspection by Prince Henry (Anthony Pagden, *Peoples and Empires: A Short History of European Migration, Exploration, and Conquest, from Greece to the Present* (New York: Modern Library, 2001), 102).

44. Gomes Eanes de Zurara, *The Chronicle of the Discovery and Conquest of Guinea*, 2 vols. (London: Hakluyt Society, 1896–1899), 81–83.

45. Jennings, *The Christian Imagination*, 25.

46. Pagden, *Lords of All the World*, 47, 94Anthony Pagden, *Lords of All the World: Ideologies of Empire in Spain, Britain, and France, c. 1500-1800* (New Haven: Yale University Press, 1995), 74. Some theologians reached for justifications from the just war tradition, as presented by Juan Ginés de Sepúlveda. These rested on a precarious argument in self-defense of the "salvation of the Christian republic," but even this relied on a connection between religious inferiority (*inculti*) and racial inferiority (*inhumani*). See Pagden *Lords of All the World*, 100, quoting Juan Ginés de Sepúlveda, *Johannis Genesii Sepulvedae Opera*, vol. 4 (Madrid, 1780), 99. Sepúlveda famously debated Bartolomé de las Casas over the intelligence and, really, humanity, of the Native Americans, despite Las Casas's support for Spanish colonialism and belief in the superiority of European civilization.

47. Roger Bastide, "Color, Racism, and Christianity," in *White Racism: Its History, Pathology, and Practice*, ed. B. N. Schwarts and R. Disch (New York: Dell, 1970), 270–285), 281; cited in Perkinson, *White Theology*, 61.

48. Perkinson, *White Theology*, 68.

49. Jennings, *The Christian Imagination*, 105.

50. Jennings, *The Christian Imagination*, 228. He quips, in these colonial encounters, the dictum "*faith seeking understanding* mutates into *faith judging intelligence*"— which translates into capacity for salvation (108).

51. Jennings, *The Christian Imagination*, 59.

52. Kelly Brown Douglas, "More Than Skin Deep: The Violence of Anti-Blackness," in *Anti-Blackness and Christian Ethics*, ed. Vincent W. Lloyd and Andrew Prevot (Maryknoll, NY: Orbis Books, 2017), 6.

53. William G. Fischer, "I Shall Be Whiter Than Snow" (1872).

54. Jennings, *The Christian Imagination*, 58.

55. Jennings, *The Christian Imagination*, 8. Jennings uses the phrase "order of things" in a specialized sense, by reference to Michel Foucault, to invoke the matrix of underlying epistemological assumptions that create the norms for this period of history (Foucault, *The Order of Things: An Archaeology of the Human Sciences* (New York: Pantheon, 1970).

56. Jennings, *The Christian Imagination*, 26. Santiago Slabodsky also claims that the biological racism of the nineteenth century is a direct consequence of the colonial theology that emerged in the sixteenth century. According to his analysis, Christendom's hegemony granted theology the exclusive right to define humanity and thus judge who existed within and without this definition (Slabodsky, "It's the Theology, Stupid!: Coloniality, Anti-Blackness, and the Bounds of 'Humanity,'" in Lloyd and Prevot, *Anti-Blackness and Christian Ethics*, 30–31.)

57. William Goodell, *The American Slave Code in Theory and Practice: Its Distinctive Features Shown by Its Statutes, Judicial Decisions, and Illustrative Facts* (1853; New York: Negro Universities Press, 1969), 23.

58. Jennings, *The Christian Imagination*, 188.

59. Orlando Patterson, *Slavery and Social Death: A Comparative Study* (Cambridge, MA: Harvard University Press, 1982), 11–12.

60. Toni Morrison, *Beloved* (1987; New York: Vintage Books, 2004), 267.

61. Jeanine Hill Fletcher, *The Sin of White Supremacy: Christianity, Racism, and Religious Diversity in America* (Maryknoll, NY: Orbis Books, 2017), 45.

62. Fletcher, *The Sin of White Supremacy*, 11.

63. Saidiya Hartman, *Lose Your Mother: A Journey along the Atlantic Slave Route* (New York: Farrar, Straus and Giroux, 2007), 133.

64. Douglas, *What's Faith Got to Do with It?* (Maryknoll, NY: Orbis Books, 2005), 9.

65. Douglas, *What's Faith Got to Do with It?*, 30.

66. See, for example, Galatians 5:16–24 and 6:8 or Ephesians 2:3 (Douglas, *What's Faith Got to Do with It?*, 36). Patristics scholar Abraham P. Bos contests this generic implication of Platonic dualism within early Hellenized Christianity, exposing the way prominent early Christian thinkers like Philo, Irenaeus, Justin Martyr, and Origen invoked vague and inconsistent versions of this at best (Bos, "'Aristotelian' and 'Platonic' Dualism in Hellenistic and Early Christian Philosophy and in Gnosticism," *Vigiliae Christianae* 56, no. 3 (2002): 273–291). He argues that a more nuanced Aristotelian dualism between intellect and soul supplanted an ambiguous "Platonic dualism" after a short lifespan. Still, Bos states, Aristotle "instrumentalizes" the body which exists to serve the soul (278), and from which the soul seeks "release" (278, 282). This nuance thus does not do much to overcome the anthropological impact of a body versus mind/soul dualism or blunt the force of Douglas's argument.

67. Justo L. Gonzalez, *The Story of Christianity,* vol. 1: *The Early Church to the Dawn of the Reformation* (New York: HarperSanFrancisco, 1984), 59–64.

68. Gonzalez, *The Story of Christianity*, 60.

69. Douglas, *What's Faith Got to Do with It?*, 37.

70. See Jean Devisse, *The Image of the Black in Western Art,* vol. 2: *From the Early Christian Era to the "Age of Discovery"* (Cambridge, MA: Harvard University Press, 1990), 58–62. For examples, see Genesis 1:2–4; Exodus 10:21; 1 Samuel 2:9; Job 3:4–6; Psalm 51:7; Isaiah 8:22; Jeremiah 4:28; Luke 11:35–36; John 1:5; Romans 1:21; 2 Corinthians 6:14; Colossians 1:13; Revelation 7:13–14. Devisse's genealogy of how blackness accrued negative meanings identifies Jerome as key in the Latin tradition to promulgating black as the color of sin (59).

71. Heng, *The Invention of Race*, 186.

72. Jennings, *The Christian Imagination*, 112.

73. Madeline Caviness, "From the Self-Invention of the Whiteman in the Thirteenth Century to the Good, the Bad, and the Ugly," *Different Visions: A Journal of New Perspectives on Medieval Art* 1 (September 2008): 22.

74. Carter, *Race*, 90.

75. Susanna Heschel, *The Aryan Jesus: Christian Theologians and the Bible in Nazi Germany* (Princeton, NJ: Princeton University Press, 2008), 22.

76. Douglas, *What's Faith Got to Do with It?*, 38. For the continued impact of "hierarchical dualisms" in Christian thought, see Elizabeth T. Vasko, *Beyond Apathy: A Theology for Bystanders* (Minneapolis: Fortress, 2015), 14.

77. Douglas, *What's Faith Got to Do with It?*, 12. Douglas again claims this originated with theological resources from Christianity's "closed monotheism," by which she means its antagonistic exclusiveness.

78. Douglas, *What's Faith Got to Do with It?*, 14.

79. "In Western Europe, at least until the twelfth century," Devisse claims, "there were simply no black people except in some very limited areas" (*Image of the Black in Western Art*, 51).

80. Fletcher, *The Sin of White Supremacy*, 11.

81. Skin tone "came to function as a universal evaluative tool to measure human hierarchy" (M. Shawn Copeland, "Race," in *Blackwell Companion to Modern Theology*, ed. Gareth Jones (Malden, MA: Blackwell, 2004), 501).

82. Fletcher, *The Sin of White Supremacy*, 27.

83. Daniel Boyarin, *The Unconverted Self: Jews, Indians, and the Identity of Christian Europe* (Chicago: University of Chicago Press, 2009), 1–2. Theologians Willie Jennings and J. Kameron Carter have recently focused on supersessionism as the primary culprit in the development of white supremacy. They both stand in the center of what has been called "the new black theology," though both resist the moniker. The chief commonalities of this movement, distinct from conventional black theology, is the effort to place the origins of racism theologically at the foot of supersessionism, and seek to retrieve pre-Enlightenment theological resources to free us from modern racism. For one of the first descriptions of this theological shift, see Jonathan Tran, "The New Black Theology: Retrieving Ancient Sources to Challenge Racism," *Christian Century*, February 8, 2012, https://www.christian-century.org/article/2012-01/new-black-theology.

84. See Luther's 1543 treatise, "On the Jews and Their Lies."

85. Denise Kimber Buell, "Early Christian Universalism and Modern Racism," in *The Origins of Racism in the West*, ed. Miriam Eliav-Feldon, Benjamin Isaac, and Joseph Ziegler (Cambridge: Cambridge University Press, 2009), 111–112; See also Buell, *Why This New Race* (New York: Columbia University Press, 2005).

86. As Terrence Keel describes it, the early church's conception of peoplehood "at the same time understood themselves to be superior to other forms of social membership by virtue of their claims to have knowledge about the destiny of all humanity" (Keel, *Divine Variations*, 8).

87. Buell, "Early Christian Universalism and Modern Racism," 130. See also Cohen, *The Beginnings of Jewishness: Boundaries, Varieties, Uncertainties* (Berkeley: University

of California Press, 1999), 175–197, and Gay Byron, *Symbolic Blackness and Ethnic Difference in Early Christian Literature* (New York: Routledge, 2002).

88. Immanuel Kant, *Immanuel Kants Schriften VIII*, Ausgabe der Königlich Preussischen (Deutschen) Akademie der Wissenschaften (Berlin: W. De Gruyter, 1900f), 100; cited by Robert Bernasconi, "Who Invented the Concept of Race: Kant's Role in the Enlightenment Construction of Race," in Bernasconi, *Race*, 14.

89. Bernasconi, "Who Invented the Concept of Race," 14; Kant, *Observations on the Feeling of the Beautiful and Sublime,* trans. John T. Goldwaithe (Berkeley: University of California Press, 1973), 113. For other sources on Kant's role in the development of racism, see Robert Bernasconi, "Kant as an Unfamiliar Source of Racism," in *Philosophers on Race: Critical Essays*, ed. Julie K. Ward and Tommy Lee Lott (Malden, MA: Blackwell, 2002), 145–166; Emmanuel Chukwudi Eze, "The Color of Reason: The Idea of 'Race' in Kant's Anthropology," in *Postcolonial African Philosophy: A Critical Reader*, ed. Emmanuel Chukwudi Eze (Malden, MA: Blackwell, 1997), 103–140; Thomas E. Hill Jr. and Bernard Boxill, "Kant and Race," in *Race and Racism*, ed. Bernard Boxill (Oxford: Oxford University Press, 2001), 448–471; and Charles W. Mills, "Kant's Untermenschen," in *Black Rights / White Wrongs: The Critique of Racial Liberalism* (New York: Oxford University Press, 2017).

90. Carter, *Race*, 4. As Carter helpfully clarifies, it was with Kant and other Enlightenment thinkers that white supremacy and the supersessionism that gave rise to it received their most robust formation. In Carter's words, "something quite new" occurs in this period as anti-Jewishness "gets linked to biology and to the newly emerging theories of race, on the one hand, and to discourses of nation, on the other" (398n2).

91. Carter, *Race*, 112.

92. Jonathan M. Hess, *Germans, Jews, and the Claims of Modernity* (New Haven, CT: Yale University Press, 2002), 153.

93. Immanuel Kant, *Religion and Rational Theology*, trans. Allen W. Wood, ed. George Di Giovanni, (Cambridge: Cambridge University Press, 1996), 119.

94. Carter, *Race*, 117.

95. Carter, *Race*, 117.

96. Kant, *Religion and Rational Theology*, 276.

97. Carter, *Race*, 81.

98. Walter D. Mignolo, *The Darker Side of Western Modernity: Global Futures, Decolonial Options* (Durham, NC: Duke University Press, 2011), 80.

99. John Adams, "Letter from John Adams to Abigail Adams, August 14, 1776," Massachusetts Historical Society, http://www.masshist.org, as quoted in Kelly Brown Douglas, *Stand Your Ground: Black Bodies and the Justice of God* (Maryknoll, NY: Orbis Books, 2015), 13.

100. Douglas, *Stand Your Ground*, 13.

101. Douglas, *What's Faith Got to Do With It?*, 45.

102. Lisa Sowle Cahill, *Love Your Enemy: Discipleship, Pacifism, and Just War Theory* (Minneapolis: Fortress, 1994), 145–147.

103. Carter, *Race*, 54. See Michel Foucault, *"Society Must Be Defended": Lectures at the College de France, 1975–1976*, trans. David Macey (New York: Picador, 2003).

104. William T. Cavanaugh, *Theopolitical Imagination: Christian Practices of Space and Time* (New York: Bloomsbury Academic, 2013), 9.

105. William T. Cavanaugh, *Torture and Eucharist* (Malden, MA: Blackwell, 1998), 196.

106. Douglas, *Stand Your Ground*, 60.

107. Douglas, *Stand Your Ground*, 56.

108. Darryl M. Trimiew, "The Social Gospel Movement and the Question of Race," in *The Social Gospel Today*, ed. Christopher H. Evans (Louisville, KY: Westminster John Knox Press, 2001), 29.

109. Walter Rauschenbusch, "The Problem of the Black Man," *American Mission Association* 68 (March 1914): 732. According to Glenn Bucher, "It was then falsely assumed that racism, too, had been exterminated or at least delivered a terminal death blow. Not only did socially aware Christians fail to recognize the limits of the Civil War, but they also assumed that the Civil War aftermath was the South's problem to attend to and solve. And so, by deduction, they concluded that they were exonerated from the problem of continuing racism" (Bucher, "Social Gospel and Racism," *Union Seminary Quarterly Review* 28, no. 2 (Winter 1973): 146–157, 147).

110. Traci C. West, "Constructing Ethics: Reinhold Niebuhr and Harlem Women Activists," *Journal of the Society of Christian Ethics* 24, no. 1 (2004): 29–49, 33.

111. Reinhold Niebuhr, *Man's Nature and His Communities: Essays on the Dynamics and Enigmas of Man's Personal and Social Existence* (1965; Eugene, OR: Wipf and Stock, 2012), 12.

112. Reinhold Niebuhr, *Reflections on the End of an Era* (New York: Charles Scribner's Sons, 1934), 285–286.

113. West, "Constructing Ethics," 35.

114. Preston Williams, "The Social Gospel and Race Relations: A Case Study of a Social Movement," in *Toward a Discipline of Social Ethics: Essays in Honor of Walter George Muelder*, ed. Paul Deats Jr. (Boston: Boston University Press, 1972), 233, 236. Early social gospelers including Josiah Strong exhibited blatant racism. He wrote of Anglo-Saxons as the "final completion of races" in the competition of "survival of the fittest" (Strong, *Our Country: Its Possible Future and Its Present Crisis* (Cambridge, MA: Harvard University Press, 1963), 215).

115. Rauschenbusch, "The Problem of the Black Man," 733.

116. Williams, "The Social Gospel and Race Relations," 236.

117. Rauschenbusch, "The Problem of the Black Man," 732.

118. Karen V. Guth, "Laying Claim to Martin Luther King Jr. and the Civil Rights Legacy: An Ethical Assessment of Social Gospel Historiography," *Journal of Religious Ethics* (forthcoming). I thank Karen for introducing me to many of these sources on Rauschenbusch.

119. Martin Luther King Jr., *Stride toward Freedom: The Montgomery Story* (1958; Boston: Beacon, 2010), 87.

120. Walter Rauschenbusch, *Christianity and the Social Crisis* (New York: Harper-Collins, 2007), 422.

121. Rauschenbusch, *Christianity and the Social Crisis*, 142.

122. Glenn R. Bucher, "Social Gospel and Racism," *Union Seminary Quarterly Review* 28, no. 2 (Winter 1973): 146.

123. Walter Rauschenbusch, "Belated Races and the Social Problems," *Methodist Review Quarterly* 63 (April 1914): 252–259.

124. Rauschenbusch, "Belated Races and the Social Problems," 254.

125. Rauschenbusch, "The Problem of the Black Man," 733.

126. Williams, "The Social Gospel and Race Relations," 236.

127. Williams, "The Social Gospel and Race Relations," 237.

128. Rauschenbusch, "Belated Races and the Social Problems," 253–254.

129. Rauschenbusch, "Belated Races and the Social Problems," 253.

130. Trimiew, "The Social Gospel Movement and the Question of Race," 28.

131. Reinhold Niebuhr, *Christian Realism and Political Problems* (New York: Charles Scribner's Sons, 1953), 119.

132. Reinhold Niebuhr, "The Problem of a Protestant Social Ethic," *Union Seminary Quarterly Review* 15 (November 1959): 2, 7, and 11.

133. Reinhold Niebuhr, *Moral Man and Immoral Society: A Study in Ethics and Politics* (New York: Charles Scribner's Sons, 1932), 253.

134. Niebuhr, *Moral Man and Immoral Society*, 253.

135. Reinhold Niebuhr, "The Race Problem" (1942), in *Reinhold Niebuhr: Major Works on Religion and Politics*, ed. Elisabeth Sifton (New York: Library of America, 2015), 652.

136. James Cone, *The Cross and the Lynching Tree* (Maryknoll, NY: Orbis Books, 201), 48.

137. Reinhold Niebuhr, "What Resources Can the Christian Church Offer to Meet the Crisis in Race Relations?" (1956), in *Reinhold Niebuhr: Major Works on Religion and Politics*, ed. Elisabeth Sifton (New York: Library of America, 2015), 677.

138. Niebuhr, "The Race Problem," 652.

139. Cone, *The Cross and the Lynching Tree*, 43.

140. Reinhold Niebuhr, "The Supreme Court on Segregation in the Schools" (1954), in *Love and Justice: Selections from the Shorter Writings of Reinhold Niebuhr*, ed. D. B. Robertson (1957; Louisville, KY: Westminster/John Knox Press, 1992), 150.

141. Niebuhr, *Moral Man and Immoral Society*, 254, 209.

142. Niebuhr, "Nullification," *New Leader*, March 5, 1956, 4.

143. Robert Bellah, "Christian Realism," *Theology Today* 26, no. 4 (January 1970): 369.

144. Cone, *The Cross and the Lynching Tree*, 41.

145. Herbert O. Edwards, "Racism and Christian Ethics in America," *Katallagete* (Winter 1971): 18.

146. Niebuhr, *Man's Nature and His Communities*, 18.

147. Niebuhr, *Moral Man and Immoral Society*, 254.

148. Reinhold Niebuhr, "The Church in the World," *Theology Today* 15, no. 4 (January 1959): 542.

149. Niebuhr, "What Resources Can the Christian Church Offer to Meet the Crisis in Race Relations?," 677.

150. Niebuhr would later, in his attempt to distance himself from his theological fore-bears, come to assure his readers that this backwardness was historical rather than biological, but by placing the blame for black suffering and the source of white prejudice on the cultural backwardness of black people rather than exclusively on white sinfulness, he implicated African Americans in their own oppression. See Edwards, "Racism and Christian Ethics in America," 19.

151. West, "Constructing Ethics," 42, citing Niebuhr's "The Religion of Communism," *Atlantic Monthly*, April 1931, 464.

152. West, "Constructing Ethics," 42.

153. West, "Constructing Ethics," 36, 37.

154. Cone, *God of the Oppressed*, 220.

155. Niebuhr, "What Resources Can the Christian Church Offer to Meet the Crisis in Race Relations," 676.

156. Reinhold Niebuhr, *The Children of Light and the Children of Darkness* (New York: Charles Scribner's Sons, 1944), 139.

157. Reinhold Niebuhr, "The Confession of a Tired Radical" (1928), in Robertson, *Love and Justice*, 121.

158. Niebuhr, *The Children of Light and the Children of Darkness*, 140.

159. Reinhold Niebuhr, *Nature and Destiny of Man* (1941; Louisville, KY: Westminster John Knox Press, 1996), 117, 178, 220.

160. Niebuhr, "Confession of a Tired Radical," 124.

161. West, "Constructing Ethics," 40.

162. See Niebuhr, "The Confession of a Tired Radical," 121.

163. Cone, *The Cross and the Lynching Tree*, 159.

164. Referenced in James K. A. Smith, *Awaiting the King: Reforming Public Theology* (Grand Rapids: Baker Academic, 2017), 181.

165. Fletcher, *The Sin of White Supremacy*, 81.

CHAPTER 3

1. "White American theologians," observes Elizabeth Johnson, "rarely cross over to analyze the gospel in the light of the consciousness of black people struggling

for human dignity, equality, and freedom" (*Quest for the Living God: Mapping Frontiers in the Theology of God* (New York: Bloomsbury, 2007), 124). Likewise, as Elaine Robinson notes in *Race and Theology*, "Despite the consistency and unanimity of [black theological] voices in regard to the importance of naming the reality of racism in theology and demonstrating how racialized discourse and practice functions to uncover, analyze, and dismantle white privilege and white supremacy, few white theologians today include or address these concerns" ((Nashville: Abingdon Press, 2012), 42). Robinson acknowledges that only "a handful" of white theologians in the United States have attempted to address these concerns in depth; she names Frederick Herzog, Peter Hodgson, and James Perkinson as the few examples. We might add Gary Dorrien to this list with his recent publications of *The New Abolition: W. E. B. Du Bois and the Black Social Gospel* (New Haven, CT: Yale University Press, 2015), and *Breaking White Supremacy: Martin Luther King Jr. and the Black Social Gospel* (New Haven, CT: Yale University Press, 2017), as well as other authors whom I reference throughout this book, including Katie Grimes, Jennifer Harvey, Jeanine Hill Fletcher, Mary McClintock Fulkerson, Karen Teel, Jennifer McBride, Timothy McGee, and Lauren Winner, plus the writers of several in-progress or recently completed dissertations.

2. See Jeffrey Stout, *Democracy and Tradition* (Princeton, NJ: Princeton University Press, 2004), 140–161. Stout claims, "Stanley Hauerwas is surely the most prolific and influential theologian now working in the United States," adding that this influence is strongest in seminaries which are training future theologians and church leaders (140, 118).

3. James Cone, "Theology's Great Sin: Silence in the Face of White Supremacy," *Black Theology* 2, no. 2 (2004): 139–152.

4. One might consider philosophers or other theologians who also present a declension narrative of modernity. They all, in their own ways, highlight the fragmenting losses of tradition, community, and narrative, among other traits. But in giving a critical account of modernity or of the development of the Self under the conditions of modernity, without addressing its darker side of colonialism and white supremacy, the story they tell is incomplete and misleading. I address one such philosopher, Alasdair MacIntyre, later in this chapter.

5. James K. A. Smith, *Awaiting the King: Reforming Public Theology* (Grand Rapids: Baker, 2017), 165, 208.

6. Ryan Andrew Newson, *Inhabiting the World: Identity, Politics, and Theology in Radical Baptist Perspective* (Macon, GA: Mercer University Press, 2018), 135, 134. Both of these theologians in personal conversations have confessed that they do believe that white supremacy is not only a problem emanating from outside the church (though I'm not sure if they'd endorse my claim of the church's role in its origins) and regret the language used in their books does not fully convey this truth.

7. Smith, *Awaiting the King*, 188, 190, 204.

8. Exceptions are noteworthy, and two ecclesiological works by white theologians are exceptional in both content and quality: Mary McClintock Fulkerson, *Places of Redemption: Theology for a Worldly Church* (New York: Oxford University Press, 2007), and Jennifer McBride, *The Church for the World: A Theology of Public Witness* (New York: Oxford University Press, 2011). Both books identify whiteness unequivocally as an ecclesiological problem, and also provide deep critical and constructive ethnographic analyses of the way racial dynamics operate within particular congregations.

9. Karen Teel, "Whiteness in Catholic Theological Method," *Journal of the American Academy of Religion* 87, no. 2 (2019): 401–433, 412.

10. James Cone, *God of the Oppressed*, New revised edition. (Maryknoll, NY: Orbis Books, 1997), 43.

11. H. Richard Niebuhr, *The Responsible Self: An Essay in Christian Moral Philosophy* (New York: Harper & Row, 1963), 96. See chapter 1 for more on Niebuhr's thought in this area.

12. See Stout, *Democracy and Tradition*.

13. See James Davison Hunter, *To Change the World: The Irony, Tragedy, and Possibility of Christianity in the Late Modern World* (New York: Oxford University Press, 2010).

14. Stanley Hauerwas, *Wilderness Wanderings: Probing Twentieth-Century Theology and Philosophy* (Boulder, CO: Westview Press, 1997), 225. Coming of age in Texas, Hauerwas worked alongside his bricklayer father. On the job he began as a laborer, a job generally reserved for African American workers who assisted the mostly white skilled bricklaying crew with the more mundane, difficult, and less-skilled tasks of moving around brick and mortar. As a "white guy who did the work of blacks," he claims a bond with his fellow laborers.

15. This article was claimed to be "lost to history" for nearly forty years, and Hauerwas himself did not possess a copy when I first approached him in 2015. This claim is made in both Jonathan Tran's essay "Time for Hauerwas's Racism," in *Unsettling Arguments: A Festschrift on the Occasion of Stanley Hauerwas's 70th Birthday,* ed. Charles R. Pinches, Kelly S. Johnson, and Charles M. Collier (Eugene, OR: Cascade Books, 2012), and James Samuel Logan, *Good Punishment?: Christian Moral Practice and U.S. Imprisonment* (Grand Rapids: Eerdmans, 2008). I obtained a copy of the article directly from the *Augustana Observer* archives in winter 2015.

16. Stanley Hauerwas, "The Ethics of Black Power," *Augustana Observer*, February 5, 1969, 3, 7. Hauerwas later references this article as "The Ethics of Black Power," as does *The Hauerwas Reader*, eds. John Berkman and Michael Cartwright (Durham, NC: Duke University Press, 2001). In the printed version of the *Augustana Observer* itself, the piece is tagged by the more descriptive headlines of "White Christian Liberals Resentful" and "Hauerwas on Black Power: Movement Morally Sound." Hauerwas recently reprinted the piece, this time calling it "An Ethical Appraisal of Black Power," as part of a new article, "Race: Fifty Years Later," *CrossCurrents* 68

no. 1 (2018): 38–53. I do not find much new in that essay to analyze here, except to highlight the fact that Hauerwas concludes it with attention to the melancholy of the black narrative and a sharper call for confession as the only appropriate theological response by white Christians.

17. Hauerwas, "Ethics of Black Power," 3.
18. Hauerwas, "Ethics of Black Power," 7. I leave Hauerwas's race and gender terminology unchanged so that I do not whitewash any mistakes or insensitivities that we may perceive today.
19. Hauerwas, "Ethics of Black Power," 7.
20. Hauerwas cites his encounters with the works of Mennonite theologian John Howard Yoder and then philosopher Alasdair MacIntyre as instrumental in the development and maturation of his theology. For Hauerwas's own reflections on their influence, see Stanley Hauerwas, *Hannah's Child: A Theologian's Memoir* (Grand Rapids: Eerdmans, 2010), 116–121, 160–161, and numerous other occasions in this book and others.
21. Stanley Hauerwas and Romand Coles, *Christianity, Democracy, and the Radical Ordinary: Conversation between a Radical Democrat and a Christian* (Eugene, OR: Cascade Books, 2008), 98.
22. Hauerwas and Coles, *Christianity, Democracy, and the Radical Ordinary*, 96n22.
23. Hauerwas, *Wilderness Wanderings*, 234.
24. Hauerwas, *Wilderness Wanderings*, 230.
25. Stanley Hauerwas, *A Better Hope: Resources for a Church Confronting Capitalism, Postmodernity, and America* (Grand Rapids: Brazos, 2000), 142.
26. Hauerwas, *A Better Hope*, 142.
27. Hauerwas, *A Better Hope*, 143.
28. See C. Eric Lincoln, *Coming through the Fire: Surviving Race and Place in America* (Durham, NC: Duke University Press, 1996), 133–134, and Lincoln, *Exclusion and Embrace: A Theological Exploration of Identity, Otherness, and Reconciliation* (Nashville: Abingdon, 1996), 136. "Eternal present" is a reference to Michael Ignatieff, *The Warrior's Honor: Ethnic War and the Modern Conscience* (New York: Henry Holt and Co., 1997), 186. This also aligns with the insights of many contemporary theologians doing research into the effects of trauma and traumatic memory. For a good example, see Shelly Rambo, *Spirit and Trauma: A Theology of Remaining* (Louisville, KY: Westminster John Knox Press, 2010).
29. Hauerwas, *A Better Hope*, 150–151.
30. Hauerwas, *A Better Hope*, 151.
31. Hauerwas and Coles, *Christianity, Democracy, and the Radical Ordinary*, 89. For examples of criticisms of Hauerwas's allergy to concepts of justice, democracy, and rights, see Gloria Albrecht, *The Character of Our Communities: Toward an Ethics of Liberation for the Church* (Nashville: Abingdon, 1995); Jeffrey Stout, *Democracy and Tradition*; and Esther Reed, *The Ethics of Human Rights: Contested Doctrinal and Moral Issues* (Waco, TX: Baylor University Press, 2007), among others.

32. Hauerwas and Coles, *Christianity, Democracy, and the Radical Ordinary* 99.

33. Stanley Hauerwas, interview with the author, Durham, NC, February 25, 2015. Cited with permission.

34. Hauerwas and Coles, *Christianity, Democracy, and the Radical Ordinary*, 90.

35. Hauerwas and Coles, *Christianity, Democracy, and the Radical Ordinary*, 98.

36. See James Cone, "Christian Faith and Political Praxis," *Encounter* 43, no. 2 (1992): 129–141, and Cone, *God of the Oppressed*, 36–56.

37. Derek Woodard-Lehman, "Body Politics and the Politics of Bodies: Racism and Hauerwasian Theopolitics," *Journal of Religious Ethics* 36, no. 2 (2008): 295–320.

38. Woodard-Lehman, "Body Politics and the Politics of Bodies," 312.

39. Logan, *Good Punishment?*, 223.

40. Tran, "Time for Hauerwas's Racism," 250–251.

41. Tran, "Time for Hauerwas's Racism," 254–255.

42. Tran, "Time for Hauerwas's Racism," 255.

43. Hauerwas, *Wilderness Wanderings*, 225.

44. Hauerwas, *Wilderness Wanderings*, 225.

45. Hauerwas, *Wilderness Wanderings*, 225n1.

46. Hauerwas, *A Better Hope*, 140.

47. James W. Perkinson, *White Theology: Outing Supremacy in Modernity* (New York: Palgrave Macmillan, 2004), 38.

48. Perkinson, *White Theology*, 41.

49. James Cone, *A Black Theology of Liberation*, 20th anniversary ed. (Maryknoll, NY: Orbis Books, 1990), 219. For a critique of Hauerwas's inattention to empirical congregations see Nicholas Healy, *Hauerwas: A Very Critical Introduction* (Grand Rapids: Eerdmans, 2014), 109.

50. Hauerwas, *Wilderness Wanderings*, 225.

51. Charles H. Long, *Significations: Signs, Symbols, and Images in the Interpretation of Religion* (Minneapolis: Fortress Press, 1986), 165.

52. Hauerwas, interview with author.

53. Hauerwas, interview with author.

54. Toni Morrison, "Unspeakable Things Unspoken: The Afro-American Presence in American Literature," in *The Black Feminist Reader*, ed. Joy James and T. Denean Sharpley-Whiting (Malden, MA: Blackwell, 2000), 11.

55. A charitable reader might argue that Hauerwas's long-standing aversion to universality itself precludes him from stepping into another's story. He worries that in accepting what he calls the "standard account" of universal and objective rationality, "we accept the odd position of viewing our stories as if they were anyone's or at least capable of being lived out by anyone" (Hauerwas, *Truthfulness and Tragedy: Further Investigations in Christian Ethics* (Notre Dame, IN: University of Notre Dame Press, 1977), 23). This sense that we float above the particular narratives of our histories and contexts and can simply dip into other's narratives as we choose reinforces his reservations about claiming the black story as his own.

56. James Baldwin, *Notes of a Native Son* (Boston: Beacon, 1955), 42.

57. James Baldwin, *No Name in the Street* (New York: Vintage, 1972), 165.

58. Alasdair MacIntyre famously defines a tradition as "an historically extended, socially embodied argument, and an argument precisely in part about the goods which constitute that tradition" (*After Virtue: A Study in Moral Theory*, 2nd ed. (Notre Dame, IN: Notre Dame University Press, 1984), 222).

59. Hauerwas often speaks of story in the singular—a tradition is constituted by its one, formative story—neglecting the ways multiple stories overlap and interact in the moral and communal development of an agent. Exceptions to this in his work include essays in *A Community of Character: Toward a Constructive Christian Social Ethic* (Notre Dame, IN: University of Notre Dame Press, 1981) and *Unleashing the Scriptures: Freeing the Bible from Captivity to America* (Nashville: Abingdon, 1993).

60. Alasdair MacIntyre, "Epistemological Crises, Dramatic Narrative, and the Philosophy of Science," in *Why Narrative? Readings in Narrative Theology*, ed. Stanley Hauerwas and L. Gregory Jones (Grand Rapids: Eerdmans, 1989): 146. Narrative is central to a tradition's understanding of itself and ability to negotiate problems and new encounters because it (1) provides a solution to previously intractable problems within a tradition, (2) furnishes a explanation of the problem, that is, what rendered the tradition incoherent, and (3) does so in a way that suggests the continuity of these new concepts and structures with the tradition's previous ones (MacIntyre, *Whose Justice? Which Rationality?* (Notre Dame, IN: Notre Dame University Press, 1989), 362). The phrase "tournament of narratives" comes from James William McClendon, *Ethics: Systematic Theology*, vol. 1 (Nashville: Abingdon, 2002), 149.

61. MacIntyre, *After Virtue*, xii. The moral inquirer of one tradition must uncover an epistemological crisis, or narrative incoherence, within another tradition: "The rational superiority of that tradition to rival traditions is held to reside in its capacity not only for identifying and characterizing the limitations and failures of that rival tradition as judged by that rival tradition's own standards, limitations, and failures which that rival tradition itself lacks the resources to explain or understand, but also for explaining and understanding those limitations and failures in some tolerably precise way" (MacIntyre, *Three Rival Versions of Moral Enquiry: Encyclopaedia, Genealogy, and Tradition* (Notre Dame, IN: University of Notre Dame Press, 1990), 181).

62. MacIntyre, *Three Rival Versions*, 5.

63. MacIntyre, *Three Rival Versions*, 81.

64. Willie Jennings, *The Christian Imagination* (New Haven, CT: Yale University Press, 2011), 83. See chapter 2 of this volume for a fuller account of this argument.

65. MacIntyre, of course, defines tradition as an ongoing internal argument of a community, suggesting the ability of traditions and communities to course-correct (*After Virtue*, 206; *Whose Justice? Which Rationality?*, 101). Yet European Christianity's failure to correct for its colonialist, racist logics calls this into question.

66. Jennings, *The Christian Imagination*, 107.

67. Willie Jennings, "The Traditions of Race Men," *South Atlantic Quarterly* 112, no. 4 (Fall 2013): 613–624, 616.

68. Ryan Andrew Newson attempts to soften this hypercompetitive description of MacIntyre in an effort to make him more palatable to critics like Jennings (see "Alasdair MacIntyre and Radically Dialogical Politics (*Political Theology* 17, no. 3 (2016): 243–263). Newson argues that MacIntyre's often-neglected later work in *Dependent Rational Animals* depicts a more sanguine MacIntyre. Here MacIntyre is more hopeful about cross-traditioned dialogue based on a recognition of our dependence on one another. Newson contends that the notion of tradition does not necessarily preclude constructive dialogue across diverse communities in search of a common good.

69. Stout, *Democracy and Tradition*, 179.

70. Stanley Hauerwas, *The Work of Theology* (Grand Rapids: Eerdmans, 2015), 5.

71. Hauerwas, *The Work of Theology*, 26.

72. MacIntyre, *Three Rival Versions*, 5.

73. Hauerwas, interview with the author.

74. For further critique of Hauerwas's agonistic, MacIntyrean understanding of narrative, see Healy, *Hauerwas*), 107

75. This fear and defensiveness were manifest in what Robert P. Jones calls the "death rattle" of white Christian America's handle on its position of power in the white, evangelical support of Donald Trump's election (see Jones, *The End of White Christian America* (New York: Simon & Schuster, 2016), and Jones, "The Rage of White Christian America," *New York Times*, November 10, 2016).

76. See Kathryn Tanner's alternative, pluralistic account of communities as the intersection of many formative stories in *Theories of Culture: A New Agenda for Theology* (Minneapolis: Fortress Press, 1997), 95, 98.

77. Baldwin, *Notes of a Native Son*, 21.

78. Emilie M. Townes, *Womanist Ethics and the Cultural Production of Evil* (New York: Palgrave Macmillan, 2006), 72.

79. For this "colony" mentality, see Stanley Hauerwas and William H. Willimon, *Resident Aliens: Life in the Christian Colony* (Nashville: Abingdon, 1989). For a criticism of this "battened-down-hatches" ecclesiology and its relationship to white supremacy, see Katie Walker Grimes, *Christ Divided: Antiblackness as Corporate Vice* (Minneapolis: Fortress, 2017).

80. James Logan, "Liberalism, Race, and Stanley Hauerwas," *CrossCurrents* 55, no. 4 (Winter 2006): 525.

81. Townes, *Womanist Ethics and the Cultural Production of Evil*, 113.

82. Karen Teel, "Whiteness in Catholic Theological Method," *Journal of the American Academy of Religion* 87, no. 2 (2019): 401–433, 406. A few theologians have accepted this task. Teel identifies whiteness in Catholic theology, Shawn Kelley investigates racism in the founding of modern biblical studies, and Tom Beaudoin

and Katherine Turpin unmask the ways the field of practical theology emerged within a white supremacist context and highlight characteristics of "white theology." See Teel, "Whiteness in Catholic Theological Method"; Shawn Kelley, *Racializing Jesus: Race, Ideology, and the Formation of Modern Biblical Scholarship* (New York: Routledge, 2002); and Tom Beaudoin and Katherine Turpin, "White Practical Theology," in *Opening the Field of Practical Theology*, ed. Kathleen A. Cahalan and Gordon S. Mikosi (Lanham, MD: Rowman & Littlefield, 2014), 251–269). Teel examines the triadic method of granting a general premise as self-evident, withholding particular relevant information, and then judging what information is relevant in order to determine the outcome of one's scholarship as indicative of white racist thinking in white theology. Similarly, Beaudoin and Turpin identify five characteristics of white theology: focus on the individual, belief in progress, promotion of white supremacy, value of orderliness, and assumption of meritocracy.

83. Hauerwas, *A Better Hope*, 142. For a similar argument from another white thinker, see Wendell Berry, *The Hidden Wound* (Berkeley, CA: Counterpoint, 1989).

84. Stanley Hauerwas, *The Character of Virtue: Letters to a Godson* (Grand Rapids: Eerdmans, 2018), 71. On this topic and referencing Hauerwas's memoir, James Logan adds, "Since Hauerwas does in fact appear to know that the habits of racism have been deeply written into the narrative of his own life, he ought to also know, then, that the story of 'the struggle' is as much *his* story as it was King's story" ("Liberalism, Race, and Stanley Hauerwas," *CrossCurrents* 55, no. 4 (Winter 2006): 525–526). Logan further claims, "King and Hauerwas were raised (from experientially different yet profoundly interrelated perspectives) deep within the story of corrupted racial intimacy" (527).

85. Hauerwas, *The Work of Theology*, 16.

86. Hauerwas, "Ethics of Black Power," 3.

87. Stanley Hauerwas, *The Peaceable Kingdom: A Primer in Christian Ethics* (Notre Dame, IN: University of Notre Dame Press, 1983), 1.

88. See Cone, *God of the Oppressed*, 14, 42–48.

89. Kathryn Tanner, *Theories of Culture: A New Agenda for Theology* (Minneapolis: Fortress, 1997), 95, 98.

90. Willis Jenkins, *The Future of Ethics: Sustainability, Social Justice, and Religious Creativity* (Washington, DC: Georgetown University Press, 2013), 101.

91. Healy, *Hauerwas*, 109.

CHAPTER 4

1. Michael Wurtham, interview with the author, Atlanta, GA, October 12, 2012.

2. Shanan Jones material comes from interviews with the author, Atlanta, GA, November 25, 2008, and October 12, 2012.

3. Raphael G. Warnock, *The Divided Mind of the Black Church: Theology, Piety, and Public Witness* (New York: New York University Press, 2014), 177.

4. James Cone, *God of the Oppressed* (Maryknoll, NY: Orbis Books, 1997), 52, emphasis added.

5. See James Evans, *We Have Been Believers: An African American Systematic Theology* (Minneapolis: Fortress, 1993), 7–8. He invokes the term "story-shaped" on pg. 29.

6. James Cone, "The Story Context of Black Theology," *Theology Today* 32, no. 2 (July 1975): 146.

7. Evans, *We Have Been Believers*, 8.

8. James Cone, *A Black Theology of Liberation* (Maryknoll, NY: Orbis Books, 1986), 11.

9. James Cone, interview with the author, New York, February 16, 2016, and April 12, 2016.

10. James Cone, *Said I Wasn't Gonna Tell Nobody* (Maryknoll, NY: Orbis Books, 2019), 35–36.

11. Cone, *Said I Wasn't Gonna Tell Nobody*, 97.

12. Cone, *Said I Wasn't Gonna Tell Nobody*, 39.

13. James Cone, *My Soul Looks Back* (Maryknoll, NY: Orbis Books, 2004), 18.

14. Cone, interview with the author.

15. Cone, *My Soul Looks Back*, 23.

16. Cone, "Story Context of Black Theology," 145.

17. See Richard Delgado, "Storytelling for Oppositionists and Others: A Plea for Narrative," *Michigan Law Review* 87 (1989): 2411–2441, and my discussion of story and counternarrative in chapter 1 of this volume.

18. Cone, *A Black Theology of Liberation*, 229.

19. James Cone, *Black Theology and Black Power* (Maryknoll: NY, Orbis Books, 1969), 63. Cone asserts that the contours of the church are not limited by ethnic or political boundaries; it "includes all who respond in faith to the redemptive act of God in Christ with a willingness to share in God's creative activity in the world" (65).

20. Cone, *A Black Theology of Liberation*, 230, 231, 232.

21. James Cone, *Speaking the Truth: Ecumenism, Liberation, and Black Theology* (Grand Rapids: Eerdmans, 1986), 123.

22. Cone, *Black Theology and Black Power*, 67. "If the Church is a continuation of the Incarnation, and if the Church and Christ are where the oppressed are," Cone writes, "then Christ and his Church must identify totally with the oppressed to the extent that they too suffer for the same reasons persons are enslaved" (69).

23. Cone, *Speaking the Truth*, 123.

24. James Cone, *For My People* (Maryknoll, NY: Orbis Books, 1986), 182. According to Cone, the gospel is "not in the abstract metaphysical world of reason which only theologians . . . and other privileged intellectuals inhabit" (Cone, "The Cry of Black Blood," Martin Luther King Lecture at Duke Divinity School, Durham, NC, April 1, 2015).

25. Cone, *For My People,* 181.

26. Cone, "Christian Faith and Political Praxis," *Encounter* 43, no. 2 (1982): 129–141, 130.

27. Cone, *A Black Theology of Liberation*, 22.

28. Cone, *A Black Theology of Liberation*, 85.

29. Cone, *Black Theology and Black Power*, 73.

30. Cone, *A Black Theology of Liberation*, 176.

31. Cone, *For My People*, 116.

32. Cone, interview with the author.

33. Cone, *For My People*, 99. The historical and social context of the black community formed many historically black churches into their own public communal spaces. Evelyn Brooks Higginbotham suggests that the lack of institutions open to African Americans necessitated that the black church become "the most logical institution for the pursuit of racial self-help ... an agency of social control, forum of discussion and debate, promoter of education and economic cooperation, and an arena for the development of leadership" (Higginbotham, *Righteous Discontent* (Cambridge: Harvard University Press, 1993), 7, 10, 5). Writing co-temporally with Cone's early work, Joseph Washington claims, "Negro churches are the only natural communities universal enough to command the loyalty and respect of the majority of Negro masses. They alone are so extensive as to form unity in political power" (Joseph R. Washington Jr., *The Politics of God: The Future of Black Churches* (Boston: Beacon, 1969), 201).

34. Cone, *Black Theology and Black Power*, 9.

35. Cone, *For My People*, 107.

36. In Cone's words, "The black church gradually became an instrument of escape instead of, as formerly, an instrument of protest" (*Black Theology and Black Power*, 104).

37. James Cone, *Martin and Malcolm and America: A Dream or a Nightmare?* (Maryknoll, NY: Orbis Books, 1991), 25.

38. Cone, *Black Theology and Black Power*, 105.

39. Cone, *Black Theology and Black Power*, 106.

40. James Cone, "Black Theology and the Black Church: Where Do We Go from Here?," *CrossCurrents* 27, no. 2 (Summer 1977): 147–156.

41. Cone, *Black Theology and Black Power*, 114.

42. Cone, *Said I Wasn't Gonna Tell Nobody*, 85.

43. Cone, *A Black Theology of Liberation*, 225.

44. Cone, *My Soul Looks Back*, 66.

45. Cone, *My Soul Looks Back*, 89.

46. Cone, *For My People*, 116.

47. Cone, "Story Context of Black Theology," 145.

48. Cone, "Story Context of Black Theology," 146.

49. Cone, "Story Context of Black Theology," 150.

50. James Cone, *The Spirituals and the Blues* (Maryknoll, NY: Orbis Books, 1972), 79. For more on "signifying," see Tim Sensing, "African American Preaching," *Journal of the American Academy of Ministry* 7 (Winter/Spring 2001): 38–53, as well as the classic text by Henry Louis Gates Jr., *The Signifying Monkey: A Theory of African-American Literary Criticism* (New York: Oxford University Press, 1988).

51. Andrew Prevot, *Thinking Prayer: Theology and Spirituality amid the Crisis of Modernity* (Notre Dame, IN: University of Notre Dame Press, 2015), 293.

52. Cone, "Story Context of Black Theology," 149, 150. These claims resonate with Hauerwas's insistence that "the test of each story is the sort of person it shapes" (Hauerwas, *Truthfulness and Tragedy: Further Investigations in Christian Ethics* (Notre Dame, IN: University of Notre Dame Press, 1977), 35).

53. Evans, *We Have Been Believers*, 30.

54. Cone, "Story Context of Black Theology," 147.

55. Cone, *God of the Oppressed*, 40, 38.

56. Cone, *For My People*, 148, quoting Gustavo Gutiérrez, *The Power of the Poor in History* (Maryknoll, NY: Orbis Books, 1983), 90–91.

57. Cone, *God of the Oppressed*, 126.

58. Cone, "The Cry of Black Blood."

59. Cone, *God of the Oppressed*, 15.

60. James Cone, *The Cross and the Lynching Tree* (Maryknoll, NY: Orbis Books, 2010), 150.

61. Reflecting on this shift, he writes, "In [*The Spirituals and the Blues*] I began my journey back home. . . . I wanted to wash my theology in the blood of my people. To write an authentic black liberation theology I would have to let the blood of the people speak" ("The Cry of Black Blood").

62. Cone, *Said I Wasn't Gonna Tell Nobody*, 41.

63. Cone, *God of the Oppressed*, 17, 29. In this vein, he lists the sources of black theology as black experience, black history, black culture, revelation, and Scripture.

64. Kelly Brown Douglas, *The Black Christ* (Maryknoll, NY: Orbis Books, 1994), 83.

65. Several of Cone's early critics, including his brother Cecil, levied this charge, leading to this shift in his sources (see Cecil Cone, *The Identity Crisis in Black Theology* (Nashville: AMEC Press, 1975), 142; Albert Cleage, *Black Christian Nationalism: New Directions for the Black Church* (New York: William Morrow, 1972); and Gayraud Wilmore, *Black Religion and Black Radicalism: An Interpretation of the Religious History of Afro-American People* (Maryknoll, NY: Orbis Books, 1983), 217–218). Critiques of his continued debt to white theologians or European models of theology have also arisen from black theologians focusing on the dismissal of African religion in black theology, other black theologians arguing that his concept of blackness is bound to whiteness, and womanist theologians highlighting the neglect of black women's experience. I attend to the latter two types of criticism later in this chapter.

66. Cone, *Said I Wasn't Gonna Tell Nobody*, 94.

67. Cone, *Said I Wasn't Gonna Tell Nobody*, 15.

68. Cone, *The Spirituals and the Blues*, 4.

69. Cone, *For My People*, 173.

70. A tension between the particular and the universal is present in Cone's thought, as is evident in some of his intentionally paradoxical observations, such as, "God's universal will [is] to liberate particular oppressed people" (Cone, *God of the Oppressed*,

135). But it is also true in his claims. While insisting on the particularity, even contextual and communal limits, of all theological claims, Cone himself makes universal claims—the claim that all theology is particular is itself a universal claim. For now I only want to observe this tension; I return to it in more depth later in the chapter.

71. Cone, *A Black Theology of Liberation*, 202.

72. Cone, *A Black Theology of Liberation*, 219. Cf. Bonhoeffer, *Dietrich Bonhoeffer Works (English)* (hereafter *DBWE*), vol. 8: *Letters and Papers from Prison*, ed. John W. de Gruchy, trans. Reinhard Krauss, Nancy Lukens, Lisa E. Dahill, and Isabel Best (Minneapolis: Fortress, 2010), 362.

73. Cone, *Black Theology and Black Power*, 68. Cone was certainly not the first to make this claim. A few earlier references in American history were Robert Alexander Young in his 1829 *Ethiopian Manifesto*; Henry McNeal Turner, who called God a "Negro" in an 1898 speech; and, of course, Countee Cullen in his 1928 poem titled "The Black Christ."

74. Bonhoeffer, *DBWE* 8:362.

75. Cone, "The Cry of Black Blood." In his posthumously published memoir, Cone claims that he writes "on behalf of all those whom the Salvadoran theologian and martyr Ignacio Ellacuría called the 'crucified peoples of history'" (Cone, *Said I Wasn't Gonna Tell Nobody*, 132).

76. Cone, *A Black Theology of Liberation*, 27, 28.

77. Cone, "The Cry of Black Blood."

78. Cone, *A Black Theology of Liberation*, 214.

79. Cone, *A Black Theology of Liberation*, 204.

80. Cone, *God of the Oppressed*, 109.

81. Cone, *Black Theology and Black Power*, 69.

82. Cone, *God of the Oppressed*, 134. According to James Evans, for Cone, "blackness is a symbol in the Tillichian sense of the term; that is, it both points to and participates in a reality outside itself" (Evans, *We Have Been Believers*, 103).

83. Evans, *We Have Been Believers*, 103–104.

84. Cone, *Black Theology and Black Power*, 120. Cone's was not the only version of the black Christ, and therefore of blackness, in early black theology. Albert Cleage contended that Jesus was ethnically black, constructing an argument from genealogical data (*The Black Messiah* (Kansas City: Sheed and Ward, 1969). J. Deotis Roberts offered a more universal image of the Black Christ, arguing that Christ comes to everyone in their own context, so Christ is black for black people, white for white people (*Liberation and Reconciliation: A Black Theology* (Philadelphia: Westminster Press, 1971), and Roberts, *Black Political Theology* (Philadelphia: Westminster Press, 1974)). For a comparative assessment of all three versions of the black Christ, see Douglas, *The Black Christ*, 53–77.

85. Victor Anderson, *Beyond Ontological Blackness: An Essay in African American Religious and Cultural Criticism* (New York: Continuum, 1995), 11.

86. Anderson, *Beyond Ontological Blackness*, 14.

87. Anderson, *Beyond Ontological Blackness*, 103. J. Deotis Roberts consistently challenged Cone's concept of blackness, concerned that Christ not be overidentified with a particular group. Roberts worried that Cone's black theology simply replicated the Christological captivity of white theology's blond-haired, blue-eyed Christ (Roberts, *Black Political Theology* (Philadelphia: Westminster Press, 1974), 119).

88. Bantam also contends that Cone "distill[s] the totality of Jesus' person and ministry into the negotiation of a politically oppressive reality" in such a way that "Jesus' redemptive work is overwhelmed by Cone's experiential framework" (Bantam, *Redeeming Mulatto: A Theology of Race and Christian Hybridity* (Waco, TX: Baylor University Press, 2010), 5, 4).

89. Anderson, *Beyond Ontological Blackness*, 92.

90. Anderson, *Beyond Ontological Blackness*, 91. Cone responds to this charge by critiquing his own early writings for emerging out of a negative reaction to whites rather than a positive reaction to the self-determination of the black community (Cone, *For My People*, 87).

91. Anderson, *Beyond Ontological Blackness*, 117. Also, "Black theology constructs its new being on the dialectical structures that categorical racism and white racial ideology bequeathed [it]" (87). Anderson asks, "At what point do thriving and flourishing enter the equation of suffering and resistance? An existence that is bound existentially only by the dimensions of struggle and resistance or survival, it seems to me, constitutes a less than fulfilling human existence. We all want more than to survive: that is a minimal requirement of a fulfilled life. We also want to thrive and flourish" (112).

92. J. Kameron Carter, *Race: A Theological Account* (New York: Oxford University Press, 2008), 171.

93. Carter, *Race*, 190.

94. Delores Williams, *Sisters in the Wilderness: The Challenge of Womanist God-Talk* (Maryknoll, NY: Orbis Books, 1993), 243.

95. Jacquelyn Grant, "Black Theology and the Black Woman," in *Black Theology: A Documentary History*, vol. 1: *1966–1979*, ed. Gayraud Wilmore and James Cone (Maryknoll, NY: Orbis Books, 1979), 418–433.

96. Williams, *Sisters in the Wilderness*, 40.

97. Kelly Brown Douglas, "Womanist Theology: What Is Its Relationship to Black Theology?," in Wilmore and Cone, *Black Theology*, 1:295.

98. M. Shawn Copeland, "Race," in *Blackwell Companion to Modern Theology*, ed. Gareth Jones (Malden, MA: Blackwell, 2012), 508, and Copeland, *Enfleshing Freedom: Body, Race, and Being* (Minneapolis: Fortress, 2009), 8.

99. Cone admits that he oscillates between referring to *blackness* and *whiteness* in literal and symbolic ways, yet claims he does this intentionally as a disruptive force to the way race is often employed in reductionistic modes in racial discourse (Cone, interview with the author).

100. Timothy, "Against (White) Redemption: James Cone and the Christological Disruption of Racial Discourse and White Solidarity," *Political Theology* (January 2017): 550. McGee lays out a fourfold index of Cone's usage of racial terms: blackness and whiteness as identifying characteristics, historical experience, identification, and representative symbol (548).

101. A synecdoche functions as a metonym, representing a larger concept or entity while directing attention to the crucial characteristic of that larger concept. (For metonyms, see George Lakoff and Mark Johnson, *Metaphors We Live By* (Chicago: University of Chicago Press, 1980), 37–38).

102. James Cone, "Why God Is Black: All Together Podcast Featuring Dr. James Cone," interview by Paul Rauschenbusch, *All Together*, HuffPost Religion, January 16, 2015, https://www.huffpost.com/entry/god-is-black-james-cone_n_6487012.

103. Douglas, *The Black Christ*, 58. See Robinson B. James, "A Tillichian Analysis of James Cone's Black Theology," *Perspectives in Religious Studies* 1 (1974): 15–28.

104. Cone, *A Black Theology of Liberation*, 20th anniversary ed., (Maryknoll, NY: Orbis Books, 1990), 204n5. As Kelly Brown Douglas notes, "Cone's version of the Black Christ is not exclusive. All people, Black and White, can receive salvation from Christ if they accept the challenge to meet Christ in the struggle for freedom" (Douglas, *The Black Christ*, 77).

105. Cone, "Why God Is Black."

106. Cone, *Black Theology and Black Power,* 151.

107. Cone, *A Black Theology of Liberation*, 124. In his call for whites to become black Cone seems to be drawing on a tension that James Baldwin noted: "The white man's unadmitted—and apparently, to him, unspeakable—private fears and longings are projected onto the Negro. The only way he can be released from the Negro's tyrannical power over him is to consent, in effect, to become black himself" (Baldwin, *The Fire Next Time* (New York: Vintage, 1962), 96).

108. Cone, *Black Theology and Black Power*, 150.

109. Cone, *God of the Oppressed*, 217.

110. Prevot, *Thinking Prayer*, 323.

111. McGee, "Against (White) Redemption," 557.

112. James Cone and William Horden, "Dialogue on Black Theology," *Christian Century*, September 15, 1971, 1085; cited in McGee, "Against (White) Redemption," 555.

113. Renee Leslie Hill, "Disrupted/Disruptive Moments: Black Theology and Black Power 1969/1999," in *Black Faith and Public Talk: Critical Essays on James Cone's Black Theology and Black Power*, ed. Dwight N. Hopkins (Maryknoll, NY: Orbis Books, 1999), 140.

114. Prevot, *Thinking Prayer*, 310.

115. Cone, "Story Context of Black Theology," 145.

116. Cone, "Story Context of Black Theology," 146.

117. Cone, "Story Context of Black Theology," 150.

118. Cone, "Story Context of Black Theology," 149, 150.

119. This understanding of Cone's ideal of blackness closely follows the way M. Shawn Copeland describes racial formation in *Enfleshing Freedom* and her short article, "Race," in the *Blackwell Companion to Modern Theology*. For her, race is both a socially structured phenomenon and an objectification of fleshly realities that result in bodily enacted white domination.

120. Cone, *A Black Theology of Liberation*, New, revised ed. (1997), 144n5.

121. Copeland, *Race*, 15. Willie Jennings applies this concept to whiteness, claiming that it "must be analyzed not simply as substantiation of European hegemonic gestures but more precisely in its identity-facilitating characteristics, its judgment-constituting features, and its global deployments of embodied visions of the true, the good, and the beautiful" (*The Christian Imagination* (New Haven, CT: Yale University Press, 2011), 290).

122. Linda Martín Alcoff, *Visible Identities: Race, Gender, and the Self* (New York: Oxford University Press, 2006), 102.

123. Copeland notes that, generally, the darker your skin tone, the less you earn, the shorter your lifespan, the poorer your health, the more likely you are to be incarcerated or a refugee (*Enfleshing Freedom*, 67).

124. Cone, *Black Theology and Black Power*, 147–148.

125. Jacquelyn Grant, *White Women's Christ and Black Women's Jesus: Feminist Christology and Womanist Response* (Atlanta: Scholars Press, 1989), 202, referencing Anna Cooper, *A Voice from the South by a Black Woman of the South* (Xenia, OH, 1892).

126. Evans, *We Have Been Believers*, 30.

127. Evans, *We Have Been Believers*, 30.

128. Robert McAfee Brown, "My Story and 'The Story,'" *Theology Today* 32, no. 2 (1975): 166–173, 172; cited in Evans, *We Have Been Believers*, 31.

129. James Logan, *Good Punishment?: Christian Moral Practice and U.S. Imprisonment* (Grand Rapids: Eerdmans, 2008), 222.

130. Mary McClintock Fulkerson and Martha Mount Shoop, *A Body Broken, A Body Betrayed: Race, Memory, and Eucharist in White-Dominated Churches* (Eugene, OR: Cascade Books, 2015), 14.

131. Cone, interview with the author.

132. This claim resonates with the experience of Willie Jennings, who laments "the resistance of theologians to think *theologically* about their [own] identities" (*The Christian Imagination,* 7).

133. James W. Perkinson, *White Theology: Outing Supremacy in Modernity* (New York: Palgrave Macmillan, 2004), 28. He adds, "Although Cone is careful to clarify that blackness is not itself a marker of innocence, but rather of the kind of condition a God of the oppressed chooses to occupy with incarnate flesh and spirit: black people can still sin and betray their calling, but black culture and

suffering, on the current landscape of race, are a privileged place of encounter with the God of the least" (28–29).

134. Perkinson, *White Theology*, 29.

135. Perkinson, *White Theology*, 29.

136. Cone, *Black Theology and Black Power*, 150.

137. Judith Butler, *Frames of War: When Is Life Grievable?* (Brooklyn, NY: Verso, 2009), 170.

138. Cone, "The Cry of Black Blood."

139. Cone, interview with the author.

140. Cone, *God of the Oppressed*, 222. In *God of the Oppressed*, he allows that this conversion event is indeed rare (221).

141. Cone, *God of the Oppressed*, 242–243.

142. Cone, *God of the Oppressed*, 221; Alan Richardson, *A Theological Word Book of the Bible* (New York: Macmillan, 1960), 191. According to Prevot, "Cone contends that this conversion to a practically embodied black spirituality is not only necessary but also nearly sufficient to bring about genuine fellowship among white and black people" (*Thinking Prayer*, 321).

CHAPTER 5

1. Frederick Douglass, *Narrative of the Life of Frederick Douglass, An American Slave* (Boston: Anti-Slavery Office, 1835).

2. Jonathan Tran, "Moral Innovation and Ambiguity in Asian American Christianity," *Theology Today* 75, no. 3 (2018): 347–357, 357.

3. Kelly Brown Douglas, *What's Faith Got to Do with It? Black Bodies / Christian Souls* (Maryknoll, NY: Orbis Books, 2005), xiii.

4. Tran, "Moral Innovation and Ambiguity," 356.

5. Tran, "Moral Innovation and Ambiguity," 357.

6. James Cone, *For My People* (Maryknoll, NY: Orbis Books, 1986), 203.

7. James Cone, interview with the author, New York, February 16, 2016, and April 12, 2016.

8. James Cone, *God of the Oppressed* (Maryknoll, NY: Orbis Books, 1997), 216–217.

9. Michael Lipka, "Many U.S. Congregations Are Still Racially Segregated, but Things Are Changing," Pew Research Center, December 8, 2014, www.pewresearch.org/fact-tank/2014/12/08/many-u-s-congregations-are-still-racially-segregated-but-things-are-changing).

10. Alexis de Tocqueville, *Democracy in America,* trans. Gerald E. Bevan (1835; New York: Penguin Books, 2003), 339–352. Tocqueville claimed that this indirect influence of religion—its shaping of mores within families and like-minded communities—signaled the principal political impact of religion, enough to cause him to claim religion as America's first political institution. For a

contemporary account of congregations as echo chambers, see Robert D. Putnam and David E. Campbell, *American Grace: How Religion Divides and Unites Us* (New York: Simon and Schuster, 2012).

11. For more on specific church practices that may contribute to the implicit racial prejudice that white churches often perpetuate, see Mary McClintock Fulkerson and Martha Mount Shoop, *A Body Broken, A Body Betrayed: Race, Memory and Eucharist in White-Dominated Churches* (Eugene, OR: Cascade Books, 2015), 37–53.

12. Jennifer Harvey, *Dear White Christians: For Those Still Longing for Racial Reconciliation* (Grand Rapids: Eerdmans, 2014).

13. Harvey, *Dear White Christians*, 19.

14. Barbara Ransby, *Ella Baker and the Black Freedom Movement: A Radical Democratic Vision* (Chapel Hill: University of North Carolina Press, 2003), 319.

15. Ransby, *Ella Baker and the Black Freedom Movement*, 319–320.

16. Michael O. Emerson and Christian Smith, *Divided by Faith: Evangelical Religion and the Problem of Race in America* (New York: Oxford University Press, 2000), 76, 77.

17. Emerson and Smith, *Divided by Faith*, 76–77.

18. For more on the need for racially exclusive places for minorities, see Beverly Tatum, *Why Are All the Black Kids Sitting Together in the Cafeteria? And Other Conversations about Race* (New York: Basic Books, 2007).

19. Gerardo Marti, *A Mosaic of Believers: Diversity and Innovation in a Multiethnic Church* (Bloomington: Indiana University Press, 2005).

20. See Korie L. Edwards, *The Elusive Dream: The Power of Race in Interracial Churches* (Oxford: Oxford University Press, 2008); Penny Edgell Becker, "Making Inclusive Communities: Congregations and the 'Problem' of Race," *Social Problems* 45, no. 4 (1998): 451–472; Kathleen E. Jenkins, "Intimate Diversity: The Presentation of Multiculturalism and Multiracialism in a High-Boundary Religious Movement," *Journal for the Scientific Study of Religion* 42, no. 3 (2003): 393–409; Gregory C. Stanczak, "Strategic Ethnicity: The Construction of Multi-Racial/Multi-Ethnic Religious Community," *Ethnic and Racial Studies* 29, no. 5 (2006): 856–881; and Brad Christerson, Korie L. Edwards, and Michael O. Emerson, *Against All Odds* (New York: New York University Press, 2005).

21. Evelyn Brooks Higginbotham, *Righteous Discontent: The Women's Movement in the Black Baptist Church, 1880–1920* (Cambridge, MA: Harvard University Press, 1993), 7, 10, 5. See also Mary Patillo-McCoy, "Church Culture as a Strategy of Action in the Black Community," *American Sociological Review* 63 (1998): 767–784.

22. Harvey, *Dear White Christians*, 60.

23. Ta-Nehisi Coates, *Between the World and Me* (New York: Spiegel and Grau, 2015), 103.

24. Ta-Nehisi Coates, "The Case for Reparations," *The Atlantic*, June 2014, www.theatlantic.com/magazine/archive/2014/06/the-case-for-reparations.

25. Coates, *Between the World*, 115.

26. Coates, *Between the World*, 151. For another example, a 2016 *Washington Post* opinion piece, during the height of the Black Lives Matter movement, argued that the time has come for black people to stop talking to whites about race altogether. Poet Zack Linly wrote, "We need to stop arguing with them because, in the end, they aren't invested like we are." He contends that attempting to educate white people will ultimately prove fruitless because "they've gone their whole lives being the default for social and cultural normalcy and never really had to think critically about race at all" (Linly, "It's Time to Stop Talking about Racism with White People," *Washington Post*, September 7, 2016, www.washingtonpost.com/posteverything/ wp/2016/09/07/its-time-to-stop-talking-about-racism-with-white-people).

27. Robin DiAngelo similarly observes, "Universalism assumes that whites and people of color have the same realities, the same experiences in the same contexts, . . . the same responses from others, and assumes that the same doors are open to all" ("White Fragility," *International Journal of Critical Pedagogy* 3, no. 3 (2011): 59).

28. Harvey, *Dear White Christians*, 59.

29. Harvey, *Dear White Christians*, 77.

30. James Cone, *Black Theology and Black Power* (Maryknoll, NY: Orbis Books, 1969), 144.

31. Cone, *Black Theology and Black Power*, 145.

32. The concept of reconciliation may one day prove retrievable, but as Willie Jennings writes, "Before we theologians can interpret the depths of the divine action of reconciliation we must first articulate the profound deformities of Christian intimacy and identity in modernity" (Jennings, *Christian Imagination* (New Haven, CT: Yale University Press, 2010), 10).

33. See, for example, popular Christian author Jim Wallis's *America's Original Sin: Racism, White Privilege, and the Bridge to a New America* (Grand Rapids: Brazos, 2016).

34. James Cone, *Said I Wasn't Gonna Tell Nobody* (Maryknoll, NY: Orbis Books, 2018), 18.

35. Ryan Andrew Newson, *Inhabiting the World: Identity, Politics, and Theology in Radical Baptist Perspective* (Macon, GA: Mercer University Press, 2018), 131.

36. Newson, *Inhabiting the World*, 132.

37. Reinhold Niebuhr, *Nature and Destiny of Man,* vol. 1 (1939; Louisville, KY: Westminster John Knox Press, 1996), 178.

38. Niebuhr, *Nature and Destiny of Man*, 181.

39. Marjorie Suchocki, *The Fall to Violence: Original Sin in Relational Theology* (New York: Continuum, 1994), 84. She does this for several reasons, most importantly that identifying anxiety as the root cause of sin limits sin to "pride" in Niebuhr's work. This overlooks the central role of violence in human behavior and needlessly vilifies many positive aspects of anxiety (83), which is not far from Hauerwas's account of original sin. According to him, rebellion against God, in order to know good from evil and control our own destiny, was the direct

cause of enmity and alienation (Hauerwas, *The Peaceable Kingdom* (Notre Dame, IN: University of Notre Dame Press, 1983), 46–49).

40. Suchocki contends that an innate aggression precedes anxiety and violence precedes pride. But if violence emerges as a means to survival, as she argues, then it seems this violence is also related to a concern over finitude. I think we should have no problem seeing in our present context how propensities toward both violence and anxiety present themselves as root causes of racism. Surely anxiety over human finitude causes violence over resources, *and* violence causes more anxiety. The point of human transcendence, at which Suchocki says violence becomes sin, is also the point at which she says anxiety is present (*Fall to Violence*, 98). All of this is to say, I think Suchocki and Niebuhr converge to produce mutually enhancing accounts. Though Suchocki's account is grounded in relational/process theology, I don't think one needs to ascribe to all aspects of process theology to appreciate this account.

41. In his fascinating book *Sapiens*, historian Yuval Noah Harari argues that, with a few genetic exceptions, *Homo sapiens* replaced other *Homo* (human) groups as they expanded out of East Africa around seventy thousand years ago. At that time, "They drove the Neanderthals and all other human species not only from the Middle East, but from the face of the earth" (*Sapiens: A Brief History of Humankind* (New York: HarperCollins, 2015), 21). Noting that "tolerance is not a Sapiens trademark," Harari insists that whether due to incompatibility, environmental factors, or genocide, "no sooner had [Sapiens] arrived at a new location than the native [human] population became extinct" (18). In line with Suchocki's account, Harari ponders whether the *Homo sapiens'* encounter with Neanderthals resulted in "the first and most significant ethnic-cleansing campaign in history" (18).

42. Walter Rauschenbusch, *A Theology for the Social Gospel* (1917; Nashville: Abingdon, 1996), 60.

43. Suchocki, *Fall to Violence*, 113.

44. Erin Kidd, "The Subject of Conceptual Mapping: Theological Anthropology across Brain, Body, and World," *Open Theology* 4 (2018): 133. Again, for the science behind these claims, see the work of Andy Clark and David Chalmers, or of philosopher George Lakoff.

45. Rauschenbusch, *Theology for the Social Gospel*, 61.

46. Suchocki, *Fall to Violence*, 118.

47. Suchocki, *Fall to Violence*, 109.

48. Cone, *God of the Oppressed*, 201. In *Beyond Apathy*, Elizabeth Vasko similarly claims that violence touches every human being in ways that prevent bystanders from claiming innocence (Vasko, *Beyond Apathy: A Theology for Bystanders* (Minneapolis: Fortress, 2015)). Anna Floerke Scheid helpfully distinguishes between three types of violence—degrading violence, structural violence, and assault violence—in *Just Revolution: A Christian Ethic of Political Resistance and Social Transformation* (New York: Lexington Books, 2015), lamenting that theological attention to violence is often limited to what she calls "assault" violence,

ignoring the other equally harmful forms. Finally, Saidiya Hartmen offers a chilling account of the ways violence can also appear in the form of empathy, silence, absence, or benevolence—especially when it involves racial systems (Hartman, *Scenes of Subjection: Terror, Slavery, and Self-Making in Nineteenth-Century America* (Oxford: Oxford University Press, 1997)).

49. William Stringfellow, *An Ethic for Christians and Other Aliens in a Strange Land* (Eugene, OR: Wipf and Stock, 2004), 129.

50. Suchocki, *Fall to Violence*, 123.

51. Kidd, "The Subject of Conceptual Mapping," 133.

52. M. Shawn Copeland, "Overcoming Christianity's Lingering Complicity," In the Shadow of Charleston: Politics, Religion, and White Supremacy: *Syndicate Theology* (2015), www.syndicate.network/symposia/theology/in-the-shadow-of-charleston.

53. This aversion to universal rationality lies at the core of both Hauerwas's and Cone's commitment to a distinctive communal vision of theological and ethical formation and activism—their respective ecclesiologies. Hauerwas laments the modern temptation to "demand a universal standpoint so that the self may reach a point from which it can judge and choose objectively among competing particularistic stories" (*The Hauerwas Reader*, ed. John Berkman and Michael Cartwright (Durham, NC: Duke University Press, 2001), 250). Hauerwas repeatedly criticizes modernity's attempt to produce a people who believe "they have no story except the story they chose when they thought they had no story." He goes on to say that this results in the false belief that "we should be held responsible only for the things we freely chose when we knew what we were doing" (Hauerwas and Jean Varnier, *Living Gently in a Violent World: The Prophetic Witness of Weakness* (Downers Grove, IL: InterVarsity Press, 2008), 92). Likewise, Cone insists that all human inquiries into truth—like theology—must begin with "the human situation as perceived from a particular standpoint of a given people" as its point of departure (Cone, *For My People*, 172).

54. Sean Larsen, "How I Think Hauerwas Thinks about Theology," *Scottish Journal of Theology* 69, no. 1 (2016): 27.

55. Walter D. Mignolo, *The Darker Side of Western Modernity: Global Futures, Decolonial Options* (Durham, NC: Duke University Press, 2011), 100.

56. Dietrich Bonhoeffer, *Performing the Faith: Dietrich Bonhoeffer and the Practice of Nonviolence* (Grand Rapids: Brazos, 2004).

57. Cone, *Black Theology and Black Power* and *Said I Wasn't Gonna Tell Nobody*. In the latter work, Cone references Bonhoeffer's notion of cheap grace as a way to understand white Christians' reluctance to see the cross as a symbol of liberation and political resistance (135). Cone's appeals to Bonhoeffer remain consistent and frequent throughout his entire career: citing him six times in *A Black Theology of Liberation*, twice in *God of the Oppressed*, once in *Martin and Malcolm and America*, and four times in *The Cross and the Lynching Tree*—and not one of these references is negative. Bonhoeffer's account of cheap and costly grace constitutes an essential theological framework for Cone's work.

58. James Cone, *A Black Theology of Liberation* (New York: J.P. Lippencott Co., 1970), 28.

59. One must be careful when making any comparison to the context of Nazi Germany or appealing to that context for guidance for one's own. I link carefully the two contexts of Third Reich/Holocaust and American white supremacy. As historian Victoria Barnett rightly cautions, the temptation to make quick comparisons to Nazi Germany "may deflect attention from the very American roots of much of what we are seeing" (Collegeville Institute, "Theology in Uncertain Times: An Interview with Bonhoeffer Scholar Victoria J. Barnett," *Bearings Online*, July 17, 2018, collegevilleinstitute.org/bearings/theology-in-uncertain-times). This comparison does not take anything away from the particular history and story of white supremacy and the way it has taken particular forms in the American context. Theologian Beverly Mitchell has demonstrated the connections and commonalities between the Holocaust and chattel slavery in *Plantations and Death Camps: Religion, Ideology, and Human Dignity* (Minneapolis: Fortress, 2009). Because both contexts are rooted in Christian supersessionism, Shawn Copeland argues that "the memory of the Jewish Jesus and the memory of the black (chattel) body coalesce as memories of a past that is not over, that must be encountered and confronted in the here" (Copeland, *Knowing Christ Crucified: The Witness of African American Religious Experience* (Maryknoll, NY: Orbis Books, 2018), 97).

60. James Cone, *The Cross and the Lynching Tree* (Maryknoll, NY: Orbis Books, 2010), 42, 47, 157.

61. Dietrich Bonhoeffer, *Dietrich Bonhoeffer Works (English)* (hereafter *DBWE*), vol. 10: *Barcelona, Berlin, New York, 1928–1931*, ed. Clifford J. Green, trans. Douglas W. Stott (Minneapolis: Fortress, 2008), 360, 373.

62. See Reggie Williams, *Bonhoeffer's Black Jesus: Harlem Renaissance Theology and an Ethic of Resistance* (Waco, TX: Baylor University Press, 2014).

63. Williams, *Bonhoeffer's Black Jesus*, 23.

64. Williams, *Bonhoeffer's Black Jesus*, 22, and Bonhoeffer, *DBWE* 10:265. He even identified his friendship with African Americans the "most important" event of his stay in America. He witnessed the moral failings of the church during a road trip through the southern United States, commenting that the way southerners treated African Americans was "repugnant," and adding, "and the pastors are no better than the others" (Charles Marsh, *Strange Glory: A Life of Dietrich Bonhoeffer* (New York: Alfred A. Knopf, 2016), 115, 133).

65. Williams, *Bonhoeffer's Black Jesus*, 78, 81, 26.

66. Bonhoeffer, *DBWE*, vol. 8: *Letters and Papers from Prison*, ed. John W. de Gruchy, trans. Reinhard Krauss, Nancy Lukens, Lisa E. Dahill, and Isabel Best (Minneapolis: Fortress, 2010), 58 (from an April 22, 1944, letter to Eberhard Bethge).

67. Williams, *Bonhoeffer's Black Jesus*, 98. Gary Dorrien also observes Powell's influence on Bonhoeffer. He records that Powell often focused his sermons on the

sermons of Jesus in the Gospels, especially his social justice–minded passages like Matthew 25, and also on Jesus's pacifistic love ethic, frequently heralding heroes like Gandhi. All of these themes played a large part in Bonhoeffer's writing after his return to Germany (Dorrien, *The New Abolition: W. E. B. Du Bois and the Black Social Gospel* (New Haven, CT: Yale University Press, 2015), 440–441). Miguel de la Torre claims that Bonhoeffer's famous notion of "cheap grace" originated with Powell (*Embracing Hopelessness* (Minneapolis: Fortress Press, 2017), 114).

68. Bonhoeffer, "After Ten Years," in *DBWE* 8:52.

69. Cone, *Said I Wasn't Gonna Tell Nobody*, 10.

70. Bonhoeffer, *DBWE*, vol. 1, *Sanctorum Communion,* ed. Clifford J. Green, trans. Reinhard Krauss and Nancy Lukens (Minneapolis: Fortress, 1998), 150.

71. Vasko, *Beyond Apathy*, 18. She continues, "Often white guilt depends upon the fear or stigmatization of being called a racist instead of the moral impetus to acknowledge harm done, make reparations, and work toward structural change" (107).

72. Robin DiAngelo, *White Fragility: Why It's So Hard for White People to Talk about Racism* (Boston: Beacon Press, 2018), 135. I noticed as I was workshopping this chapter that white readers of this section appreciated this take on guilt and readers of color were often split over it. Many of the latter agreed with my tactical choice and shared my concern that white guilt immobilizes action. But others worried that disavowing "guilt" failed to challenge the affective dimension of white supremacy—white people ought to feel shame for our history of white supremacy and our current participation in it. I share this worry and wrestled with this section, leaving it to each reader to judge.

73. Jennifer McBride, *The Church for the World: A Theology of Public Witness* (New York: Oxford University Press, 2011), 9.

74. Dietrich Bonhoeffer, *DBWE*, vol. 6: *Ethics*, ed. Clifford J. Green, trans. Reinhard Krauss, Charles C. West, and Douglas W. Stott (Minneapolis: Fortress, 2005), 134–145.

75. Bernd Wannenwetsch, "'Responsible Living' or 'Responsible Self'? Bonhoefferian Reflections on a Vexed Moral Notion," *Studies in Christian Ethics* 18, no. 3 (2005): 125–140, 133.

76. For Reinhold, responsibility was the appropriate action resulting from moral calculation among any number of inevitably flawed options; for him, responsibility in a sinful world emerged out of social conflict. "All responsibility," he wrote, "is exercised in a field where partial and fragmentary values are supported against contending forces, and the ultimate exercise of responsibility may involve the guilt of the destruction of life" (Reinhold Niebuhr, *Our Moral and Spiritual Resources for International Cooperation*, US Department of State Publication 6230, February 1956, 23; cited in Robin Lovin, "Reinhold Niebuhr and Dietrich Bonhoeffer on Responsibility," in *Engaging Bonhoeffer: The Influence and Impact of Bonhoeffer's Life and Thought*, ed. Matthew D. Kirkpatrick (Minneapolis: Fortress Press, 2016), 58, 63).

77. H. Richard Niebuhr, *The Responsible Self: An Essay in Christian Moral Philosophy* (New York: Harper and Row, 1963), 64.

78. Cone, interview with the author.

79. Bonhoeffer, *DBWE* 8:388.

80. Wannenwetsch, "'Responsible Living' or 'Responsible Self'?," 138. Likewise, as Jennifer McBride contends, "Unlike the social ethics of Reinhold Niebuhr, in which there is 'eternal conflict between the necessities of historical action and the ethic of Jesus,' Bonhoeffer's ethic of Christological conformation 'is not crushed by conflicts of principle'" (McBride, *The Church for the World*, 142; referencing Bonhoeffer, *DBWE* 6:229, 238).

81. Bonhoeffer, *DBWE* 8:362.

82. I mentioned earlier that Hauerwas, while indebted to Bonhoeffer, repudiates an ethic based on actions that are deemed "responsible" (Hauerwas, *Peaceable Kingdom*, especially pp. 135–151). Yet Hauerwas seems to allow the Niebuhrs' versions of responsibility as reasonableness to spoil the term (as well as speculation that it is meant to justify violence). Hauerwas does not engage or directly critique Bonhoeffer's concept; he simply ignores it. If he were to engage, I think he would find a concept compatible with his own ethical vision. For Bonhoeffer, responsibility is not reasonableness, but "consists above all in a response, shaped by the concrete, historical relationships and encounters in which we find ourselves" (Guide de Graaff, "Overcoming Ethical Abstraction: Peaceableness, Responsibility, and the Rejection of Foundationalism in Bonhoeffer and Hauerwas," in Kirkpatrick, *Engaging Bonhoeffer*, 92). It is a concept that grows out of Bonhoeffer's Christology, determined by how Christ is taking form in the world, not one that emerges from a social conflict or moral calculation. De Graaff argues for the compatibility of Hauerwas and Bonhoeffer here, insisting that Hauerwas's emphasis on character formation is an "awareness of the real scope of [one's] moral responsibility" (de Graaff, "Overcoming Ethical Abstraction," 90). Hauerwas's avoidance of Bonhoeffer's concept of responsibility is likely predicated on the way many scholars view Bonhoeffer's account of the "responsible life" as providing an explanation for his involvement in tyrannicide. Thus, for a theologian as committed to nonviolence as Hauerwas, responsibility and pacifism appear to be at odds. Yet de Graaff also attempts to resolve this tension: "Hauerwas observes our perennial temptation to remove the other who resists us or puts our security at risk, often through violent means, and thus secure our own security without having to take responsibility for that other. But peaceableness is in fact taking on responsibility for one another, enemy included. We do not annihilate the other, we do not abandon him. We must over-accept the other, despite the risks, and that is responsibility" (de Graaff, "Overcoming Ethical Abstraction," 90).

83. Bonhoeffer, *DBWE* 6:99.

84. Cone, *A Black Theology of Liberation*, 167–168, referring to Bonhoeffer's *Creation and Fall: A Theological Exposition of Genesis 1–3, DBWE* 3, ed. John W. de Gruchy, trans. Douglas Stephen Bax, (Minneapolis: Fortress Press, 2004).

85. Bonhoeffer, *DBWE* 6:255, 256.

86. Bonhoeffer, *DBWE* 6:257.

87. Bonhoeffer, *DBWE* 6:219, 222. See the connection in Bonhoeffer's German between *Verantwortlichkeit* [responsibility], and *Antwort* [answer].

88. Bonhoeffer, *DBWE* 6:261.

89. Bonhoeffer, *DBWE* 6:261.

90. Bonhoeffer, *DBWE* 6:261, 264.

91. Bonhoeffer, *DBWE* 6:57.

92. Bonhoeffer, *DBWE* 6:275.

93. McBride, *The Church for the World*, 13. She argues that "Too often the concept of accepting guilt is linked directly to Bonhoeffer's involvement in the Abwehr's conspiracy against Hitler, and so it is removed from the realm of everyday discipleship" (13). Similarly, Matthew Puffer effectively argues that scholars have overemphasized the "short-lived thought experiment" in Bonhoeffer's writing of actively embracing guilt. This is a concept that appears only in one eight-page section of Bonhoeffer's corpus and seems to be revised in later essays (Matthew Puffer, "Three Rival Versions of Moral Reasoning: Interpreting Bonhoeffer's Ethics of Lying, Guilt, and Responsibility," *Harvard Theological Review* 112, no. 2 (2019): 160–183, references to pp. 161 and 176).

94. Guido de Graaff, *Politics in Friendship: A Theological Account* (New York: Bloomsbury, 2014), 193.

95. Cone, *A Black Theology of Liberation* (New York: Lippencott and Co., 1970), 27.

96. Bonhoeffer, *DBWE*, vol. 4: *Discipleship*, ed. John D. Godsey and Geffrey B. Kelly, trans. Reinhard Krauss and Barbara Green (Minneapolis: Fortress, 2003), 43–56.

97. Cone, *Said I Wasn't Gonna Tell Nobody,* 135.

98. Cone, *A Black Theology of Liberation*, 219.

99. Bonhoeffer, *DBWE* 6:268; Cone, *God of the Oppressed*, 222.

100. Bonhoeffer, *DBWE* 1:51, 48.

101. Bonhoeffer, *DBWE* 1:51, 49.

102. Bonhoeffer, *DBWE* 1:49.

103. Wannenwetsch, " 'Responsible Living' or 'Responsible Self'?," 132.

104. Michael DeJonge, *Bonhoeffer's Reception of Luther* (Oxford: Oxford University Press, 2017), 163.

105. Bonhoeffer, *DBWE* 6:268–269. This counters the popular idea that Bonhoeffer's concept of responsibility was a way of justifying tyrannicide.

106. Stacey Floyd-Thomas, *Mining the Motherlode: Methods in Womanist Ethics* (Cleveland: Pilgrim Press, 2006), 34.

107. Katie G. Cannon, *Black Womanist Ethics* (Atlanta: Scholars Press, 1988), 75.

108. Cannon, *Black Womanist Ethics,* 76.

109. Karen Teel, *Racism and the Image of God* (New York: Palgrave Macmillan, 2010), 57.

110. Bonhoeffer, *DBWE* 1:38. Bonhoeffer reiterates the point in *Ethics,* explaining that Christ takes form in the world as the church (*DBWE* 6:96).

111. Bonhoeffer, *DBWE* 6:232.

112. Bonhoeffer, *DBWE* 6:69. He continues, "What distinguishes responsibility from violation is this very fact of recognizing other people as responsible persons."

113. Emilie Townes, "To Be Called Beloved," in *Womanist Theological Ethics: A Reader,* ed. Katie Geneva Cannon, Emilie M. Townes, and Angela D. Sims (Louisville, KY: Westminster John Knox Press, 2011), 185.

114. Townes, "To Be Called Beloved," 185. Reggie Williams adds that empathy easily becomes distorted because in its traditional sense—and its dependence on perception—it can be "prone to projection, in which the dominant, self-determining, autonomous persons within the social hierarchy bounce their image off the fungible body of fixed, commodified human subjects, only to see their own reflection returned to them." In these situations of inequality, notes Williams, empathy "can be distorted to make it another way of keeping the subject in subjection, requiring an imagined white body overlaying a black one to humanize it" (Williams, *Bonhoeffer's Black Jesus,* 3–4).

115. Melinda McGarrah Sharp, *Misunderstanding Stories: Toward a Postcolonial Pastoral Theology* (Eugene, OR: Pickwick Publications, 2013), 145. Thank you to Amy Canosa for pointing me to this source.

116. Bonhoeffer, *DBWE* 6:99.

117. Bonhoeffer, *DBWE* 6:101.

118. Bonhoeffer, *DBWE* 6:93. As Lisa Dahill notes, "To the extent that Christians participate in his form, being conformed to him, they too take on the role of *Stellverter* [vicarious representative] of others and of Christ in the world" (Dahill, *Reading from the Underside of Selfhood: Bonhoeffer and Spiritual Formation* (Eugene, OR: Pickwick, 2009), 188.

119. Copeland, *Syndicate.*

120. J. Kameron Carter, "Bonhoeffer and Blackness," 20th Annual Bonhoeffer Lectures in Public Ethics, McCormick Seminary, Chicago, IL, June 1, 2019.

121. Michael P. DeJonge, "The Place of Race in Bonhoeffer's Resistance Reasoning," 20th Annual Bonhoeffer Lectures in Public Ethics, McCormick Seminary, Chicago, IL, June 1, 2019; DeJonge, in *Bonhoeffer's Reception of Luther,* argues that the mistreatment of Jews "was not for Bonhoeffer directly a confessional issue. The direct confessional issues were the gracious character of the gospel, the church as the community defined by God's gracious word, the ministry of all believers, and the character of temporal and spiritual authority. The mistreatment of Jews was for Bonhoeffer a tragedy, a blight on the state, . . . and it was

reason for humanitarian action, but it was not a matter of confession" (DeJonge, *Bonhoeffer's Reception of Luther* (New York: Oxford University Press, 2017), 221).

122. DeJonge, *Bonhoeffer's Reception of Luther*, 223.

123. See Bonhoeffer, "The Church and the Jewish Question," in *DBWE*, vol. 12: *Berlin: 1932–1933*, ed. Larry L. Rasmussen, trans. Douglas W. Stott, Isabel Best, and David Higgins (Minneapolis: Fortress, 2009), 362–364, 367–370.

124. DeJonge offers a complex historical account of the traditional Lutheran division between "gospel" issues and *adiaphora*, or "indifferent" issues. Only matters pertaining to salvation, explicitly justification by grace in Bonhoeffer's Lutheran context, were gospel issues, and only gospel issues were of proper theological significance. Questions like the wearing of clergy vestments were *adiaphora*, and not properly of theological concern. Only in situations of dire emergency—moments of persecution, potential schism, or extreme heresy—could the church invoke a *status confessionis* (a circumstance in which the essence of the gospel or the church is under attack) and declare *adiaphora* issues to be gospel issues (see DeJonge, *Bonhoeffer's Reception of Luther*, 196–206). Thus, in normal circumstances, for Bonhoeffer, race was an issue indifferent to theology. DeJonge comments, "In 'The Church and the Jewish Question,' Bonhoeffer says race is not a central theological category but rather an adiaphoron" (225).

125. Bonhoeffer writes that the "Aryan paragraph . . . is a '*status confessionis*' for the church" ("The Jewish-Christian Question as Status Confessionis," in *DBWE* 12:372). See also "The Church and the Jewish Question," in *DBWE* 12:366.

126. DeJonge, *Bonhoeffer's Reception of Luther*, 225.

127. Bonhoeffer, *DBWE* 12:272, 273.

128. After decades of hagiographic attention to Bonhoeffer's concern for Jewish people during the Reich, scholars are beginning to question this narrative. For example, historian Victoria Barnett argues that "there is relatively little evidence in [Bonhoeffer's] writings that the plight of the European Jews was his primary motive for participating in . . . the resistance" (Victoria J. Barnett, "Dietrich Bonhoeffer's Relevance for a Post-Holocaust Christian Theology," in *Bonhoeffer and Interpretive Theory: Essays on Methods and Understanding*, ed. Peter Frick (Frankfurt: Peter Lang, 2013), 215–216).

129. Bonhoeffer, *DBWE* 6:105.

130. Bonhoeffer, *DBWE* 8:52.

131. Bonhoeffer, *DBWE* 6:138.

132. This claim stretches Bonhoeffer's definition of *grenzfall*. He was clear in every reference to the borderline case in *Ethics* that these are uncommon occurrences in which we experience a conflict between ethical norms (Bonhoeffer, *Ethics, DBWE* 6:195, 273, and 366, and in *DBWE*, vol. 16: *Conspiracy and Imprisonment, 1940–1945*, ed. Mark Brocker, trans. Lisa E. Dahill (Minneapolis: Fortress, 2006), 608). Yet, if we agree with Robin Lovin and Matthew Puffer that, in our context in twenty-first-century America, our ordinary lives generate and

experience such conflicts, then we might accurately describe the situation of the white church today as an emergency. The moral complexity of life dictates that conflicts between ethical norms are not as uncommon as Bonhoeffer believed; rather, according to Lovin, "the conflict is part of life" (Robin Lovin, *Christian Realism and the New Realities* (New York: Cambridge University Press, 2008), 202 (also pp. 104–107)); see also Matthew Puffer, "The 'Borderline Case' in Bonhoeffer's Political Theology," in *A Spoke in the Wheel: The Political in the Theology of Dietrich Bonhoeffer*, ed. Kirsten Busch Nielsen, Ralf K. Wüstenberg, and Jens Zimmerman (Gütersloh: Gütersloher Verlagshau, 2013), 257–269, 268). Specifically, in the case of white supremacy, white Christians face a moral conflict between our commitment to a church institution and tradition soaked in white supremacy and our commitment to the oppressed and marginalized. This conflict surely generates the emergency situation that Bonhoeffer describes, and places us in a position of responsibility. Out of this responsibility, Cone's call to action—to conversion, to become black—emerges.

133. Bonhoeffer, *DBWE* 8::389.
134. Bonhoeffer, *DBWE* 8:389.
135. Bonhoeffer, *DBWE* 8:389.
136. Bonhoeffer, *DBWE* 8:389.
137. Bonhoeffer, *DBWE* 8:490.
138. Eberhard Bethge, *Dietrich Bonhoeffer: A Biography*, rev. ed. (Minneapolis: Fortress, 2003), 744.
139. Stanley Hauerwas, *Community of Character: Towards a Constructive Christian Social Ethic* (Notre Dame, IN: University of Notre Dame Press, 1981), 3.
140. Katie M. Grimes, "Breaking the Body of Christ: The Sacraments of Initiation in a Habitat of White Supremacy," *Political Theology* 18, no. 1 (2017): 22–43, 37.
141. Grimes, "Breaking the Body of Christ," 40.
142. See Bryan Massengale, "*Vox Victimarum Vox Dei*: Malcolm X as a 'Classic' for Catholic Theological Reflection," *Catholic Theological Society of America* 65 (2010): 83–84.
143. Paul tells the church in Corinth, "Now you are the body of Christ and individually members of it" (1 Corinthians 12:27), and likewise to the Romans, "We, who are many, are one body in Christ, and individually we are members one of another" (Romans 12:5). This image is also used in Ephesians 4 and 5, and Colossians 1 and 3.
144. Bonhoeffer, "Lectures on Christology," in *DBWE* 12:323, italics in original. Alternative translation from *Christ the Center*, trans. E. H. Robertson (San Francisco: Harper Collins, 1978), 59. Bonhoeffer reiterates the point in *Ethics*, explaining that Christ takes form in the world as the church (*DBWE* 6:96).
145. Bonhoeffer, DBWE 1:127.
146. Copeland, *Enfleshing Freedom: Body, Race, and Being* (Minneapolis: Fortress Press, 2010), 81.

147. Copeland, *Enfleshing Freedom*, 83.
148. Copeland, *Enfleshing Freedom*, 83.
149. Copeland, *Enfleshing Freedom*, 127.

CHAPTER 6

1. James Cone, *Black Theology and Black Power* (Maryknoll, NY: Orbis Books, 1969), 150.
2. Eduardo Bonilla-Silva, *Racism without Racists: Color-Blind Racism and the Persistence of Racial Inequality in America* (New York: Rowman & Littlefield, 2009), 96.
3. Mary McClintock Fulkerson and Martha Mount Shoop, *A Body Broken, A Body Betrayed: Race, Memory, and Eucharist in White-Dominated Churches* (Eugene, OR: Cascade Books, 2015), 1.
4. Fulkerson and Mount Shoop, *A Body Broken*, 2, 11.
5. See Emilie Townes, *Womanist Ethics and the Cultural Production of Evil* (New York: Palgrave Macmillan, 2006), 111–138.
6. George Yancey, *Christology and Whiteness: What Would Jesus Do?* (London: Routledge, 2012), 5, emphasis added.
7. Stanley Hauerwas, *A Community of Character: Toward a Constructive Christian Social Ethic* (Notre Dame, IN: University of Notre Dame Press, 1983), 83.
8. James K. A. Smith, *Awaiting the King: Reforming Public Theology* (Grand Rapids: Baker, 2017), 190.
9. Smith, *Awaiting the King*, 221.
10. Lauren F. Winner, *The Dangers of Christian Practice: On Wayward Gifts, Characteristic Damage, and Sin* (New Haven, CT: Yale University Press, 2018), 167.
11. Winner, *The Dangers of Christian Practice*, 16.
12. Orlando Paterson, *Slavery and Social Death: A Comparative Study* (Cambridge, MA: Harvard University Press, 1982), 8–9.
13. Katie Grimes, "Breaking the Body of White Supremacy: The Sacraments of Initiation in a Habitat of White Supremacy" *Political Theology* 18, no. 1 (2017): 24. See also Brandy Daniels, "Is There No Gomorrah? Christian Ethics, Identity, and the Turn to Ecclesial Practices: Where's the Difference?" *Journal of the Society of Christian Ethics* 39, no. 2 (2020).
14. M. Shawn Copeland, *Enfleshing Freedom: Body, Race, and Being* (Minneapolis: Fortress, 2009), 109.
15. Copeland, *Enfleshing Freedom*, 126.
16. Copeland, *Enfleshing Freedom*, 100, 104.
17. Copeland, *Enfleshing Freedom*, 127.
18. Mary McClintock Fulkerson, *Places of Redemption: Theology for a Worldly Church* (Oxford: Oxford University Press, 2007), 35.

19. Fulkerson, *Places of Redemption*, 157, 214.

20. Fulkerson, *Places of Redemption*, 233.

21. Fulkerson, *Places of Redemption*, 234.

22. Stanley Hauerwas and Samuel Wells, "The Gift of the Church and the Gifts God Gives It," in *The Blackwell Companion to Christian Ethics*, 2nd ed. (Malden, MA: Blackwell, 2011), 13.

23. Cone, *Black Theology and Black Power*, 150. As I take my cue from Cone, I also move beyond him with increasing attention to the critiques and proposals of womanist ethics, as well as feminist and secular scholars in my account of practices. I noted the ways womanist theology critiques and presses beyond Cone, especially with a more nuanced understanding of the multiplicity and intersectionality of oppression. For examples, see Marcia Riggs, "The Logic of Interstructured Oppression: A Black Womanist Perspective," in *Redefining Sexual Ethics: A Sourcebook of Essays, Stories, and Poems*, ed. Susan E. Davies and Eleanor Humes Haney (Cleveland: Pilgrim Press, 1991), 97–102; and Emilie Townes, "Living in the New Jerusalem," in *A Troubling in My Soul: Womanist Perspectives on Evil and Suffering*, ed. Emilie Townes (Maryknoll, NY: Orbis Books, 1993), 79–91.

24. Matthew 15:21–28 and Mark 7:24–30. The terms *Canaanite* and *Syrophoenician* are not synonymous designations (Matthew employs one and Mark the other). *Canaanite* is a more encompassing term but identifies her as a descendant of the preconquest Canaanite inhabitants, like the Samaritan woman at the well in John 4. The point is that she is a Gentile and "representative of the despised indigenous population with which Israel was not supposed to fraternize" (Douglas R. A. Hare, *Matthew: Interpretation* (Louisville, KY: Westminster/John Knox Press, 1993), 178).

25. Earlier in Matthew's Gospel, Jesus had forbidden his followers from giving what is holy to dogs—a deeply offensive image for outsiders in the ancient world. See Matthew 7:6 and Revelation 22:15, noted in the *New Oxford Annotated Bible*, 3rd ed., ed. Michael Coogan (New York: Oxford University Press, 2001), 17 New Testament, and *The Jewish Annotated New Testament*, ed. Amy-Jill Levine and Marc Zvi Brettler (New York: Oxford University Press, 2011), 75.

26. Jason Byassee, "Honorary Jews," sermon in Duke University Chapel, Durham, NC, August 14, 2011, available at https://chapel.duke.edu/2011-sermons-archive. Many interpreters point to the fact that both Mark and Matthew use the diminutive form of the term, κυναρίοις, which denotes household puppies rather than wild canines in an attempt to soften the blow of Jesus's words. However, this hermeneutical maneuver does not work since there was no diminutive term in Jesus's Aramaic (M. Eugene Boring, *Matthew: The New Interpreter's Bible*, vol. 8 (Nashville: Abingdon, 1995), 336).

27. Ranjini Wickramaratne Rebera, "The Syrophoenician Woman: A South Asian Feminist Perspective," in *A Feminist Companion to Mark*, ed. Amy-Jill Levine with Marianne Blickenstaff (Sheffield: Sheffield Academic Press, 2001), 101–110, 103; see also Joel Marcus, *Mark 1–8: The Anchor Bible* (New York: Doubleday, 1999), 468.

28. Kwok Pui-Lan, *Discovering the Bible in the Non-Biblical World* (Eugene, OR: Wipf and Stock, 2003), 71–83; Surekha Nelavala, "Smart Syrophoenician Woman: A Dalit Reading of Mark 7:24–31," *Expository Times* 118, no. 2 (2006): 64–69; Zhang Jing, "Beyond What She Said: On the Syrophoenician Woman," *Chinese Theological Review* 20 (2007): 102–136; Musa W. Dube, *Postcolonial Feminist Interpretation of the Bible* (St. Louis, MO: Chalice Press, 2000), 127–201. Thank you to Ashleigh Elser for pushing me to attend to the "difficult" stories and to Joe Lenow for alerting me to these sources.

29. Kelly Brown Douglas, *The Black Christ* (Maryknoll, NY: Orbis Books, 1994), 91.

30. Marilyn McCord Adams, *Christ and Horrors: The Coherence of Christology* (Cambridge, MA: Cambridge University Press, 2006), 79.

31. This leads Elizabeth Struthers Malbon to conclude that the "Markan Jesus is shown as learning from a Gentile woman about inclusive community," imagining Jesus telling this woman, "What you say brings me up short" (Malbon, *Hearing Mark: A Listener's Guide* (Harrisburg, PA: Trinity Press, 2002), 47).

32. Angela D. Sims, *Lynched: The Power of Memory in a Culture of Terror* (Waco, TX: Baylor University Press, 2016), 90–91; Clarence Kidd and Margie Kidd Campbell, interviewed by Sims, August 18, 2009, in Benton, Louisiana.

33. Sims, *Lynched*, 93.

34. Peter McLaren, "Whiteness Is . . . the Struggle for Postcolonial Hybridity," in *White Reign: Deploying Whiteness in America*, ed. Joe L. Kincheloe, Shirley R. Steinberg, Nelson M. Rodriguez, and Ronald E. Chennault (New York: St. Martin's Press, 1998), 63–75, 66.

35. Saidiya Hartman, *Lose Your Mother: A Journey along the Atlantic Slave Route* (New York: Farrar, Straus and Giroux, 2007), 133.

36. Sims, *Lynched*, 446.

37. Sims, *Lynched*, 56.

38. Sims, *Lynched*, 57.

39. Alice Walker, *Living by the Word: Essays* (San Diego: Harcourt Brace, 1988), 63.

40. Stanley Hauerwas, *Christian Existence Today: Essays on Church, World, and Living in Between* (Durham, NC: Duke University Press, 1994), 94.

41. Kelly Brown Douglas, *Stand Your Ground: Black Bodies and the Justice of God* (Maryknoll, NY: Orbis Books, 2015), 221.

42. M. Shawn Copeland, *Knowing Christ Crucified: The Witness of African American Religious Experience* (Maryknoll, NY: Orbis Books, 2018), 87.

43. Copeland, *Knowing Christ Crucified*, 97.

44. Hamil R. Harris, "D.C.'s Calvary Baptist Church Celebrates 150 Years," *Washington Post*, June 8, 2012, http://www.washingtonpost.com/local/dcs-calvary-baptist-church-celebrates-150-years/2012/06/08 (italics added). This story was repeated— "Calvary, founded more than 150 years ago by abolitionists"—in another article in 2017 (Michael Alison Chandler, "Couple hired at D.C. Baptist church among a growing number called to co-pastor in nation's pulpits," *Washington Post*, January

14, 2017, http://www.washingtonpost.com/news/acts-of-faith/wp/2017/01/14/gay-couple-hired-at-calvary-baptist-in-dc-among-a-growing-number-of-spouses-called-to-co-pastor-at-nations-churches). I am a member of Calvary.

45. John Appiah-Duffell, et al., "Understanding Calvary's Origin Story: In the Beginning," Sermon, Calvary Baptist Church, Washington, DC, June 16, 2019, http://www.calvarydc.org/sermons/sunday-june-16.

46. John Appiah-Duffell, et al., "Understanding Calvary's Origin Story: In the Beginning."

47. Elijah Zehyoue, "Understanding Calvary's Origin Story: In the Beginning."

48. Donald B. Cole, *A Jackson Man: Amos Kendall and the Rise of American Democracy* (Baton Rouge: Louisiana State University Press, 2004), 63, 200. Thank you to John Appiah-Duffell, et al., for the research into this and for providing me with this source.

49. Maria Swearingen, "Understanding Calvary's Origin Story: In the Beginning."

50. Cole, *A Jackson Man*, 239. When Daniel was taken and freed by an abolitionist, Kendall was furious that someone would "steal and hide my property." He added, "My Democracy has not been able to reconcile black and white." It is not known what happened to Daniel, but soon after this incident, Kendall bought two more slaves.

51. James Baldwin, *Price of the Ticket: Collected Nonfiction, 1948–85* (New York: St. Martin's Press, 1985), xix.

52. From Acts 9:1–25.

53. Brittany E. Wilson, *Unmanly Men: Refigurations of Masculinity in Luke–Acts* (New York: Oxford University Press, 2015), 189. The political reflections on Wilson's book in this subsection come from an unpublished lecture by Luke Bretherton, "On Conversion."

54. George K. A. Bell, *The Kingship of Christ: The Story of the World Council of Churches* (Middlesex: Penguin, 1954), 34.

55. Guido de Graaff, *Politics in Friendship: A Theological Account* (New York: Bloomsbury, 2014), 138–139; Peter Raina, *Bishop George Bell—The Greatest Churchman: A Portrait in Letters* (London: Churches Together in Britain and Ireland, 2006), 235. Guido de Graaff explains, "Thus Bonhoeffer's repentance was vicarious, rather than representative. . . . Instead of claiming to atone for the atrocities perpetrated by Germany, he declared that he would stand by his compatriots, willing to suffer with them the burden of their guilt that pressed on them, both individually and collectively" (De Graaff, *Politics in Friendship*, 186).

56. Dietrich Bonhoeffer, *Dietrich Bonhoeffer Works (English)* (hereafter *DBWE*), vol. 6: *Ethics*, ed. Clifford J. Green, trans. Reinhard Krauss, Charles C. West, and Douglas W. Stott (Minneapolis: Fortress, 2005), 142.

57. Winner, *The Dangers of Christian Practice*, 91.

58. Jennifer McBride, *The Church for the World: A Theology of Public Witness* (New York: Oxford University Press, 2011), 81.

59. According to Gregory Jones, the church confesses "in order to renarrate our lives (often by having it renarrated to us by others)" (Jones, *Embodying Forgiveness: A Theological Analysis* (Grand Rapids: Eerdmans, 1995), 184).

60. Charles Mathewes, *Republic of Grace: Augustinian Thoughts for Dark Times* (Grand Rapids: Eerdmans, 2010), 211–212, 210.

61. Bonhoeffer, *DBWE 6*:88.

62. McBride, *The Church for the World*, 82.

63. Jennifer McBride, *The Church for the World*, 65; Bonhoeffer, *DBWE*, vol. 8: *Letters and Papers from Prison,* ed. John W. de Gruchy, trans. Reinhard Krauss, Nancy Lukens, Lisa E. Dahill, and Isabel Best (Minneapolis: Fortress, 2010), 479–480.

64. Bonhoeffer, *DBWE 6*:80.

65. McBride, *The Church for the World*, 66–67.

66. Bonhoeffer, *DBWE*, vol. 4: *Discipleship,* ed. John D. Godsey and Geffrey B. Kelly, trans. Reinhard Krauss and Barbara Green (Minneapolis: Fortress, 2003), 90.

67. "We Repent," Mount Vernon Place United Methodist Church, http://www.mvpumc.org/we-repent.

68. Rev. Donna Claycomb Sokol, "Unlocking the Treasure," sermon, Mount Vernon Place United Methodist Church, Washington, DC, October 8, 2017, quoting H. Shelton Smith, *In His Image, But . . .* (Durham, NC: Duke University Press, 1972), 37.

69. Smith, *In His Image*, 44.

70. Smith, *In His Image*, 112.

71. Smith, *In His Image*, 113.

72. Sokol, "Unlocking the Treasure," drawing on Royce Thompson, ed., *History of Mount Vernon Place United Methodist Church, 1850–1976* (Washington, DC: Mount Vernon Place United Methodist Church Trustees, 1977).

73. Sokol, "Unlocking the Treasure."

74. John 8:32.

75. Luke 19:1–10.

76. Laurie Kellman, "McConnell on Reparations for Slavery: 'Not a Good Idea,'" *Associated Press*, June 18, 2019, http://www.apnews.com/e79abc3b64e7400e-a961f2fe99a73dc6. Shortly after McConnell's statement, NBC News reported that he descended from slave owners (Corky Siemaszko, "Sen. Mitch McConnell's Great-Great-Grandfathers Owned 14 Slaves, Bringing Reparations Issue Close to Home," *NBC News*, July 8, 2019, http://www.nbcnews.com/politics/congress/mitch-mcconnell-ancestors-slave-owners-alabama-1800s-census).

77. Ta-Nehisi Coates, "House Testimony," transcript reprinted in *The Atlantic*, June 2019, http://www.theatlantic.com/politics/archive/2019/06/ta-nehisi-coates-testimony-house-reparations-hr-40.

78. A 2005 UN resolution titled "Basic Principles and Guidelines on the Right to a Remedy and Reparation for Victims of Gross Violations of International Human Rights Law and Serious Violations of International Humanitarian Law" identified five forms of reparation: (1) *restitution*, by which victims are restored (where

possible) to the original situation before the violation; (2) *compensation*, by which victims receive for any "economically assessable damage" an amount "proportional to the gravity of the violation and the circumstances of each case"; (3) *rehabilitation*, by which "medical and psychological care" and "legal and social services" are delivered; (4) *satisfaction*, by which a "public apology"—a public "acceptance of responsibility . . . restoring the dignity . . . reputation and . . . rights" of victims—is offered, including or memorials; and (5) *guarantees of nonrepetition*, including "mechanisms for preventing and monitoring social conflicts and their resolution" (Van Boven/Bassiouni Principles of the Commission on Human Rights, Resolution 2005/35 of April 19, 2005, UN Doc. E/CN.4/RES/2005/35, specifically Articles 18–23). These principles were adopted by the UN Human Rights Council and subsequently by the General Assembly. They are cited by Grace Y. Kao, "Reparations in Asian American Contexts: When 'Sorry' Isn't Enough," presentation at the Georgetown University Religion, Culture, and Politics Workshop, Washington, DC, January 25, 2019.

79. Coates, "House Testimony."

80. Ta-Nehisi Coates, "The Case for Reparations," in *We Were Eight Years in Power* (New York: One World, 2017), 163–210, 174 (all citations from the book version). "The Case for Reparations" was originally published in *The Atlantic*, June 2014, http://www.theatlantic.com/magazine/archive/2014/06/the-case-for-reparations.

81. See Ira Katznelson, *When Affirmative Action Was White: An Untold History of Racial Inequality* (New York: Norton, 2005), 36–44.

82. Melvin L. Oliver and Thomas M. Shapiro, *Black Wealth / White Wealth: A New Perspective on Racial Inequality* (New York: Routledge, 2006), 150.

83. Hartman, *Lose Your Mother*, 6. For an account of the policies and legal decisions that foreclosed racial equality in the immediate postbellum period see Saidiya Hartman, *Scenes of Subjection: Terror, Slavery, and Self-Making in Nineteenth-Century America* (New York: Oxford University Press, 1997), 125–206.

84. Coates, *We Were Eight Years in Power*, 205.

85. Coates, *We Were Eight Years in Power*, 177.

86. Martha Minow, *Between Vengeance and Forgiveness: Facing History after Genocide and Mass Violence* (Boston: Beacon Press, 1998), 102. See also Miroslav Volf, *Exclusion and Embrace: A Theological Exploration of Identity, Otherness, and Reconciliation* (Nashville: Abingdon, 1996).

87. Grace Kao notes that in the context of reparations to interned Japanese Americans, "many Japanese Americans ultimately embraced the reparations package provided to them, in large part because the U.S. had bundled together what they had interpreted as meaningful symbolic and material forms of redress" (Kao, "Reparations in Asian American Contexts").

88. Georgetown University and Princeton Theological Seminary come to mind. There may be others, especially by the time of publication.

89. It is telling that one of the few successful examples I could find does not involve reparations to African Americans. In 1991 the General Synod of the United Church of Christ issued a formal apology to native Hawaiians for their complicity in the illegal overthrow of the Kingdom of Hawaii. Two years later UCC president Reverend Paul Sherry formally repented on behalf of the entire denomination for the ways the church had too often confused "the ways of the West with the ways of Christ," while pledging reparations of $1.25 million to native institutions for redress (Paul Sherry, quoted in J. Bennett Guess, "Forgiveness Is Not Forgetting," La Salette Missionaries, http://www.lasalette.org/about-la-salette/reconciliation/reconciliation-resources/944-forgiveness-is-not-forgetting; cited by Kao, "Reparations in Asian American Contexts"). The Hawaii Conference of the UCC gave an additional twenty-eight thousand dollars to each of the forty-eight native Hawaiian churches in existence during the overthrow, or its successors, committed $1.5 million to the newly created Pu'a Foundation to serve the native Hawaiian community, and transferred six parcels of land to native Hawaiian churches (Eric K. Yamamoto, *Interracial Justice: Conflict and Reconciliation in Post–Civil Rights America* (New York: New York University Press, 2000), 61, 65).

90. M. Dion Thompson, "Diocese of Maryland Takes Up Reparations," The Episcopal Church, May 16, 2016, http://www.episcopalchurch.org/library/article/diocese-maryland-takes-reparations.

91. "Diocese of Maryland Resolution on Racial Reconciliation Passes Unanimously at 235th Diocesan Convention," Episcopal News Service, June 4, 2019, http://www.episcopalnewsservice.org/pressreleases/diocese-of-maryland-resolution-on-racial-reconciliation-passes-unanimously-at-235th-diocesan-convention. Earlier in 2019 the bishop of Maryland, the Right Reverend Eugene Sutton, an African American clergyperson, wrote a letter to the diocese again urging reparations: "We must come to acknowledge that there can be no love without justice, and there can be no justice without some form of repairing an injustice. . . . Through reparations, we can be leaders in the long-awaited process of reconciliation, of creating God's dream for us—a truly *Beloved Community*" ("Bp. Sutton Urges Reparations in Maryland," Episcopal Diocese of Maryland, May 1, 2019, http://www.episcopalmaryland.org/wp.../sites/.../Reparations-Pastoral-Letter-May-2019).

CONCLUSION

1. James Cone, *Said I Wasn't Gonna Tell Nobody: The Making of a Black Theologian* (Maryknoll, NY: Orbis Books, 2018), 170–171.

2. Martin Luther King Jr., "Where Do We Go from Here?" in *A Testament of Hope: The Essential Writings and Speeches of Martin Luther King Jr.*, ed. James Melvin Washington (New York: HarperOne, 1986), 245.

3. Miguel de la Torre, *Embracing Hopelessness* (Minneapolis: Fortress Press, 2017), 142, 5–6.

4. De la Torre, *Embracing Hopelessness*, 140. He offers a somewhat sketchy critique of Jürgen Moltmann, simultaneously arguing that Moltmann espouses a white European universalism in his utopian and triumphal eschatology as well as promotes a self-limiting God that collapses hope into assurance of eternal life (25, 51). I have no interest here in assessing his reading of Moltmann, nor of critiquing Moltmann himself.

5. Vincent Lloyd, "For What Are Whites to Hope?," *Political Theology* 17, no. 2 (2016): 168–181, 171.

6. Lloyd, "For What Are Whites to Hope?," 174.

7. Lloyd, "For What Are Whites to Hope?," 175. Lloyd also has in mind here "theologies of hope" produced by scholars like Jürgen Moltmann. While I am using Lloyd and de la Torre to make a unified point, I should note two differences between their texts. First, de la Torre wants to distinguish hopelessness from despair, preferring the equation of desperation leading to hopelessness, while Lloyd contends that despair leads to hopelessness (141). I do not feel the need to choose sides in what seems like a semantic quibble. Next, de la Torre proposes hopelessness as a strategy for marginalized and oppressed communities, while Lloyd is challenging white people. I am repurposing some of the insights of de la Torre to also make an argument about white Christians because I think his insights usefully align with Lloyd's argument.

8. Stanley Hauerwas, *Approaching the End: Eschatological Reflections on Church, Politics, and Life* (Grand Rapids: Eerdmans, 2013), 157.

9. Lloyd, "For What Are Whites to Hope?," 178, drawing on Søren Kierkegaard's *The Sickness unto Death*.

10. King, "Where Do We Go from Here?," 250–251.

11. This is one of Paul's favorite images for the church. See 1 Corinthians 12:27; Romans 12:5; Ephesians 4 and 5; and Colossians 1 and 3.

12. This is Luke's favorite name for the early church, the label the community gave to itself, twice from the mouth of Paul. See Acts 9:2; 19:9; 19:23; 22:4; 24:14; 24:22.

13. Gillian Rose, *Mourning Becomes the Law: Philosophy and Representation* (Cambridge: Cambridge University Press, 1996), 38.

14. Dietrich Bonhoeffer, *Dietrich Bonhoeffer Works (English)*, vol. 6,: *Ethics*, ed. Clifford J. Green, trans. Reinhard Krauss, Charles C. West, and Douglas W. Stott (Minneapolis: Fortress, 2005), 224–225.

15. Augustine, *Enarrationes in psalmos*, on Psalm 54.3; trans. Michael McCarthy, in "An Ecclesiology of Groaning: Augustine, the Psalms, and the Making of Church," *Theological Studies* 66 (2005): 35. See also Augustine, *Exposition of the Psalms,* trans. Maria Boulding (New York: New City, 2000–2004).

Selected Bibliography

Alcoff, Linda Martìn. *Visible Identities: Race, Gender, and the Self*. New York: Oxford University Press, 2006.

Alexander, Michelle. *The New Jim Crow: Mass Incarceration in the Age of Colorblindness*. New York: New Press, 2010.

Anderson, Carol. *White Rage: The Unspoken Truth of Our Racial Divide*. New York: Bloomsbury, 2017.

Anderson, Victor. *Beyond Ontological Blackness: An Essay in African American Religious and Cultural Criticism*. New York: Continuum, 1995.

Baldwin, James. *The Fire Next Time*. New York: Vintage, 1962.

———. *No Name in the Street*. New York: Vintage, 1972.

———. *Notes of a Native Son*. Boston: Beacon Press, 1955.

———. *Price of the Ticket: Collected Nonfiction, 1948–85*. New York: St. Martin's Press, 1985.

Bantum, Brian. *Redeeming Mulatto: A Theology of Race and Christian Hybridity*. Waco, TX: Baylor University Press, 2010.

Barber, William J., II, and Jonathan Wilson-Hartgrove. *The Third Reconstruction: Moral Mondays, Fusion Politics, and the Rise of a New Justice Movement*. Boston: Beacon Press, 2016.

Barnett, Victoria J. "Dietrich Bonhoeffer's Relevance for a Post-Holocaust Christian Theology." In *Bonhoeffer and Interpretive Theory: Essays on Methods and Understanding*. Edited by Peter Frick, 213–238 Frankfurt: Peter Lang, 2013.

Bartlett, Robert. *The Making of Europe*. Princeton, NJ: Princeton University Press, 1994.

Beaudoin, Tom, and Katherine Turpin. "White Practical Theology." In *Opening the Field of Practical Theology*. Edited by Kathleen A. Cahalan and Gordon S. Mikosi, 251–269. Lanham, MD: Rowman & Littlefield, 2014.

Becker, Penny Edgell. "Making Inclusive Communities: Congregations and the 'Problem' of Race." *Social Problems* 45, no. 4 (1998): 451–472.

Berger, Peter, and Thomas Luckman. *The Social Construction of Reality: A Treatise in the Sociology of Knowledge*. Garden City, NY: Anchor Books, 1966.

Bernasconi, Robert. "Kant as an Unfamiliar Source of Racism." In *Philosophers on Race: Critical Essays.* Edited by Julie K. Ward and Tommy Lee Lott, 145–166. Malden, MA: Blackwell, 2002.

———. "Who Invented the Concept of Race?" In *Race.* Edited by Robert Bernasconi, 11–36. Malden, MA: Blackwell, 2001.

Berry, Wendell. *The Hidden Wound.* Berkeley, CA: Counterpoint, 1989.

Bethge, Eberhard. *Dietrich Bonhoeffer: A Biography.* Revised ed. Minneapolis: Fortress, 2003.

Bonhoeffer, Dietrich. *Dietrich Bonhoeffer Works (English).* Vol. 1: *Sanctorum Communion.* Edited by Clifford J. Green, translated by Reinhard Krauss and Nancy Lukens. Minneapolis: Fortress, 1998.

———. *Dietrich Bonhoeffer Works (English).* Vol. 4: *Discipleship.* Edited by John D. Godsey and Geffrey B. Kelly, translated by Reinhard Krauss and Barbara Green. Minneapolis: Fortress, 2003.

———. *Dietrich Bonhoeffer Works (English).* Vol. 6: *Ethics.* Edited by Clifford J. Green, translated by Reinhard Krauss, Charles C. West, and Douglas W. Stott. Minneapolis: Fortress, 2005.

———. *Dietrich Bonhoeffer Works (English).* Vol. 8: *Letters and Papers from Prison.* Edited by John W. de Gruchy, translated by Reinhard Krauss, Nancy Lukens, Lisa E. Dahill, and Isabel Best. Minneapolis: Fortress, 2010.

———. *Dietrich Bonhoeffer Works (English).* Vol. 10: *Barcelona, Berlin, New York: 1928– 1931.* Edited by Clifford J. Green, translated by Douglas W. Stott. Minneapolis: Fortress, 2008.

———. *Dietrich Bonhoeffer Works (English).* Vol. 12: *Berlin: 1932–1933.* Edited by Larry L. Rasmussen, translated by Douglas W. Stott, Isabel Best, and David Higgins. Minneapolis: Fortress, 2009.

———. *Dietrich Bonhoeffer Works (English).* Vol. 16: *Conspiracy and Imprisonment: 1940– 1945.* Edited by Mark Brocker, translated by Lisa E. Dahill. Minneapolis: Fortress, 2006.

Bonilla-Silva, Eduardo. *Racism without Racists: Color-Blind Racism and the Persistence of Racial Inequality in America.* Lanham, MD: Rowman & Littlefield, 2006.

Bouie, Jamelle. "The Enlightenment's Dark Side." *Slate,* June 5, 2018.

Boyarin, Daniel. *The Unconverted Self: Jews, Indians, and the Identity of Christian Europe.* Chicago: University of Chicago Press, 2009.

Braxton, Brad R. "Lifting the Veil: The *Shoah* and the *Maafa* in Conversation." *Perspectives in Religious Studies* 38, no. 2 (2011): 185–193.

Bretherton, Luke. "Exorcising Democracy: The Theo-Political Challenge of Black Power." *Journal of the Society of Christian Ethics* 38, no.1 (2018): 3–24.

Bucher, Glenn R. "Social Gospel and Racism." *Union Seminary Quarterly Review* 28, no. 2 (Winter 1973): 146–157.

Buell, Denise Kimber. "Early Christian Universalism and Modern Racism." In *The Origins of Racism in the West*. Edited by Miriam Eliav-Feldon, Benjamin Isaac, and Joseph Ziegler, 109–131. Cambridge: Cambridge University Press, 2009.

———. *Why This New Race*. New York: Columbia University Press, 2005.

Butler, Judith. *Frames of War: When Is Life Grievable?*. Brooklyn, NY: Verso, 2009.

Cahill, Lisa Sowle. *Love Your Enemy: Discipleship, Pacifism, and Just War Theory*. Minneapolis: Fortress, 1994.

Cannon, Katie G. *Black Womanist Ethics*. Atlanta: Scholars Press, 1988.

Castagno, Angelina E. "Multicultural Education and the Protection of Whiteness." *American Journal of Education* 120, no. 1 (2013): 101–128.

Carter, J. Kameron. *Race: A Theological Account*. New York: Oxford University Press, 2008.

Cavanaugh, William T. *Theopolitical Imagination: Christian Practices of Space and Time*. New York: Bloomsbury Academic, 2013.

———. *Torture and Eucharist*. Malden, MA: Blackwell, 1998.

Caviness, Madeline. "From the Self-Invention of the Whiteman in the Thirteenth Century to the Good, the Bad, and the Ugly." *Different Visions: A Journal of New Perspectives on Medieval Art*, no. 1 (September 2008), http://differentvisions.org/issue-one/.

Christerson, Brad, Korie L. Edwards, and Michael O. Emerson. *Against All Odds*. New York: New York University Press, 2005.

Clark, Andy. *Supersizing the Mind: Embodiment, Action, and Cognitive Extension*. Oxford: Oxford University Press, 2008.

Clark, Andy, and David Chalmers. "The Extended Mind." *Analysis* 58, no. 1 (January 1998): 7–19.

Cleage, Albert. *The Black Messiah*. Kansas City: Sheed and Ward, 1969.

Coates, Ta-Nehisi. *Between the World and Me*. New York: Spiegel & Grau, 2015.

———. "The Case for Reparations." *The Atlantic*, June 2014, https://www.theatlantic.com/magazine/archive/2014/06/the-case-for-reparations/361631/.

———. "The First White President." *The Atlantic*, October 2017, https://www.theatlantic.com/magazine/archive/2017/10/the-first-white-president-ta-nehisi-coates/537909/.

———. "Ta-Nehisi Coates's Testimony on Reparations." *The Atlantic*, June 2019, https://www.theatlantic.com/politics/archive/2019/06/ta-nehisi-coates-testimony-house-reparations-hr-40/592042/.

Cone, James H. "Black Theology and the Black Church: Where Do We Go from Here?" *Cross=Currents* 27, no. 2 (Summer 1977): 147–156.

———. *Black Theology and Black Power*. Maryknoll, NY: Orbis Books, 1997.

———. *A Black Theology of Liberation*. Maryknoll, NY: Orbis Books, 1986.

———. *A Black Theology of Liberation*, 20th anniversary edition. Maryknoll, NY: Orbis Books, 1990.

———. "Christian Faith and Political Praxis." *Encounter* 43, no. 2 (Spring 1982): 129–141.

———. *The Cross and the Lynching Tree*. Maryknoll, NY: Orbis Books, 2011.

———. "The Cry of Black Blood." Martin Luther King Lecture at Duke Divinity School, Durham, NC, April 1, 2015.

———. *For My People*. Maryknoll, NY: Orbis Books, 1984.

———. *God of the Oppressed*. Maryknoll, NY: Orbis Books, 1973.

———. Interview by the author. New York, February 16, 2016, and April 12, 2016.

———. "Martin, Malcolm, and Black Theology." In *How Long This Road: Race, Religion, and the Legacy of C. Eric Lincoln*. Edited by Alton B. Pollard and Love Henry Whelchel Jr., 119–130. New York: Palgrave Macmillan, 2003.

———. *My Soul Looks Black*. Maryknoll, NY: Orbis Books, 2004.

———. *Said I Wasn't Gonna Tell Nobody: The Making of a Black Theologian*. Maryknoll, NY: Orbis Books, 2019.

———. *Speaking the Truth: Ecumenism, Liberation, and Black Theology*. Grand Rapids: Eerdmans, 1986.

———. *The Spirituals and the Blues*. Maryknoll, NY: Orbis Books, 1972.

———. "The Story Context of Black Theology." *Theology Today* 32, no. 2 (July 1975): 144–150.

———. "Theology's Great Sin: Silence in the Face of White Supremacy." *Black Theology* 2, no. 2 (2004): 139–152.

———. "Why God Is Black: All Together Podcast Featuring Dr. James Cone." Interview by Paul Rauschenbusch. *All Together*, HuffPost Religion. January 16, 2015, https://www.huffpost.com/entry/god-is-black-james-cone_n_6487012.

Copeland, M. Shawn. *Enfleshing Freedom: Body, Race, and Being*. Minneapolis: Fortress, 2009.

———. *Knowing Christ Crucified: The Witness of African American Religious Experience*. Maryknoll, NY: Orbis Books, 2018.

———. "Overcoming Christianity's Lingering Complicity," *In the Shadow of Charleston: Syndicate Theology* (2015), https://syndicate.network/symposia/theology/in-the-shadow-of-charleston/.

———."Race." In *Blackwell Companion to Modern Theology*. Edited by Gareth Jones, 499–511. Malden, MA: Blackwell, 2004.

Dahill, Lisa. *Reading from the Underside of Selfhood: Bonhoeffer and Spiritual Formation*. Eugene, OR: Pickwick, 2009.

Daniels, Brandy. "Is There No Gomorrah? Christian Ethics, Identity, and the Turn to Ecclesial Practices: Where's the Difference?" *Journal of the Society of Christian Ethics* 39, no. 2 (2019): 287–302.

De Graaff, Guido. "Overcoming Ethical Abstraction: Peaceableness, Responsibility, and the Rejection of Foundationalism in Bonhoeffer and Hauerwas." In *Engaging Bonhoeffer: The Influence and Impact of Bonhoeffer's Life and Thought*. Edited by Matthew D. Kirkpatrick, 115–138. Minneapolis: Fortress, 2016.

———. *Politics in Friendship: A Theological Account*. New York: Bloomsbury, 2014.

DeJonge, Michael. *Bonhoeffer's Reception of Luther*. Oxford: Oxford University Press, 2017.

De La Torre, Miguel. *Embracing Hopelessness*. Minneapolis: Fortress, 2017.

Delgado, Richard. "Storytelling for Oppositionists and Others: A Plea for Narrative." *Michigan Law Review* 87, no. 8 (1989): 2411–2441.

Derman-Sparks, Louise, Patricia Ramsey, and Julie Olsen Edwards. *What If All the Kids Are White?: Anti-Bias Multicultural Education with Young Children and Families*. New York: Teachers College Press, 2006.

Devisse, Jean. *The Image of the Black in Western Art*. Vol. 2: *From the Early Christian Era to the "Age of Discovery."* Cambridge, MA: Harvard University Press, 1990.

DiAngelo, Robin. "White Fragility." *International Journal of Critical Pedagogy* 3, no. 3 (2011): 54–70.

———. *White Fragility: Why It's So Hard for White People to Talk about Racism*. Boston: Beacon Press, 2018.

Dorrien, Gary. *The New Abolition: W. E. B. Du Bois and the Black Social Gospel*. New Haven, CT: Yale University Press, 2015.

Douglas, Kelly Brown. *The Black Christ*. Maryknoll, NY: Orbis Books, 1994.

———. "More Than Skin Deep: The Violence of Anti-Blackness." In *Anti-Blackness and Christian Ethics*. Edited by Vincent W. Lloyd and Andrew Prevot, 3–18. Maryknoll, NY: Orbis Books, 2017.

———. *Stand Your Ground*. New York: Orbis Books, 2017.

———. *What's Faith Got to Do with It? Black Bodies / Christian Souls*. Maryknoll, NY: Orbis Books, 2005.

———. "Womanist Theology: What Is Its Relationship to Black Theology?" In *Black Theology: A Documentary History*. Vol. 2. Edited by Gayraud Wilmore and James Cone, 290–299. Maryknoll, NY: Orbis Books, 1979.

Dyer, Richard. *White: Essays on Race and Culture*. New York: Routledge, 1997.

Edwards, Herbert O. "Racism and Christian Ethics in America." *Katallagete* (Winter 1971): 15–24.

Edwards, Korie L. *The Elusive Dream: The Power of Race in Interracial Churches*. Oxford: Oxford University Press, 2008.

Edwards, Korie L., Brad Christerson, and Michael O. Emerson. "Race, Religious Organizations, and Integration." *Annual Review of Sociology* 39 (July 2013): 211–228.

Emerson, Michael O., and Christian Smith. *Divided by Faith: Evangelical Religion and the Problem of Race in America*. New York: Oxford University Press, 2000.

Evans, James. *We Have Been Believers: An African American Systematic Theology*. Minneapolis: Fortress, 1993.

Eze, Emmanuel Chuckwudi. "The Color of Reason: The Idea of 'Race' in Kant's Anthropology." In *Postcolonial African Philosophy: A Critical Reader*. Edited by Emmanuel Chukwudi Eze, 103–140. Malden, MA: Blackwell, 1997.

Eze, Emmanuel Chuckwudi, ed. "Introduction." In *Race and the Enlightenment: A Reader*, 1–9. Oxford: Blackwell, 1997.

Feagin, Joe R. *The White Racial Frame: Centuries of Racial Framing and Counter Framing*, 2nd edition. New York: Routledge, 2013.

Feagin, Joe R., and Eileen O'Brien. *White Men on Race: Power, Privilege, and the Shaping of Cultural Consciousness*. Boston: Beacon Press, 2004.

Fletcher, Jeanine Hill. *The Sin of White Supremacy: Christianity, Racism, and Religious Diversity in America*. Maryknoll, NY: Orbis Books, 2017.

Floyd-Thomas, Stacey. *Mining the Motherlode: Methods in Womanist Ethics*. Cleveland: Pilgrim Press, 2006.

Frankenburg, Ruth. *The Social Construction of Whiteness: White Women, Race Matters*. Minneapolis: University of Minnesota Press, 1993.

Fulkerson, Mary McClintock. *Places of Redemption: Theology for a Worldly Church*. New York: Oxford University Press, 2007.

Fulkerson, Mary McClintock, and Marcia Mount Shoop. *A Body Broken, A Body Betrayed: Race, Memory and Eucharist in White-Dominated Churches*. Eugene, OR: Cascade Books, 2015.

Gates, Henry Louis, Jr. *The Signifying Monkey: A Theory of African-American Literary Criticism*. New York: Oxford University Press, 1988.

Goetz, Rebecca Anne. *The Baptism of Early Virginia: How Christianity Created Race*. Baltimore: Johns Hopkins University Press, 2012.

Gonzalez, Justo L. *The Story of Christianity*. Vol. 1: *The Early Church to the Dawn of the Reformation*. New York: HarperSanFrancisco, 1984.

Grant, Jacquelyn. "Black Theology and the Black Woman." In *Black Theology: A Documentary History, 1966–1979*. Vol. 1. Edited by Gayraud Wilmore and James Cone, 418–433. Maryknoll, NY: Orbis Books, 1979.

———. *White Women's Christ and Black Women's Jesus: Feminist Christology and Womanist Response*. Atlanta: Scholars Press, 1989.

Grimes, Katie W. "Breaking the Body of Christ: The Sacraments of Initiation in a Habitat of White Supremacy." *Political Theology* 18, no. 1 (2017): 22–43.

Grimes, Katie Walker. *Christ Divided: Antiblackness as Corporate Vice*. Minneapolis: Fortress, 2017.

Guth, Karen V. "Laying Claim to Martin Luther King Jr. and the Civil Rights Legacy: An Ethical Assessment of Social Gospel Historiography," *Journal of Religious Ethics* 48.1 (March 2020): 1–19.

Gutiérrez, Gustavo. *A Theology of Liberation: History, Politics and Salvation*. Maryknoll, NY: Orbis Books, 1988, orig. 1973.

Habermas, Jürgen. *Legitimation Crisis*, trans. Thomas McCarthy. Boston: Beacon Press, 1975.

Hannaford, Ivan. *Race: The History of an Idea in the West*. Baltimore: Johns Hopkins University Press, 1996.

Harnack, Adolf von. *The Mission and Expansion of Christianity*. Vol. 2, translated by James Moffatt. New York: G. P. Putnam's Sons, 1908.

Hartman, Saidiya. *Lose Your Mother: A Journey along the Atlantic Slave Route*. New York: Farrar, Straus & Giroux, 2008.

———. *Scenes of Subjection: Terror, Slavery, and Self-Making in Nineteenth-Century America*. Oxford: Oxford University Press, 1997.

Harvey, Jennifer. *Dear White Christians: For Those Still Longing for Racial Reconciliation*. Grand Rapids: Eerdmans, 2014.

Hauerwas, Stanley. *Approaching the End: Eschatological Reflections on Church, Politics, and Life*. Grand Rapids: Eerdmans, 2013.

———. *A Better Hope: Resources for a Church Confronting Capitalism, Postmodernity, and America*. Grand Rapids: Brazos, 2000.

———. *The Character of Virtue: Letters to a Godson*. Grand Rapids: Eerdmans, 2018.

———. *Christian Existence Today: Essays on Church, World, and Living in Between*. Durham, NC: Duke University Press, 1994.

———. *A Community of Character: Toward a Constructive Christian Social Ethic*. Notre Dame, IN: University of Notre Dame Press, 1981.

———. "Ethics of Black Power." *Augustana Observer*, February 5, 1969, 5 and 7.

———. *Hannah's Child: A Theologian's Memoir*. Grand Rapids: Eerdmans, 2010.

———. Interview by the author. Durham, NC, February 25, 2015.

———. *The Peaceable Kingdom: A Primer in Christian Ethics*. Notre Dame, IN: University of Notre Dame Press, 1983.

———. *Truthfulness and Tragedy: Further Investigations in Christian Ethics*. Notre Dame, IN: University of Notre Dame Press, 1977.

———. *Wilderness Wanderings: Probing Twentieth-Century Theology and Philosophy*. Boulder, CO: Westview Press, 1997.

———. *The Work of Theology*. Grand Rapids: Eerdmans, 2015.

Hauerwas, Stanley, and Romand Coles. *Christianity, Democracy, and the Radical Ordinary: Conversation between a Radical Democrat and a Christian*. Eugene, OR: Cascade Books, 2008.Hauerwas, Stanley, and Jean Varnier. *Living Gently in a Violent World: The Prophetic Witness of Weakness*. Downers Grove, IL: InterVarsity Press, 2008.

Hauerwas, Stanley, and Samuel Wells. "The Gift of the Church and the Gifts God Gives It." In *The Blackwell Companion to Christian Ethics*, 2nd edition, 13–27. Malden, MA: Blackwell Publishing, 2011.

Hauerwas, Stanley, and William H. Willimon. *Resident Aliens: Life in the Christian Colony*. Nashville: Abingdon, 1989.

Healy, Nicholas. *Hauerwas: A Very Critical Introduction*. Grand Rapids: Eerdmans, 2014.

Heng, Geraldine. *The Invention of Race in the European Middle Ages*. New York: Cambridge University Press, 2018.

Heschel, Susanna. *The Aryan Jesus: Christian Theologians and the Bible in Nazi Germany*. Princeton, NJ: Princeton University Press, 2008.

Hess, Jonathan M. *Germans, Jews, and the Claims of Modernity*. New Haven, CT: Yale University Press, 2002.

Higginbotham, Evelyn Brooks. *Righteous Discontent*. Cambridge, MA: Harvard University Press, 1993.

Hill, Thomas E., Jr., and Bernard Boxill. "Kant and Race." In *Race and Racism*. Edited by Bernard Boxill, 448–471. Oxford: Oxford University Press, 2001.

Hochschild, Adam. *Bury the Chains: Prophets and Rebels in the Fight to Free an Empire's Slaves*. Boston: Mariner Books, 2006.

Hopkins, Dwight, ed. *Black Faith and Public Talk: Critical Essays on James Cone's Black Theology and Black Power*. Maryknoll, NY: Orbis Books, 1999.

Hunter, James D. *To Change the World: The Irony, Tragedy, and Possibility of Christianity in the Late Modern World*. New York: Oxford University Press, 2010.

Jenkins, Willis. *The Future of Ethics: Sustainability, Social Justice, and Religious Creativity*. Washington, DC: Georgetown University Press, 2013.

Jennings, Willie. *The Christian Imagination*. New Haven, CT: Yale University Press, 2011.

———. "The Traditions of Race Men." *South Atlantic Quarterly* 112, no. 4 (Fall 2013): 613–624.

Jones, Robert P. *The End of White Christian America*. New York: Simon & Schuster, 2016.

———. "The Rage of White Christian America." *New York Times*, November 10, 2016.

Kant, Immanuel. *Observations on the Feeling of the Beautiful and Sublime,* translated by John T. Goldwaithe. Berkeley: University of California Press, 1973.

———. *Religion and Rational Theology*. translated by Allen W. Wood. Edited by George Di Giovanni. Cambridge: Cambridge University Press, 1996.

Keel, Terrence. *Divine Variations: How Christian Thought Became Racial Science*. Stanford, CA: Stanford University Press, 2018.

Kelley, Shawn. *Racializing Jesus: Race, Ideology and the Formation of Modern Biblical Scholarship*. New York: Routledge, 2002.

Kidd, Erin. "The Subject of Conceptual Mapping: Theological Anthropology across Brain, Body, and World." *Open Theology* 4, no. 1 (2018): 117–135.

King, Martin Luther, Jr. *Stride toward Freedom: The Montgomery Story*. Boston: Beacon Press, 2010.

———. "Where Do We Go from Here?" In *A Testament of Hope: The Essential Writings and Speeches of Martin Luther King, Jr.* Edited by James Melvin Washington, 245–252. New York: HarperOne, 1986.

Larsen, Sean. "How I Think Hauerwas Thinks about Theology." *Scottish Journal of Theology* 69, no. 1 (2016): 20–38.

Lincoln, C. Eric. *Coming through the Fire: Surviving Race and Place in America*. Durham, NC: Duke University Press, 1996.

Lloyd, Vincent. "For What Are Whites to Hope?" *Political Theology* 17, no. 2 (2016): 168–181.

Lloyd, Vincent, and Andrew Prevot, editors. *Anti-Blackness and Christian Ethics.* Maryknoll, NY: Orbis Books, 2017.

Logan, James. *Good Punishment?: Christian Moral Practice and U.S. Imprisonment.* Grand Rapids: Eerdmans, 2008.

———. "Liberalism, Race, and Stanley Hauerwas," *CrossCurrents* 55, no. 4 (Winter 2006): 522–533.

Long, Charles H. *Significations: Signs, Symbols, and Images in the Interpretation of Religion.* Minneapolis: Fortress, 1986.

Lovin, Robin. *Christian Realism and the New Realities.* New York: Cambridge University Press, 2008.

———. "Reinhold Niebuhr and Dietrich Bonhoeffer on Responsibility." In *Engaging Bonhoeffer: The Influence and Impact of Bonhoeffer's Life and Thought.* Edited by Matthew D. Kirkpatrick, 65–86. Minneapolis: Fortress, 2016.

MacIntyre, Alasdair. *After Virtue: A Study in Moral Theory,* 2nd edition. Notre Dame, IN: Notre Dame University Press, 1984.

———. *Three Rival Versions of Moral Enquiry: Encyclopedia, Genealogy, and Tradition.* Notre Dame, IN: University of Notre Dame Press, 1990.

———. *Whose Justice? Which Rationality?* Notre Dame, IN: Notre Dame University Press, 1989.

Marsh, Charles. *Strange Glory: A Life of Dietrich Bonhoeffer.* New York: Alfred A. Knopf, 2016.

Mathewes, Charles. *Republic of Grace: Augustinian Thoughts for Dark Times.* Grand Rapids: Eerdmans, 2010.

McBride, Jennifer M. *The Church for the World: A Theology of Public Witness.* New York: Oxford University Press, 2011.

———. *Radical Discipleship: A Liturgical Politics of the Gospel.* Minneapolis: Fortress, 2017.

McGee, Timothy. "Against (White) Redemption: James Cone and the Christological Disruption of Racial Discourse and White Solidarity." *Political Theology* 18 no. 7 (January 2017): 542–559.

Mignolo, Walter D. *The Darker Side of Western Modernity: Global Futures, Decolonial Options.* Durham, NC: Duke University Press, 2011.

Mills, Charles W. *Black Rights / White Wrongs: The Critique of Racial Liberalism.* Oxford: Oxford University Press, 2017.

———. *The Racial Contract.* Ithaca, NY: Cornell University Press, 1997.

Minow, Martha. *Between Vengeance and Forgiveness: Facing History after Genocide and Mass Violence.* Boston: Beacon Press, 1998.

Mitchell, Beverly. *Plantations and Death Camps: Religion, Ideology, and Human Dignity.* Minneapolis: Fortress, 2009.

Morrison, Toni. *Beloved*. New York: Vintage Books, 2004 (orig. 1987).

———. "Unspeakable Things Unspoken: The Afro-American Presence in American Literature." In *The Black Feminist Reader*. Edited by Joy James and T. Denean Sharpley-Whiting, 24–56. Malden, MA: Blackwell, 2000.

Newsom, Ryan Andrew. *Inhabiting the World: Identity, Politics, and Theology in Radical Baptist Perspective*. Macon, GA: Mercer University Press, 2018.

Niebuhr, H. Richard. *The Responsible Self: An Essay in Christian Moral Philosophy*. New York: Harper & Row, 1963.

Niebuhr, Reinhold. *The Children of Light and the Children of Darkness*. New York: Charles Scribner's Sons, 1944.

———. *Christian Realism and Political Problems*. New York: Charles Scribner's Sons, 1953.

———. *The Irony of American History*. New York: Charles Scribner's Sons, 1952.

———. *Love and Justice: Selections from the Shorter Writings of Reinhold Niebuhr*. Edited by D. B. Robertson. 1957; Louisville, KY: Westminster/John Knox Press, 1992.

———. *Moral Man and Immoral Society: A Study of Ethics and Politics*. 1932; Louisville, KY: Westminster John Knox Press, 2002.

———. *The Nature and Destiny of Man: A Christian Interpretation*. New York: Charles Scribner's Sons, 1943.

———. *Reflections on the End of an Era*. New York: Charles Scribner's Sons, 1934.

———. *Reinhold Niebuhr: Major Works on Religion and Politics*. Edited by Elisabeth Sifton. New York: Library of America, 2015.

Pagden, Anthony. *Lords of All the World: Ideologies of Empire in Spain, Britain, and France, c. 1500–1800*. New Haven, CT: Yale University Press, 1995.

———. *Peoples and Empires: A Short History of European Migration, Exploration, and Conquest, from Greece to the Present*. New York: Modern Library, 2001.

Patterson, Orlando. *Slavery and Social Death: A Comparative Study*. Cambridge, MA: Harvard University Press, 1985.

Perkinson, James W. *White Theology: Outing Supremacy in Modernity*. New York: Palgrave Macmillan, 2004.

Prevot, Andrew. *Thinking Prayer: Theology and Spirituality amid the Crisis of Modernity*. Notre Dame, IN: University of Notre Dame Press, 2015.

Puffer, Matthew. "The 'Borderline Case' in Bonhoeffer's Political Theology." In *A Spoke in the Wheel: The Political in the Theology of Dietrich Bonhoeffer*. Edited by Kirsten Busch Nielsen, Ralf K. Wüstenberg, and Jens Zimmerman, 257–269. Gütersloh: Gütersloher Verlagshau, 2013.

———. "Three Rival Versions of Moral Reasoning: Interpreting Bonhoeffer's Ethics of Lying, Guilt, and Responsibility." *Harvard Theological Review* 112, no. 2 (2019): 160–183.

Putnam, Robert D., and David E. Campbell. *American Grace: How Religion Divides and Unites Us*. New York: Simon & Schuster, 2012.

Raboteau, Albert. *Slave Religion: The "Invisible" Institution in the Antebellum South.* Oxford: Oxford University Press, 1978.

Rambo, Shelly. *Resurrecting Wounds: Living in the Afterlife of Trauma.* Waco, TX: Baylor University Press, 2017.

Ransby, Barbara. *Ella Baker and the Black Freedom Movement: A Radical Democratic Vision.* Chapel Hill: University of North Carolina Press, 2003.

Rauschenbusch, Walter. "Belated Races and the Social Problems." *Methodist Review Quarterly* 63 (April 1914): 252–259.

———. *Christianity and the Social Crisis.* New York: Macmillan, 1907.

———. *Christianizing the Social Order.* New York: Macmillan, 1912.

———. "The Problem of the Black Man." *American Mission Association* 68 (March 1914): 732–733.

———. *A Theology for the Social Gospel.* New York: Abingdon Press, 1917.

Riggs, Marcia. "The Logic of Interstructured Oppression: A Black Womanist Perspective." In *Redefining Sexual Ethics: A Sourcebook of Essays, Stories, and Poems.* Edited by Susan E. Davies and Eleanor Humes Haney, 97–102. Cleveland, OH: Pilgrim Press, 1991.

Rivera, Luis N. *A Violent Evangelism: The Political and Religious Conquest of the Americas.* Louisville, KY: Westminster/John Knox Press, 1992.

Roberts, J. Deotis. *Black Political Theology.* Philadelphia: Westminster Press, 1974.

———. *Liberation and Reconciliation: A Black Theology.* Philadelphia: Westminster Press, 1971.

Rogers, Melvin. "White Supremacy, Fear and the Crisis of Legitimation." *Public Seminar*, January 1, 2017, www.publicseminar.org/2017/01/white-supremacy-fear-and-the-crises-of-legitimation.

Sharp, Melinda McGarrah. *Misunderstanding Stories: Toward a Postcolonial Pastoral Theology.* Eugene, OR: Pickwick, 2013.

Shelton, Jason E., and Michael O. Emerson. *Black and Whites in Christian America: How Racial Discrimination Shapes Religious Convictions.* New York: New York University Press, 2012.

Sims, Angela D. *Lynched: The Power of Memory in a Culture of Terror.* Waco, TX: Baylor University Press, 2016.

Smith, James K. A. *Awaiting the King: Reforming Public Theology.* Grand Rapids: Baker Academic, 2017.

Stacey, Robert C. "The Conversion of Jews to Christianity in Thirteenth-Century England." *Speculum* 67, no. 2 (April 1992): 263–283.

Stout, Jeffrey. *Democracy and Tradition.* Princeton, NJ: Princeton University Press, 2004.

Suchocki, Marjorie. *The Fall of Violence: Original Sin in Relational Theology.* New York: Continuum, 1994.

Tanner, Kathryn. *Theories of Culture: A New Agenda for Theology.* Minneapolis: Fortress, 1997.

Teel, Karen. *Racism and Image of God.* New York: Palgrave Macmillan, 2010.

———. "Whiteness in Catholic Theological Method." *Journal of the American Academy of Religion* 87, no. 2 (2019): 401–433.

Townes, Emilie. *Womanist Ethics and the Cultural Production of Evil.* New York: Palgrave Macmillan, 2006.

Townes, Emilie, editor. *A Troubling in My Soul: Womanist Perspectives on Evil and Suffering.* Maryknoll, NY: Orbis Books, 1993.

Tran, Jonathan. "Moral Innovation and Ambiguity in Asian American Christianity." *Theology Today* 75, no. 3 (2018): 347–357.

———. "The New Black Theology: Retrieving Ancient Sources to Challenge Racism." *Christian Century*, February 8, 2012, https://www.christiancentury.org/article/2012-01/new-black-theology.

———. "Time for Hauerwas's Racism." In *Unsettling Arguments: A Festschrift on the Occasion of Stanley Hauerwas's 70th Birthday.* Edited by Charles R. Pinches, Kelly S. Johnson, and Charles M. Collier. Eugene, OR: Cascade Books, 2012.

Trimiew, Darryl M. "The Social Gospel Movement and the Question of Race." In *The Social Gospel Today.* Edited by Christopher H. Evans, 27–37. Louisville, KY: Westminster John Knox Press, 2001.

Vasko, Elizabeth T. *Beyond Apathy: A Theology for Bystanders.* Minneapolis: Fortress, 2015.

Walker, Alice. *Living by the Word: Essays.* San Diego: Harcourt Brace, 1988.

Wannenwetsch, Bernd. "'Responsible Living' or 'Responsible Self'? Bonhoefferian Reflections on a Vexed Moral Notion." *Studies in Christian Ethics* 18, no. 3 (2005): 125–140.

Warnock, Raphael G. *The Divided Mind of the Black Church: Theology, Piety and Public Witness.* New York: New York University Press, 2014.

Washington, Joseph R, Jr. *Anti-Blackness in English Religion, 1500–1800.* Lewiston, NY: Edwin Mellen Press, 1984.

———. *The Politics of God: The Future of Black Churches.* Boston: Beacon Press, 1969.

Weber, Max. *Basic Concepts in Sociology.* New York: Citadel Press, 1993.

———. *Economy and Society: An Outline of Interpretive Sociology.* Oakland: University of California Press, 1978.

———. *The Theory of Social and Economic Organization.* New York: Free Press, 1964.

West, Cornel. *Prophesy Deliverance!: An Afro-American Revolutionary Christianity.* 1982; Louisville, KY: Westminster John Knox Press, 2002.

———. *Prophetic Fragments: Illuminations of the Crisis in American Religion and Culture.* Grand Rapids: Eerdmans, 1988.

West, Traci C. "Constructing Ethics: Reinhold Niebuhr and Harlem Women Activists." *Journal of the Society of Christian Ethics* 24, no. 1 (2004): 29–49.

Williams, Delores. *Sisters in the Wilderness: The Challenge of Womanist God-Talk.* Maryknoll, NY: Orbis Books, 1993.

Williams, Preston. "The Social Gospel and Race Relations: A Case Study of a Social Movement." In *Toward a Discipline of Social Ethics: Essays in Honor of Walter George Mueller.* Edited by Paul Deats Jr., 233–236. Boston: Boston University Press, 1972.

Williams, Reggie. *Bonhoeffer's Black Jesus: Harlem Renaissance Theology and an Ethic of Resistance.* Waco, TX: Baylor University Press, 2014.

Wilson, Brittany E. *Unmanly Men: Refigurations of Masculinity in Luke–Acts.* New York: Oxford University Press, 2015.

Winner, Lauren F. *The Danger of Christian Practice.* New Haven, CT: Yale University Press, 2018.

Woodard-Lehman, Derek. "Body Politics and the Politics of Bodies: Racism and Hauerwasian Theopolitics." *Journal of Religious Ethics* 36, no. 2 (2008): 295–320.

Yancy, George. *Black Bodies, White Gazes: The Continuing Significance of Race.* Lanham, MD: Rowman &Littlefield, 2008.

———. *Christology and Whiteness: What Would Jesus Do?* London: Routledge, 2012.

Index

For the benefit of digital users, indexed terms that span two pages (e.g., 52–53) may, on occasion, appear on only one of those pages.